6-17-75

EZRA TAFT BENSON
AND THE POLITICS OF AGRICULTURE:

The Eisenhower Years, 1953-1961

EZRA TAFT BENSON
AND THE POLITICS OF AGRICULTURE:

The Eisenhower Years, 1953-1961

Edward L. Schapsmeier
Illinois State University

and

Frederick H. Schapsmeier
University of Wisconsin—Oshkosh

The Interstate Printers & Publishers, Inc.
Danville, Illinois

Library of Congress Catalog Card No. 74-21896

Reorder No. 1697

To Juanita and Diana

With Love

TABLE OF CONTENTS

Page

Preface ix

Acknowledgments xiii

Introduction xv

Chapter

    I.   Winning Farm Votes in 1952 1

    II.   Ike Selects An Agriculture Secretary 12

    III.   What Manner of Man 20

    IV.   Resistance to Reform 34

    V.   Formulation of a New Farm Program 59

    VI.   The Problem of Plenty 97

    VII.   The Soil Bank 125

    VIII.   Farm Politics and the 1956 Election 160

    IX.   The President's Political Loyalty 180

    X.   Profile of Courage 217

    XI.   Richard Nixon and the 1960 Election 244

Conclusion 271

Notes 277

Select Bibliography 351

Index 371

Preface

The politics of agriculture are difficult to comprehend unless one has been projected into the role of administrator of the many complex laws that make up what we call "farm policy."

Changing times, food and fiber requirements and new world conditions have made it imperative that there be a continual review and revision of farm policy in order to meet our nation's requirements and commitments. The political pressures exerted on the Congress and the Administration by farmers, industry, and consumers, together with the problems of our import and export programs, create a political atmosphere that makes legislating difficult and at times almost impossible.

As Secretary of Agriculture during the post-war period, it became my task to administer agriculture programs in abnormal times when our country had unusual responsibilities. During the war, all possible pressure was put on

farmers to produce all of the food and fiber possible.
Price supports were provided to guarantee them against
losses should they overproduce. In the post-war years,
there was a period of adjustment. We had the responsibility
of feeding war-torn foreign nations; but at the same time,
we had to plan ahead when we would need less food and fiber
and formulate a policy for readjustment.

During the Eisenhower years, Secretary Benson had to
deal with similar problems during and after the Korean conflict. While many were criticizing our farmers for overproduction and accumulation of surpluses, Secretary Benson
said:

It would be unfair to criticize farmers
for creating surpluses. Through the second
World War and years immediately following, and
again during the Korean conflict, they were
called upon to produce every possible pound of
food and fiber. They responded with the
greatest burst of agricultural production in
history.

I had proposed a system of controls and flexible
price supports with the aim of eventually letting the law
of supply and demand take over and regulate our agriculture
production. Secretary Benson came to Congress with a

proposal to use a part of accumulated surplus agricultural products to assist in strengthening the economies of friendly countries which would assist in accomplishment of some of our foreign policy objectives. He also proposed a system of lowered price supports and acreage controls which he hoped would hold production in line and move us toward a time when supply and demand would be the controlling factor. I was in agreement with most of his proposals since we sought the same objective by similar methods. I supported a great many of the Eisenhower people and programs, but none more, I believe, than Ezra Taft Benson. I believed he was a good man serving at a good time, and I still maintain that attitude. I feel that he conscientiously worked at doing a good job for the farmers of the country, as well as the entire nation.

Clinton P. Anderson

Formerly Secretary of Agriculture
and a member of the United States Senate
from New Mexico

Acknowledgments

We are grateful to Ezra Taft Benson for making his papers available to us and to Sherman Adams for the valuable information given by him pertaining to the Eisenhower administration.

Special thanks must also go to Wayne D. Rasmussen, USDA historian and Executive Secretary of the Agricultural History Society; Alfred M. Landon of Kansas; Reed A. Benson; James T. Patterson, Professor of history at Indiana University; Leonard J. Arrington, Historian of the Church of Jesus Christ of Latter-day Saints; and James G. Patton, President Emeritus of the National Farmers Union. These gentlemen kindly consented to read this book in manuscript form. We are responsible, needless to say, for all subsequent interpretations and conclusions.

Our gratitude must also be expressed for the assistance of many archivists, librarians, and people who knew Ezra Taft Benson.

Last but not least the authors make known their appreciation to Illinois State University for a research grant, and we thank our typist, Alberta Carr, for her diligent work. Both ingredients make it possible for books to be born.

Edward L. Schapsmeier   Frederick H. Schapsmeier

Introduction

When the first Commissioner of Agriculture, Isaac Newton, issued his initial report, he considered it indispensible to see to it that "two blades of grass grow where one grew before."[1] Even after 1889, when the agriculture post was elevated to cabinet rank, early holders of this office also considered it important to find ways to increase production. It was not until after World War I that agricultural secretaries found themselves confronted with a different problem--that of surpluses. Overproduction of feed and fiber continued each decade thereafter until ironically abundance itself became a cause of concern to farmers.

This capacity of the rural sector to produce enormous amounts of agricultural commodities has, needless to say, been a perpetual blessing to the nation as a whole. Widespread famine due to underproduction is not a constant threat nor has it ever been. No country on the face of the earth succeeded so well in agriculture as did the United

States. Ample land, energetic tillers of the soil, and a dynamic technology made it possible for Americans to wage two world wars without suffering from food shortages, and then go on to feed millions of starving people during periods of postwar reconstruction.

The Great Depression of the thirties, accompanied by drought and dust storms, caused great anguish among farm people. It was as if the land was rebelling against those who depended upon it for a livelihood. When yields were bountiful during these years, profits declined even further. The Triple-A programs of the New Deal, plus other measures initiated by the administration of Franklin D. Roosevelt, provided economic mechanisms for controlling surpluses. This involved complicated devices for imposition of acreage allotments to restrict production, the establishment of a system of price supports, and controls over certain phases of marketing so that farm income might be raised.

Government intervention into agriculture continued beyond the New Deal era. Federal controls became tantamount to a form of national management for agriculture. Whereas the original economic mechanism for aiding farmers had great merit, later models became increasingly corrupted by politics. Members of Congress so tampered with the federal machinery that ultimately programs designed to help farmers were in actuality detrimental to their long-range welfare.

When Ezra Taft Benson became the Secretary of Agriculture on January 21, 1953, it was his firm intention to reverse the direction of farm policy. Viewing himself as a reformer and a genuine friend of the farmer, he sought to free agriculture from stifling controls imposed by years of political machination on the part of Congress. Truly an apostle of economic freedom, Benson soon found himself pitted against entrenched members of the farm bloc who regarded agriculture as their private domain. His term of office, therefore, is the story of eight controversial and conflict-filled years.

Not one to yield to political expediency or temporary popularity, Ezra Taft Benson was truly a man of principle. This Agriculture Secretary was above all a conscientious Mormon. As an Apostle of his church, being a member of the Council of Twelve of The Church of Jesus Christ of Latter-day Saints, he was daily sustained by an unwavering sense of duty to serve man by serving God. This he believed could be done only by adhering to what seemed morally right to him. Public service in his mind meant neither condoning irresponsibility nor pandering to political pressure. Even before the era of Watergate, Benson was involved in no unethical or suspicious "deals" and absolutely refused to even consider bestowing favors upon special interest groups offering campaign contributions in return.

Unwilling even to measure each act only by voter popularity,
he strove to live up to the motto inscribed on a plaque in
full view of all who stood before his desk. It read: "O
God give us men with a mandate higher than the ballot box."[2]

How did a Mormon leader become associated with the
politics of agriculture during the era of the Eisenhower
administration? For this answer we must pick up the campaign trail of a presidential candidate seeking farm votes.
As in most political biographies the principal subject is
drawn into the mainstream of action only after many cross
currents have muddied up the water. Ezra Taft Benson was
plunged into the maelstrom of politics with many an unseen
pitfall awaiting him. This then is the story of one man's
struggle not just to survive politically or even to succeed
against great odds, but to serve the public with unimpeach-
able integrity.

Chapter I
Winning Farm Votes in 1952

By 1952 the Republican party was truly desperate for victory on the national level. It had lost five presidential elections in a row. Herbert Hoover was the last GOP candidate actually to occupy the White House. In 1948 Governor Thomas E. Dewey of New York seemed to have the presidency within grasp, yet miraculously Harry S. Truman wrenched the victor's prize from him at the last moment. Circumstances once more made it appear a Republican could gain public approval for the highest office in the land.

From a political viewpoint General Dwight D. Eisenhower made an admirable candidate. Conqueror of Hitler's mighty Wehrmacht, NATO Commander, and president of Columbia University were impressive accomplishments for this Kansas-raised general. Outwardly genial but made of stern stuff, this folk hero spoke the language of Middle America. No press agent could have invented a better nickname than that already possessed by Eisenhower. "I like Ike" became a slogan that blended familiarity with trust. Ike's boyish grin provided the perfect touch for a candidate seeking to dispel the notion that a Republican Chief Executive would be unreliable as the people's steward.

A major concern of Midwestern Republicans was the lack of knowledge displayed by Eisenhower when it came to farm policy. To a military man such phrases as 90 per cent of parity, price supports, acreage allotments, marketing quotas, two-price systems, and production controls meant very little. But these terms were a part of the language of agricultural economics as well as being important in the lexicon of rural politics.

Since the days of Calvin Coolidge, who twice vetoed the McNary-Haugen Bill (an early attempt to deal with sur- pluses via dumping abroad), Republican administrations had been on the defensive when it came to the farm vote. For fifteen years Democrats had scored Herbert Hoover for his seemingly unfriendly attitude toward farmers. Hoover's Federal Farm Board, set up by the Agricultural Marketing Act of 1929, had collapsed under the weight of surplus wheat which accrued during the depression years.

Suffering stinging defeats at the hands of Franklin D. Roosevelt, Midwest Republicans began to support rather than criticize the idea of federal intervention on behalf of the American farmer. The Agricultural Adjustment Acts of both 1933 and 1938 set up the basic mechanism whereby the government established a floor under farm prices. Farmers were assured some semblance of parity with other sectors of the economy. Parity meant equality. The years taken to establish a ratio formula were those of 1910-1914 when farm income and outgo were most equally balanced. In an attempt to stabilize commodity prices the Triple-A of 1938 established a flexible scale whereby participating farmers would be guaranteed from 52 to 75 per cent of parity depending upon what crops were involved. This economic mechanism, which could either decrease or increase production by lowering or raising the parity ratio, functioned through a host of devices. Farmers were given certain acreage allotments to restrict output; they could accept non-recourse loans and allow the government to take their crop if market prices fell; they sometimes had to accept marketing quotas; or they could voluntarily choose to stay out of the federal programs.

What happened over the years was clear enough. Farmers became accustomed to income protection and government subsidy. Representatives of the rural community found it to their advantage politically to vote for greater appropriations and higher parity ratios. It was necessary to raise parity during both world wars and the Korean War to insure maximum production, but Congress was always reluctant to lower parity during periods of peace.

Finally in 1948 the 80th Congress did take steps to reinstate the concept of flexible parity. With the range of parity supports widened to from 60 to 90 per cent, and the base period for its computation shifted from the 1910-1914 era to the immediate preceding decade, the floor under farm income was materially lowered. In order to provide a cushion for farmers who needed time for readjusting their production a two-year grace period was allowed. In other words the new farm act would not go into effect until 1950.

Despite the fact that it was Harry Truman's Secretary of Agriculture, Clinton Anderson, who advised this needed step, the Missourian campaigned strongly against it in farm states. Needing votes desperately, the incumbent President made the rural electorate believe the Republican dominated 80th Congress was intent upon reducing farm income. Specifically Truman could point to reduced appropriations for the Commodity Credit Corporation (the federal agency responsible for storing food and fiber held by the government) and to the current decline in farm prices. Effectively the President posed as a champion of American farmers while casting Republicans in the role of hard-hearted villains.[1]

When the man from Missouri won in 1948 it made Midwestern Republicans even more wary about how their rural constituencies regarded them in terms of their position on price supports. Charles Brannan, Truman's new Secretary of Agriculture, proposed a grand scheme to cement the farm vote permanently to Democrats. The Brannan plan would continue paying the equivalent of 90 per cent of parity, but would do so by eliminating the non-recourse loans and storage facilities. Farm output was to be rigidly controlled and government payments would be in the form of direct and undisguised subsidies. Acreage allotments would be eliminated in favor of regulated units of production, i.e. bushels of wheat or bales of cotton. The whole idea was to insure high farm income while keeping prices low for urban consumers.

Brannan's proposal had great political merit but would have involved the government in a massive managerial role in agriculture. Likewise the cost to taxpayers would have been enormous. And the major farm organizations were not at all unanimous in their support for this scheme. While a Democratic Congress rejected the Brannan plan, it did pass a new Agriculture Act in 1949. With considerable Republican support the Secretary of Agriculture was given latitude to use either the old (which was higher) or new parity formula depending upon which would be more advantageous to farmers in terms of cash benefits. Also implementation of flexible price supports was postponed once more. This time until 1952.

When the year 1952 arrived it was both an election year and a time of involvement in the Korean War. Congress again temporized by voting to extend 90 per cent of parity two more years. Now flexible price supports were scheduled to go into effect in 1954.

Governor Adlai Stevenson of Illinois, the Democratic nominee, invoked the 90 per cent of parity phrase albeit with some qualifications. He promised to support this level while at the same time voicing doubts about the wisdom of including perishable products within the price support system. Scandals had already occurred relative to the destruction of produce having spoiled while in storage. Newspaper photos of potatoes (partially rotten) being made totally inedible discouraged any candidate from advocating practices of this type.

Senator Frank Carlson and Representative Clifford Hope, both of Kansas, along with Nebraska's Fred Seaton, were designated by Ike to be his farm advisors.[2] These Midwestern Republicans, backed by Governor Dan Thornton of Colorado and Governor Sherman Adams of New Hampshire, strongly urged Eisenhower likewise to endorse the principle of 90 per cent parity. The ghost of Harry Truman haunted Clifford Hope.[3] This Kansan, who was then considered a likely choice for the Agriculture Secretary post, did not want Eisenhower to make the same mistake made by Thomas E.

Dewey. As one of the earliest supporters of Ike for the
Republican nomination he importuned constantly for the GOP
candidate to declare himself unequivocally in favor of high,
rigid price supports. Hope, the ranking Republican on the
House Committee on Agriculture, felt this step was absolutely necessary for victory.[4]

The dilemma faced by Ike was simple. Conceding he
did not comprehend all the intricate aspects of farm policy,
Eisenhower nevertheless felt federal involvement in agriculture should be reduced. This meant he favored reinstatement
of flexible price supports as the first step in curtailing
the amount of government control over agriculture. But to
tell this to farm audiences in a no hedging and straightforward manner would have been tantamount to courting disaster.
Not wanting to repeat Tom Dewey's mistake, Ike chose Kasson,
Minnesota to make his stand known on the farm issue. Speaking to a large rural audience attending the National Plowing
Contest on September 6, 1952, the General made what sounded
like an ironclad pledge to the farm community. Using the
same forum which helped launch Harry Truman's victory in
1948 Eisenhower solemnly vowed: "And here and now, without
'ands,' 'ifs' or 'buts,' I say to you that I stand behind--and
the Republican party stands behind--the price support laws
now on the books. This includes the amendment to the basic
Farm Act, passed by the votes of both parties in Congress,

to continue through 1954 the price supports on basic commodities at 90 per cent of parity."[5]

   This was clever political rhetoric. To the undiscerning ear it appeared as if the GOP candidate had unequivocally endorsed the concept of high, rigid price supports. In point of fact Ike had merely committed himself to continue such a policy for the next two years, that is until the current measure expired. Once again, for the benefit of the South, Eisenhower repeated his carefully phrased promise to fulfill the letter of the law. At Memphis, Tennessee on October 6, 1952 the General spoke the reassuring words: "Here and now let me say to you what I have said to farmers elsewhere. I stand behind the price support laws now on the books. This includes the amendment to the basic farm act, approved by both parties in Congress, to continue through 1954 the price supports on basic commodities at 90 per cent of parity."[6]

   The farm plank in the Republican platform was likewise designed to be appealing without binding the party to perpetuate the New Deal system of price supports. In a seemingly forthright statement it asserted: "We favor a farm program aimed at full parity for all farm products in the market place."[7] Without being very explicit it was inferred the GOP stood for 100 per cent of parity. Later in the text this original vote-catching sentence was clarified

8

to mean that rural prosperity would be achieved when the free market was allowed to operate without federal interference. This equivocation represented both a difference within Republican ranks over what policy to follow and a desire to make political capital out of an issue no matter how much sophistry was involved.

The Democratic farm plank on the other hand proclaimed its intention to "continue to protect the producers of basic agricultural commodities under the terms of a mandatory support program at not less than ninety per cent of parity."[8] Only the hedging of presidential candidate Adlai Stevenson on the subject of perishable products added an element of uncertainty as to the scope of the Democratic party's commitment.[9]

Even while courting the farm vote with carefully couched promises Dwight D. Eisenhower did feel compelled to make known his aversion to government management of agriculture. At Kasson Ike let rural voters know that "our goal will be sound, farmer-run programs that safeguard agriculture--but do not regiment you, do not put the federal government in charge of your farms."[10] With a disarming smile the genial Eisenhower could simultaneously pledge continued federal assistance while praising the virtues of economic individualism. His credibility was simply not subject to challenge.

Issues seemed less important in the 1952 presidential campaign than did the image of the two candidates. The constantly-heard phrase "I like Ike" reflected Eisenhower's widespread appeal. "Communism, corruption, and Korea," along with the refrain: "It's time for a change," were potent but Ike's personal magnetism contributed enormously to the GOP sweep. Even as Franklin D. Roosevelt overshadowed his opponents no matter what the issues were, so Eisenhower won both the votes and hearts of his fellow countrymen. An unheralded era was about to come into existence and its architect was to be the boy from Abilene who now led the nation as the man of the hour.

Eisenhower made deep inroads in farm states as Illinois, Iowa, Oklahoma, Texas and Colorado. Previously captured by Truman in 1948 they were retaken by Ike with greater pluralities than those achieved by the Democrats. Not only did the General score well in the Midwest but he also drew Virginia, Florida and some border states into the Republican column. With 55.1 per cent of the popular vote and an electoral count of 442 the former military man had proven his vote-getting ability. Going with him to Washington would be a Republican controlled Congress, although with the narrow margin of eight in the House of Representatives and only one in the Senate.

Faced with the difficult task of selecting a cabinet the President-elect had to contend with factions having favorite candidates. One of his major concerns was to placate his defeated rival, Senator Robert A. Taft, because the Ohioan commanded great power in the Senate. People acceptable to the Taft forces would obviously have to be given some cabinet seats. Since the Midwest was Taft territory most political pundits believed the Agriculture Secretary post would be a person picked by the Senator from Ohio. While not disdainful of compromise nor unaware of the need for party unity, Ike had no intention of letting others pick his cabinet for him. He solicited advice but reserved final judgment for himself. His basic criterion was simple enough. The man for the job had to hold views compatible with his outlook on agriculture.

Chapter II
Ike Selects an Agriculture Secretary

Although the Eisenhower wing of the Republican party
was generally considered somewhat progressive, the President
definitely wanted the cooperation of its conservative core.
Through such intermediaries as Senator Everett M. Dirksen of
Illinois and Senator Frank Carlson of Kansas he arranged a
meeting with Senator Robert A. Taft.[1] The two men agreed
upon a set of guiding principles and Ike indicated a willingness to give Taft's followers due representation in his
administration. No specific selections were agreed upon,
however, and no other special commitments were made. Since
he viewed his own election as a personal triumph, the
President-elect felt he should make the final decision as to
who would sit in his cabinet.

Recommendations for Agriculture Secretary came in
from many interested parties. They included heads of farm
organizations, political advisors, and congressional leaders.

Rumors were rampant that Ike might name his own brother Milton to the post. The youngest of the Eisenhowers was quite knowledgeable on farm policy, having served many years in the Department of Agriculture during F.D.R.'s administration, but he had no desire to obtain the post. He did, however, volunteer to aid in the search and his expertise in this area would eventually play a decisive role.[2] Also prominently mentioned for the position by the press were Clifford Hope, Frank Carlson, Fred A. Seaton, and Dan Thornton. All were early Eisenhower supporters and were presumed to have an inside track.

At this stage the name of Ezra Taft Benson was seldom mentioned as a serious contender for this position. First recommended by Ken Stern, President of the American Institute of Cooperation (an enterprise to which some 1,500 farm co-ops were affiliated), Benson was strongly endorsed by those in the cooperative movement. Milton Eisenhower, in doing the footwork to check out likely prospects for the Agriculture Secretary post, quickly learned that he was also highly respected by other farm leaders.[3] Such a prominent figure as William I. Myers, Dean of the College of Agriculture at Cornell University and a leading Republican party farm advisor, was also high on Benson.

Ezra Taft Benson, a high official in the Mormon Church, had superb credentials when it came to the field of

agriculture. He held a Master's degree in Agricultural
Economics; had served in the extension service; was Executive Secretary of the National Council of Farmer Cooperatives (a federation of 4,600 co-ops) from 1939 to 1944;
became Director of the Farm Foundation from 1946 to 1950;
and presently headed the Board of Trustees of the American
Institute of Cooperation. Furthermore Benson had served
on the National Agricultural Advisory Committee during
World War II and had represented the interests of cooperatives in testimony before various congressional committees.
Of notable significance from a political point of view was
the fact that he had been a rabid Taft supporter in 1952.

When Benson's name was announced publicly as a
potential candidate for Secretary of Agriculture, other
important endorsements enhanced his chances for appointment.
No less a political personage than Thomas E. Dewey backed
him because the Utahan had served as an agricultural
advisor to him during the 1948 presidential campaign. A
most crucial source of support came when Allan B. Kline,
President of the American Farm Bureau Federation (with a
membership of one and one-half million farmers), enthusi-
astically backed Ezra Taft Benson.

Although newspaper accounts related that Senator
Taft was personally responsible for Benson's eventual
selection, this was not really the case. The Ohioan told

intimates that he would recommend his colleague Senator Frank Carlson of Kansas. But when Ike picked Benson instead, the nomination was supported wholeheartedly.[4] Ezra Taft Benson, who was incidentally a very distant relative of the Senator, had supported and admired "Mr. Republican" for years. The two men only knew each other casually, but the bond between them was in the form of a mutual compatibility on basic principles of political conservatism.

Because Ezra Taft Benson was a member of the Council of Twelve of The Church of Jesus Christ of Latter-day Saints, his interest was not focused on seeking political appointment but simply in performing his ministerial duties. As an Apostle of the Mormon Church, he was regarded as one of its General Authorities and his responsibilities were commensurate with those of other church officials in other denominations. Since the Mormons do not have a professionally trained or salaried clergy (although a few top officials are given a modest stipend because their official duties are so time-consuming), Benson had always earned his living in the secular world just as any layman might do. In this sense he was a professional agriculturalist and had developed an expertise in this field at all levels over many years. Attainment of a high-level executive position in the co-op movement by 1952 amply testified to his stature as a qualified farm leader.

15

Benson's first inkling that he was seriously being talked about for a cabinet position came when Utah's Senator Arthur V. Watkins (a fellow Mormon) informed him his name was under consideration for Secretary of Agriculture. When news of this leaked out the Utah Farm Bureau immediately added an endorsement of their favorite son. Hardly believing himself really in contention, since his state was not normally considered important agriculturally by members of the congressional farm bloc, Benson paid little attention to the discussions then transpiring in high political circles. In fact when a telephone call came for him from Ike's New York headquarters, Benson could not even be reached. He was busily pursuing his daily church work. Upon returning the call Benson was greeted by Milton Eisenhower who invited him to visit the President-elect at the Hotel Commodore. The surprised Benson did agree to talk with Ike although he still felt nothing serious would develop.

In New York City Benson was met by Milton who immediately took him out to lunch. At this time the President-elect's brother informed the astonished Utahan that he was definitely going to be offered the post of Agriculture Secretary.[5] Still dumbfounded by the sudden turn of events Ezra Taft Benson was ushered in to meet the man who would shortly be both the President and his boss. His initial

16

impression of Dwight D. Eisenhower was highly favorable. Ike's warm greeting and friendly personality made him feel quite at ease and even though he had never before met the General, they talked as if they had been long-time acquaintances.

Soon after the initial amenities were out of the way Ezra Taft Benson took it upon himself to let his host know exactly where he stood relative to basic agricultural policy. Speaking directly to the point he said, "I believe that we need to put our emphasis on research, education, and market development, and I believe, further, that farmers should be permitted to make their own decisions on their own farms with a minimum of government interference." Listening carefully Eisenhower nodded his assent, but before the President-elect could utter any comment, Benson emphasized that his beliefs were "in conflict with the philosophy of the New Deal." He added with finality that his views might also run contrary to those of some Republicans in Congress, "but that's the way I feel."[6]

"Mr. Benson," the President-elect interjected, "you'll never be asked to support a program you don't believe in."[7]

Pleased at this remark Benson quickly raised another point as to the advisability of having a clergyman in the cabinet. "What will be the reaction from other religious groups, from the people generally?"[8]

To this question Eisenhower replied: "Surely you know that we have the great responsibility to restore the confidence of our people in their government--that means we've got to deal with spiritual matters. I feel that your Church connection is a distinct asset." These words too were reassuring to Benson. "We've got a job to do," Ike insisted, "you can't refuse to serve America. I want you on my team, and you can't say no."[9]

This patriotic appeal by Eisenhower made a deep impression upon Ezra Taft Benson. He was hesitant to accept a position so closely connected with politics. Before seeing Eisenhower he had sought the private counsel of the man he most revered and respected: namely President David O. McKay, the prophet, seer, and revelator of The Church of Jesus Christ of Latter-day Saints. The aged and saintly leader of millions of Mormons advised Benson he could truly serve God by entering the cabinet. "Brother Benson," McKay announced, "my mind is clear in the matter and if the opportunity comes, I think that you should accept."[10]

With such assurances Benson reacted positively to Eisenhower's invitation and treated it as if it were a divine call to duty. After prayer and supplication to God for divine guidance, he notified the President-elect of his

willingness to take the post of Agriculture Secretary.
Knowing full well the difficulties facing him, Benson
nevertheless rejoiced that through public service he might
testify to his faith. Uppermost in his mind was the
knowledge that agricultural policy needed to be changed to
fit contemporary conditions.

Chapter III
What Manner of Man

Ezra Taft Benson, the fifteenth Secretary of Agriculture, was born on a farm in Whitney, Idaho on August 4, 1899. Of ruddy complexion this six foot, two hundred twenty pound energetic man looked much younger than his fifty-three years would indicate. With rimless glasses mounted on a cherubic face his appearance was commonplace enough except for the unusual fact that Benson's countenance reflected a striking inner composure. The son of George T. and Sarah Dunkley Benson, Ezra was the eldest of eleven children. No stranger to manual labor the young Benson did a man's job in the field while still a teen-ager. Imbued by his parents with a love of the land and raised according to the strict tenets of the Mormon faith, Ezra acquired a life-long belief in the efficacy of hard work and self-reliance.

Missing some years of elementary school because he was needed on the farm, Ezra nevertheless qualified for the Oneida Stake Academy at Preston, Idaho. At this Mormon prep school, the equivalent of a parochial school, he studied earnestly to prepare for college. Economic circumstances dictated that he alternate academic quarters with his brother Orval so that it would be possible for both to attend the Utah State Agricultural College at Logan. After three years of studying agriculture he transferred to Brigham Young University at Provo. Following several years of toil and forced interruption of his formal education, he finally received his bachelors degree from BYU in 1926.

It was while attending Utah State Agricultural College at Logan that he met his wife-to-be Flora Smith Amussen. They postponed their wedding in order for both to enlist for voluntary tours abroad as Mormon missionaries. Commencing in 1921 Ezra spent two years at Newcastle in England and soon after Flora served a year and a half in Hawaii. It was customary for members of the faith to do this as their personal contribution toward advancing the work of the church. Benson's father had actually sold part of the family farm to finance a missionary endeavor, while Ezra, at age fourteen, supported the rest of the family by keeping a dairy herd of thirty cows on the remaining acreage.

Degree in hand and duty to God's call completed, the eldest of the Benson boys exchanged nuptial vows with Flora Amussen at a solemn service in the Temple at Salt Lake City. It proved to be an ideal marriage: each was devoted to the other and both were devout in adhering to the tenets of their church.

After receiving a postgraduate scholarship to Iowa State College in Ames, Benson took his young bride with him as he began study for an advanced degree. With their meager belongings in an old pickup truck they headed toward the Midwest. Serious and willing to sacrifice, the couple lived frugally on the $70 a month stipend the scholarship paid. Dedicated and resourceful, they gratefully supplemented their daily diet with surplus produce from nearby experimental plots. Flora even found time to take some courses in home economics while her husband worked for his Master's degree. They were young, adventuresome, and accustomed to hard work--so their stay in Iowa was enjoyable and profitable to both.

In 1927 Ezra Taft.Benson was awarded an M.S. in Agricultural Economics. His thesis was entitled: "The Beef Cattle Situation in the Northern Range Area in Its Relation to the Iowa Feeder." The substance of his study dealt with economic relationships between Iowa feeders and the ranchers in Utah, Montana, Wyoming, and Colorado from

whom they bought their cattle. His findings indicated that
Cornbelt feeders buying range stock to fatten for market
would have to take cognizance of competition from new
markets in the West. Instead of habitually furnishing cattle for the Midwest, many stockmen were shipping their
livestock directly to feeders in Los Angeles, Seattle, and
other Pacific Coast cities.

Some ranchers were even beginning to finish off
their own range-fed cattle by feeding them grain before
marketing them. For the Western cattlemen this meant
selling high-grade beef on the hoof at higher prices and
it eliminated the Midwestern farmer as a middleman. "Thus
we can see," Benson concluded from his analysis of the
transition taking place, "that the channels through which
the cattle from the northern range area move on their way
to market is changing."[1] The implication for Iowa stock
feeders was obvious. They too would have to adjust to ever-
changing conditions by becoming more efficient in order to
meet the new competition.

Following his graduation from Iowa State College,
Benson and his wife returned to Idaho where Ezra and his
brother owned the family stead. For a number of years he
farmed for a living until offered a job in 1929 as county
agricultural agent working out of the University of Idaho

Extension Service. At this new vocation his work was of such good quality that he was soon given broader responsibilities as an economist and marketing specialist. By the age of thirty he had established a solid reputation over the entire Cache Valley as a first-rate agriculturist. From 1933 to 1939 he also served as executive secretary of the Idaho Cooperative Council, an organization he helped found. Through his promotional efforts the Idaho potato became known as the best variety in the world.

From 1937 to 1938, to increase his knowledge of agricultural economics, especially the intricacies of modern marketing, Benson took additional graduate work at the University of California at Berkeley. This advanced education paid off for in 1939 he was offered the position of Executive Secretary of the National Council of Farmer Cooperatives at a salary of $25,000 per year. The NCFC, with its headquarters in Washington, D.C., had thousands of affiliates throughout the country. One of the largest and most famous was the California Fruit Growers Exchange whose oranges were sold under the brand name of Sunkist.

While working hard at his new job in the nation's capital Ezra Taft Benson did not neglect the work of his church. Before long he became President of the Washington Stake and under his guidance the Mormon Church in the

District of Columbia, Virginia, and Maryland grew steadily in membership. Right at the time when new career opportunities beckoned--he was offered an important position with another farm organization at four times the salary he was earning--Benson decided to consult on this matter in Salt Lake City with the leading officials of his church. This was in 1943.

All thoughts of monetary or secular success vanished when he was informed that he had been elected to become a member of Council of Twelve.[2] At the age of forty-four he was the youngest Apostle in the Mormon Church and his selection to this high office was an honor beyond his fondest dreams. Being a member of the highest order of Mormon priesthood meant increased responsibilities but it was, as he told a General Conference of the church, a summons "greater than any call that can come from men--that can be offered by the men of the world."[3]

The close ties that bound Ezra Taft Benson to the Mormon Church were both historical and spiritual. His great-grandfather and namesake had likewise been an Apostle in the church. In 1847 this illustrious forebear had been charged by Brigham Young to form a company of faithful at Omaha and lead them to Utah. Thus a Benson took part in the famous Mormon trek which eventually took them from Nauvoo, Illinois to Salt Lake, Utah.[4] Later he was commissioned to start a pioneer colony in Cache Valley and this explains why the Benson family took up residence in Idaho near the Utah border.

The Agriculture Secretary-designate had continued in his forefathers' footsteps by laboring diligently in the vineyard of his church. Progressing through the various stages of Mormon priesthood Benson began his leadership role as President of the Boise, Idaho Stake and devoted much time to promoting youth organizations. To him the Mutual Improvement Association, his own church's agency for developing good character in its youth, and the Boy Scouts, of which he was a member of the National Executive Board, were endeavors worthy of much devotion.

Adhering rigidly to canons of religious morality, Benson neither smoked nor drank alcoholic beverages. Fasting and private meditation were a regular part of his spiritual life. He not only tithed but presented to the church his regular "fast day offering." The latter represented the money saved from abstaining from two meals on the first Sunday of each month. Funds collected from this voluntary contribution went for the care of those in need of material assistance. In this manner cooperative farms and warehouses were maintained by the church for the care of those in distress so that they would not have to live in want.

The Benson family was a close-knit group in 1952. Composed of six children of which the oldest two were boys, Reed at twenty-four was an Air Force Chaplain and Mark at twenty-three was a student at Stanford University. The four daughters included Barbara at eighteen, Beverly at fifteen, Bonnie at twelve, and little Flora Beth at eight years of age. Typical of their life styles, the Bensons had regular family nights at which time they held devotions at home. Their problems were discussed and solved as a group. They also had designated fun nights at which time they gathered around the piano and held songfests, danced together, and played games.

Mrs. Benson seemed perpetually young as she both led and joined in the festivities. Her light brown hair and green eyes were striking when paired up with a radiant personality. So that each child would learn to accept responsibility, from youth on up, she delegated certain household chores to each one. Typed and posted weekly, duties might range from cutting grass for the older boys to dusting for the bigger girls. Even tiny Flora Beth was given the task of cleaning the soap dishes in the bathroom. In this manner every child was taught to make a positive contribution to the happiness and welfare of the entire family.

Benson's personal life was impeccable and one highly
exemplary of the highest moral rectitude. Conscientious and
uncompromising when it came to doing what he believed was
right, Ezra Taft Benson always strove to be honest and to do
his job to the best of his ability. Upon accepting
Eisenhower's invitation to join the cabinet, he forthrightly
told the President-elect, "Consistent with the principles
that have guided my life, I will do my best, God being my
helper."[5]

It came naturally to Benson not even to consider his
appointment to public office fully consummated until he
received a blessing by an official of his church. At a
church conference held in Washington D.C., Elder Harold
B. Lee spoke the following words: "When a man is ordained
to the apostleship of this Church, that is not just a job,
but is a power from Almighty God, and that power will remain
in him so long as he knows that down in his soul there is
a fire of testimony and a determination to serve God at all
hazard and keep His commandments, and then there will be
given inspiration and revelation."[6]

During the course of the next eight years Ezra Taft
Benson was sustained by an inner faith rare in the realm of
public officialdom. His instincts were to be candid and
truthful, and he was not inclined to play politics for the
sake of expediency. He deeply believed his commitment to

serve his country could only be fulfilled by making his actions accountable to God. In adhering to such high principles he eschewed many of the practices common among professional politicians. He could not engage in the artifices that were stock in trade for those holding elective office. Benson could not bring himself to deliberately flatter voters or conceal his views amid meaningless verbiage. Always he presumed that what was good for the nation had priority over what was good for special interests. Not one to shirk his duty Ezra Taft Benson felt the job had sought him, not the reverse. After being in office only a short while he told a student group at Brigham Young University: "I didn't want to be Secretary of Agriculture . . . because I know something of the crossfires, the pressures, the problems, the difficulties. . . . I've always feared, in a way, getting into politics."[7]

Another concern, in and above the fact that Benson was a political anomaly, related directly to his fears that as a Mormon clergyman he might be the victim of prejudice and ignorance. He recalled that before Senator Reed Smoot was allowed to take his duly elected seat he was deliberately humiliated during weeks of grueling hearings. Others had subsequently gone to Washington as elected officials but he would be the first of his faith to hold a top cabinet post. His apprehension proved unfounded. His religious affiliation never became an issue and subsequently Mormons have served increasingly in high government positions.[8]

As with a Christian or Jew who is guided by the precepts of his religion, a political figure guided by spiritual values reflects his faith in both his political thought and actions. Among the examples of history one immediately thinks of William Jennings Bryan. He considered himself a defender of the faith and a spokesman for the common man. Ezra Taft Benson's political philosophy reflected aspects of his religious thought as well as that of the Western tradition he so admired. Central to his mode of thought was the belief that man was a free moral agent responsible to his Maker for his acts. It was his conviction that freedom, both personal and economic, was an inalienable and God-given right. Personal accountability for the moral or material consequences of freely arrived at decisions were a corollary to liberty. Any form of totalitarianism was repugnant to Benson because it abridged freedom.

The Mormons of old had created a Zion out of a desert wilderness.[9] In so doing they relied only upon strength derived from their faith and a determination to labor diligently to build a home for themselves. They were self-reliant while being their neighbor's keeper; they were rugged individualists while possessing a strong sense of community. The quick and the dead were united in spirit and the congregation on earth was conjoined by solid fellowship and a strong social ethic. This heritage, tinged with agrarianism, helped mold Ezra Taft Benson's outlook.

In dedicating a building in 1950 for the Daughters of Utah Pioneers, erected in Salt Lake City, Benson saw the saga of 1847 as one worthy of emulation. Seeking the Promised Land of religious freedom their forebears had sacrificed everything for liberty. "They believed in free agency," Benson maintained, "that freedom is a God-given inalienable right, that freedom is an eternal principle, that only free men can be happy."[10] On an earlier occasion, while addressing a Semi-Annual Conference of his church, Benson counseled against the temptation to "run to a paternalistic government for help." He further admonished, "Let us Latter-day Saints stand on our feet" since the "principles of self-help are economically, socially, and spiritually sound."[11]

Imbued with the heritage of Utah's pioneers and the agrarian way of life from which he came, Benson was sure farm life propagated virtues worthy of perpetuation. Speaking to the Dairyman's League in 1950 at their annual meeting in Syracuse, he cautioned them against allowing the federal government to encroach upon their freedom of decision making. "I declare without fear of contradiction,"

31

asserted Benson, "that our rural people are today the strongest bulwark we have against all that is aimed, not only at weakening, but at the very destruction of our American way of life."[12]

In his judgment collective action by farmers was best attained via the cooperative movement. In this manner monetary advantages were gained but not at the expense of personal freedom. He emphasized this while addressing the American Institute of Cooperation at Madison, Wisconsin in 1949. Benson contended: "These associations, brought about through cooperatives, can build and protect the morale of farmers and their families. . . . Through applications of democratic principles, they can through their cooperation be made to raise their sights economically, socially, and spiritually."[13] Expanding this theme the next year when he spoke to the same group at Logan, Utah, Ezra Taft Benson remonstrated even more strongly: "Let cooperatives and every other organization and institution teach the youth of America the world does not owe them a living. Nobody owes them anything for crops they don't grow. . . ." Emphasizing the moral danger involved in losing their individual freedom to make economic decisions, he warned that a "planned and subsidized economy weakens initiative, discourages industry, destroys character, and demoralizes the people."[14]

It was evident to Benson his first task in Washington would be to instigate needed reforms in agricultural policy. What was not so apparent to him was how resistant to change were members of the Congress with which he would have to work. His ordeal was beyond anything he would have imagined and there would be no surcease for eight years.

Chapter IV
Resistance to Reform

While making arrangements to purchase a home in
Washington, D.C., finally settling for a roomy red brick
house on the outskirts of Rock Creek Park, Ezra Taft Benson
was summoned to a preinaugural convocation of the cabinet
in New York City. Approaching Eisenhower prior to the
formal opening of the session, Benson suggested the appro-
priateness of a prayer to ask the blessing of the Almighty
on the endeavors of this gathering.

When the time came for the assemblage to be seated
for their luncheon meeting at the Hotel Commodore, the
President-elect graciously called upon his future Agriculture Secretary to offer the invocation. Benson's devotional
remarks included the following thanksgiving and supplication:

> We are deeply grateful for this glorious land
> in which we live. We know it is a land choice
> above all others--the greatest nation under

Heaven. . . . We thank Thee for liberty--
for our free agency, our way of life, and
our free institutions.

We thank Thee for the glorious Constitution of this land which has been established by noble men who Thou didst raise up
for this very purpose. . . . Help us ever,
we pray Thee, to be true and faithful to
these great and guiding principles.[1]

Ezra Taft Benson asked furthermore that each subsequent Friday cabinet meeting be opened with a petition for
divine guidance. The President, after consulting with the
others, graciously assented to a moment of silent prayer at
the start of each session.[2] For eight years that practice
was followed. The Secretary of Agriculture also made it a
habit of beginning his own staff meetings with an oral
prayer. Beseeching the Lord for spiritual strength was as
necessary for him as eating or sleeping.

Heads of the three big farm organizations praised
Ike's selection of Benson as Secretary of Agriculture.
Allan Kline of the AFBF called it a "top-notch appointment."[3]
Master of the National Grange Herschel Newsom asserted,
"President Eisenhower is to be commended on his choice."[4]
Even James G. Patton, President of the National Farmers

Union and soon to be a bitter foe, had these kind words:
"I have known Ezra Taft Benson since 1938, and while we have
disagreed on some matters I have found him both honest and
magnanimous. He will hold the balance level between farm
organizations, which is all we ask. . . . All in all, I
think this is one of the best of Mr. Eisenhower's cabinet
appointments, one which promises well."[5]

Feelings in the Senate among a few farm bloc members
were not so generous at the outset. Two Senators in particular, Milton R. Young (R.-N.D.) and Edward J. Thye (R-
Minn.) did not even attempt to disguise their disappointment
over his selection. Both felt Benson held political beliefs
incompatible to their own. When the Secretary-designate
appeared before a Senate committee seeking confirmation,
Senator Young tried hard to pry from Benson some specific
commitment relative to farm policy. After quoting what Ike
had said at Kasson, Minnesota, Young asked the pointed
question, "Do you agree with his policy?"[6] Answering promptly, Benson said, "Yes, I think the General and I are in general agreement, Senator, on this matter."[7]

Pressing on, Senator Young queried: "Senator Russell
and I on Friday of this week--and I think other Senators may
wish to join us--have a bill which is to be introduced.
This bill would extend 90 per cent price supports for basics
for three additional years. Would you care to comment on

this?"[8] "I would prefer not to, Senator."[9] Benson in no way wanted to give the slightest assent to such a proposition.

Not satisfied Senator Young responded: "You would agree, though, if General Eisenhower himself said that the party is for sustaining 90 per cent supports, and in the absence of any speeches supporting the flexible idea of supports, that his position would be for 90 per cent supports?"[10]

Dodging the trap set by his interlocutor, one which might have pledged him to a policy with which he disagreed, Benson answered, "I understand he is committed for 90 per cent support for the next two years at least."[11]

The North Dakota Senator seemed perturbed when he could not get Benson to endorse a policy of permanent 90 per cent parity. Young replied, "I wish that I could get a more clear-cut statement as to your position on these matters. It might well affect my vote in the Senate."[12] As it turned out he did not vote against Benson's eventual confirmation but instead absented himself when the roll call was taken.[13]

Upon being confirmed Ezra Taft Benson returned to his private office in the massive Department of Agriculture building and began to make plans for a major reorganization within his bureaucratic domain. To make sure the some 8,000 employees were on their toes at all times the new Secretary issued a memorandum that read in part: "As public servants, we must recognize the duty and responsibility we have to serve the public efficiently and well. The people of this country have a right to expect that everyone of us will give a full day's work for a full day's pay."[14]

Ezra Taft Benson's convictions were guided by specific articles of faith and it seemed imperative to him that he enunciate publicly the canons of his political philosophy. Putting down in explicit and clear language what amounted to a proclamation of principles, the Secretary issued for public consumption a "General Statement on Agricultural Policy." The first principle enunciated set forth the following premise: "The supreme test of any government policy, agricultural or other, should be 'How will it affect the character, morale, and well-being of our people?'"[15]

Following this assertion on the need for agricultural policy to bolster moral qualities in farmers, Benson spelled out the fundamental tenets of his conservative political creed. Warned against were the dangers of federal concentration of powers stemming from big government and the fallacy of wanting Washington to do for individuals what they should do for themselves. This meant specifically that farmers were to regard price supports as devices for the general protection and stabilization of the commodity market, and not as personal relief, private subsidies, or undesirable stimulants for producing surpluses.

This 1200-word statement also reflected some aspects of Benson's religious beliefs. It went on to declare: "Freedom is a God-given, eternal principle vouchsafed to us under the Constitution. It must be continually guarded as something more precious than life itself."[16] Any infringement upon personal liberty, in Benson's judgment, would in the long run stifle initiative, destroy character, and demoralize the people.

Believing it was his duty to speak rationally and truthfully about the problems confronting agriculture and the consequent need for basic reforms, Benson elaborated upon his views shortly thereafter. He did so in his first public speech as Agriculture Secretary to the Central Livestock Association meeting in St. Paul, Minnesota. The cattle raisers present were anxious to hear what the Secretary planned to do about falling beef prices. Not one to engage in political panegyrics or use the rhetoric of flattery to a special interest group, Benson told his audience truthfully they should produce meat for the free market and not seek government bounty. He reasoned that price supports were neither intended to be a largesse nor a device for the promotion of surpluses. They were, he asserted, devised both as an insurance against disaster and to help stabilize food supplies--that was all. With undaunted firmness Benson announced candidly he would not be stampeded into any unwise action by recent price declines.[17]

Democrats quickly fell upon Benson's remarks at St. Paul to voice partisan criticism. Senator John Sparkman of Alabama claimed the speech constituted a repudiation of all price support programs while Minnesota Representative Eugene McCarthy jibed sarcastically, "Benson is like a man standing on the bank of the river telling a drowning man that all he needs to do is to take a deep breath of air."[18]

Not a few Midwest Republicans were also displeased over Benson's plain pronouncement. Forwarding his complaint to Sherman Adams, Senator Frank Carlson of Kansas thought the St. Paul speech constituted a political blunder and bemoaned the fact that the Secretary had needlessly shaken the confidence of farmers. Only a reassuring statement by the President, he contended, could undo some of the political damage.[19] The only comment coming from the White House was a mild scolding from Ike. The President informed Benson, "I believe every word you said at St. Paul . . . , but I'm not sure you should have said it quite so soon."[20]

In order to reassess the value of all farm programs then in existence, Benson sought the assistance of specially appointed study groups and of an interim fourteen-man

National Agricultural Advisory Commission. The latter had
been established to fulfill a promise made in the Republican
farm platform. This nonpartisan body was to investigate the
farm policy and make specific legislative recommendations.
In time the NAAC was to be made a permanent organization
for the purpose of initiating needed changes in established
farm programs and originating new plans for contemporary
rural needs. More will be said of this group and its
activities.

For the first time in twenty years the GOP controlled
the Executive and Legislative branches of the government.
The desire among Republicans to throw the rascals out, as it
were, was tremendous. Hungry for patronage, avaricious
Senators looked greedily at the huge Department of Agriculture. But Ezra Taft Benson was both unaware of senatorial
prerogatives and unmindful of partisan demands. His only
concern was merit and departmental needs, so he began to
replace certain USDA employees without consulting anyone
about patronage. Upon learning about what he considered an
unacceptable practice South Dakota's Karl Mundt wasted no
time informing General Wilton B. Persons, Deputy Assistant
to the President, that there were at least a half dozen
Senators ready to lash out against Benson just as Senator
Young of North Dakota had done. Senator Mundt complained
bitterly that new appointments for the Production and

Marketing Administration were being made without consulting GOP Senators or state Republican organizations. Mundt was highly irritated at what he termed the "lack of political savvy"[21] displayed by Benson.

Iowa's Bourke B. Hickenlooper joined the chorus of criticism but absolved Benson of personal blame. Senator Hickenlooper felt strongly that PMA needed a thorough house cleaning since the Democrats had made it "one of the most vicious, partisan political groups"[22] within the Department of Agriculture. The Iowan was of the opinion Benson's political inexperience, and possibly bad advice from disloyal subordinates, had caused the confusion in selection of certain PMA state committees.

News of this intra-party discontent over patronage quickly reached the ears of Leonard Hall, Chairman of the Republican National Committee. He took speedy steps to alter the procedure relating to selection of personnel for the Production and Marketing Administration. In a special meeting in which he, Representative Hope, and Senator Aiken sat down with Benson, they worked out (and wrote out) a "Procedure Used in Selecting State PMA Committee Members."[23] This was the first of many instances where Benson would feel hindered, because of strictly political considerations, in his administration of the Department of Agriculture.

Working closely with Gabriel Hauge, the Chief Executive's Economic Advisor, Leonard Hall helped draft the text of a farm speech he wanted the President to deliver. It stressed the value of federal intervention in agriculture and reassured farmers in soothing words that the new administration was genuinely concerned about their economic welfare. Eisenhower rebuffed the two men's efforts by tossing the manuscript on his desk with the comment: "I don't believe for a minute the farmer wants the government to be his boss."[24]

Benson's initiation to political crossfire was not yet over. In another incident a Republican Congressman criticized him for the manner in which emergency relief for a drought situation was handled. Representative Frank Chelf, Chairman of the House Judiciary Committee, had requested that eleven counties in his Kentucky district be declared eligible for federal assistance. When only five were so listed by the Department of Agriculture, because they were the only ones to qualify, he sent a stinging telegram to Benson. Venting his anger, his message read in part: "While the country literally burns, you fiddle and piddle and talk about a farm program."[25] His blistering personal attack ended with a demand for the Secretary's resignation.

Fuming, Frank Chelf also wired the President telling him: "Mr. President, if . . . [Benson] remains in your cabinet he will do more harm to undermine the confidence of the farmers in your administration than anything that could happen."[26]

Ike did not like critical communications of this type and invariably passed them on to Sherman Adams for some type of reply. It was the task of the former Governor of New Hampshire, among other things, to "keep troublemakers off Eisenhower's back."[27] With skill and sagacity born of political experience Ike's top aide strove to placate complainants and preserve harmony within the administration. In an effort to smooth things out, Adams explained to the irate Kentuckian that "looking dispassionately at what Secretary Benson has accomplished, the President feels that he has done a good job."[28] Ike't top aide gently chided the Congressman for joining in the hue and cry for Benson's scalp, telling him this outcry was inspired by groups whose political philosophy was quite different from that of the Kentuckian.

Both Sherman Adams and his fellow presidential assistant General "Jerry" Persons found themselves frequently having to defend the Agriculture Secretary. Persons felt Benson's public utterances simply had to be "couched in more acceptable terms."[29] In Adams' judgment the Secretary of

Agriculture was so dedicated to basic principles that he ignored practical political considerations. Ironically Ike admired this very trait while the former New Hampshire governor regarded Benson's passion for integrity as a political liability. After serving Eisenhower for seven years the New Englander concluded, "it was this spiritual force of character that inspired the President to come to . . . [Benson's] defense time after time."[30]

From his vantage point Sherman Adams felt the Agriculture Secretary was far too inconsiderate of the political needs of rural representatives and their constituents. Experienced politicians were always prone to speak of price supports as something farmers deserved and not as handouts or wasteful federal subsidies. That was the reason the acreage allotment and production control apparatus was so complex. It provided financial assistance to farmers without making them appear to be mere recipients of government bounty. Certainly few Congressmen really thought of their constituents as being on government relief and yet Benson seemingly offended them by inferring as much when he told them to stop buying elections by inviting rural voters to sup at the public trough. By being such an outspoken critic of such well-established political practices the Secretary made it difficult for himself when he faced Congress with legislative proposals. His reforms, despite their merit,

were met with hostility and suspicion. Dwight D. Eisenhower
endorsed the ideas of the Agriculture Secretary and backed
him to the hilt, but he did not always understand why his
cabinet appointee tended to antagonize fellow Republicans.
The only criticism Ike ever made publicly about Benson was
that written in his memoirs where he commented that once the
Secretary's conclusions were formed, they "were earnestly
held and argued, though not always with the maximum of
tact."[31]

Taking advantage of a welcomed opportunity to visit
Salt Lake City, Ezra Taft Benson addressed the 123rd
General Conference of his church. Standing amidst the
splendor of the Tabernacle brought back fond memories. Un-
ashamedly he confessed: "I know, my brethren and sisters,
that the sweetest work in all the world is the work in which
we are engaged in helping to save and exalt the souls of the
children of men."[32]

Referring to the already onerous burdens of political office, Benson thanked his fellow Saints for their
sustaining prayers. He claimed that he and his colleagues
in the Department of Agriculture were officials who loved
America and believed that the Constitution embodied principles worthy of preservation. With pride he described his
top aides as "men of faith, men who are willing to join
with me weekly in prayer at our staff meetings, men who love

46

our free institutions, [and] men who want to keep America strong. . . ."[33]

Upper echelon members in the Department of Agriculture were indeed proficient in their professions. As a group they were dedicated men who tended to be active in church work. Collectively they inclined toward a conservative brand of economics and only a few had any practical experience in politics.

True D. Morse was chosen personally by Benson to be Under Secretary. Morse had once farmed for a living after graduating from the University of Missouri but eventually got into the business aspect of agriculture as the president of the Doane Agricultural Service. In 1948 he had served as chairman of the National Farm Committee for Dewey and Warren.

For the position of Assistant Secretary of Agriculture, Benson selected J. Earl Coke. The latter was a graduate from the University of California and had many years of experience as director of that state's Agricultural Extension Service.

As his own Special Assistant Benson chose a Purdue University Professor of Agricultural Economics by the name of Don Paarlberg. In 1957 Paarlberg would become an Assistant Secretary and in 1958 he was chosen by Ike to be one of his personal economic advisors. This Purdue

47

economist had been recommended to Benson by William I. Myers, Dean of the College of Agriculture at Cornell University, as an outstanding agricultural economist. It was interesting to note that when Benson interviewed Paarlberg the Secretary asked only three questions. He wanted to know if Paarlberg liked his job at Purdue, if he was happily married, and was he active in church affairs.[34] Choosing this Hoosier was a stroke of luck, since he was not only able and imaginative but possessed a pragmatic outlook which helped to provide Benson with workable ideas. Paarlberg's service as secretary to the National Agricultural Advisory Commission was invaluable and put him in a key position to influence the formulation of all policy matters.

Others included in the coterie of those close to Benson included William I. Myers who became Chairman of the National Agricultural Advisory Commission; Earl L. Butz, also a Professor of Agricultural Economics at Purdue University, designated Assistant Secretary in 1954; and John H. Davis, a product of Iowa State College who was appointed President of the Commodity Credit Corporation. Davis had been Benson's handpicked successor as Executive Secretary of the National Council of Farmer Cooperatives. By 1953 he also held the post of Executive Vice-President of the National Wool Marketing Corporation. Eventually Davis would be made Director of Commodity Marketing and Adjustment and then Assistant Secretary.

Dr. Earl L. Butz served in the Eisenhower administration only three years. Along with his duties as Assistant Secretary he was a member of the Commodity Credit Corporation board and in 1955 headed the U.S. delegation to the International Food and Agriculture Organization based in Rome. In 1957 he returned to Purdue University where he became Dean of the College of Agriculture. In 1968 he sought the GOP nomination for governor and was defeated in the primaries. That same year he was named Vice-President for Special Projects (Purdue Research Foundation) and Dean for Continuing Education. Nonacademic affiliations included directorships related to such companies as Ralston-Purina, International Mines and Minerals, J. I. Case, and Stokely-Van Camp. In 1971 President Richard M. Nixon appointed Earl Butz to succeed Clifford M. Hardin as Secretary of Agriculture.[35] In this capacity Butz continued to carry out many of the policies started by Ezra Taft Benson.[36]

Still other top-level appointees included Clarence M. Ferguson, Director of Ohio Extension Service, to be administrator of the National Extension Service (ultimately becoming Assistant Secretary) and Romeo E. Short, a former president of the Arkansas Farm Bureau and one of the founders of the Arkansas Rice Growers' Cooperative

Association, who was appointed Assistant Secretary of Agriculture in mid-July of 1953. While Dr. Karl A. Butler helped out in the transition period he did not desire a permanent post in the USDA.

The only suggestion to come from the White House regarding appointments related to the desirability of bringing blacks into government service. In accordance with the President's wishes, Benson informed Eisenhower: "Some time ago you expressed the hope that we might appoint at least one Negro in some position of leadership in the Department. We have appointed Mr. John W. Mitchell to our staff to act as leader for Negro extension work. . . ."[37]

Just prior to taking office Ezra Taft Benson had conferred with ex-President Herbert C. Hoover at the latter's Waldorf Tower residence in New York City. It was Benson's intention, immediately after assuming his duties as Agriculture Secretary, to initiate a long overdue reorganization of the USDA along the lines once recommended by the Hoover Commission Report. When word leaked out of his plans, even before specifics had been worked out, old bureau chiefs and farm bloc allies in Congress (particularly Democrats) complained that the new Secretary intended to carry out a purge. In order to get men who would agree with his policies and loyally implement them, Benson had to replace certain key personnel. Thus old-time New Dealer

M. L. Wilson lost his job as Extension Director and Claude R. Wickard was replaced as head of the Rural Electrification Administration.[38]

Testifying before the Senate Committee on Government Operations, on May 19, 1953, Benson defended his reorganization plan by declaring: "A principal purpose of Reorganization Plan No. 2 now before you is to enable us to make reasonable changes, from time to time, within the several agencies, including areas heretofore closed to us, by transfers of certain functions from one agency to another, by consolidation or merger of agency units where practicable and by any other means which will promote economy, eliminate duplication, and increase efficiency. . . ."[39]

Of major importance to Benson was the fact that he had to alter the ideological temper of his department and acquire some measure of direction over its vast operations. Cases in point were the Bureau of Agricultural Economics and the Production and Marketing Administration. Both had been largely staffed for the past twenty years by Democrats. To effectively control these New Deal oriented bureaus he needed to reduce their autonomy.

Such restructuring called for the consolidation of all departmental agencies into four main service groups: (1) Federal-State Relations; (2) Marketing and Foreign Agriculture; (3) Agricultural Stabilization; and

(4) Agricultural Credit. Two additional Assistant Secretaries and one Administrative Assistant Secretary were to be added. After Congress approved the plan, John H. Davis and Romeo E. Short were named Assistant Secretaries and Richard D. Aplin became the first Administrative Assistant Secretary.

Part of the refashioning of USDA administrative offices involved abolition of the Regional Soil Conservation Service. Its duties were to be absorbed by State Conservationists. The Bureau of Agricultural Economics was eliminated entirely as an independent agency and its functions transferred to Agricultural Research Service and to the new Agricultural Marketing Service. Also state and county committeemen of the Production and Marketing Administration were taken off regular salaries and placed on a "when-actually-employed" basis.[40] The whole thrust of the reorganization plan was to reorient the USDA away from the acreage allotment-production control policy and prepare the way for more emphasis upon marketing, expansion of overseas outlets, and increased utilization research.

Since the Republican platform had endorsed the idea of making the Farm Credit Administration an independent body, with Benson concurring, he proceeded on his own to have a bill drawn up to implement this pledge. Without consulting the White House staff, it was sent to the House

Committee on Agriculture. To further complicate matters, farm organization leaders had presented their own version of a measure to the Senate Committee on Forestry and Agriculture. Both bills went much further than White House officials deemed wise, especially since they weakened Executive control over the FCA. Bernard M. Shanley, Special Counsel to the President, suggested to Sherman Adams that True Morse be invited out to lunch informally at which time they could "go over the whole matter of the correct relationship of the Department with the Budget and White House staff."[41]

The mixup on FCA bills was ultimately settled when Shanley and other White House aides met with Benson, Senator Aiken, and Budget Director Joseph M. Dodge. It was then agreed upon that Secretary Benson would alter the USDA bill in order to protect Executive authority.[42] This was imperative since federal funds were involved and the Budget Bureau reserved the right to check on agencies dispensing government money. On August 6, 1953 the Farm Credit Act was passed and on December 4 the FCA became an independent agency of the Executive branch.

Few changes are ever made in government without someone protesting. Congressman Lee Metcalf (D-Mont.) complained directly to the President about the abolition of regional soil conservation offices. He told Eisenhower such an act would "turn back the clock to the days when the states tried in 48 different ways to go it alone in soil conservation."[43]

Another criticism of Benson's action was made when Senator Hugh Butler (R-Nebr.) grumbled to White House aides that supporters of REA had been embarrassed by Claude Wickard's sudden ouster. Whereas Butler agreed that F.D.R.'s former Agriculture Secretary should have been removed, he thought it was unwise to have done so without simultaneously naming a permanent successor. Debate about the legality of an interim head ended when Ancher Nelson was given the post.[44]

While reorganization was taking place Benson thought it his duty to prepare public opinion for future reforms. Farmers needed to know why their industry was in economic trouble. The Secretary felt it necessary to explain honestly why a rigid parity system was creating enormous difficulties. It was a matter of conscience to him that farmers be educated as to where their real interests lay. To do this Benson seldom missed an opportunity to address farm groups in order to explain to them why so many problems existed in the realm of agriculture.

Taking advantage of an invitation from the National Farm Ranch Congress of the Denver Chamber of Commerce, the Secretary explained that falling farm prices were due to the

policies of the previous administration. It was President
Truman who had encouraged high production and then permitted
markets, both domestic and foreign, to decline.

Continuing his portrayal of why existing conditions
were poor, Benson pointed to the huge holdings of the Commodity Credit Corporation. The CCC, as of the end of March,
held over a billion dollars' worth of stored commodities.
In addition to these government acquired stocks, he pointed
out, three billion dollars' worth of farm products were
currently under loan. Much of the latter he noted pessi-
mistically would eventually revert to the CCC. Accretion
of such surpluses drove down prices, Benson argued, and
therefore steps should be taken to eliminate them as a depressing factor. It was now necessary for every farmer to
adjust his output to market realities. He remonstrated:
"Our task is to see that he has these opportunities in an
atmosphere of freedom, with a minimum of government regulation and control."[45]

The economic message the Secretary of Agriculture
wanted to get over to farmers had great merit. Because of
the inflexible price support mechanism, there was little
doubt some farmers were actually raising unmarketable
varieties of wheat and cotton. With consumer preferences
in constant flux, it was certainly unreasonable to encourage
the output of undesirable products only to have the government

purchase them. The unfortunate aspect of farm policy, as it had been implemented previously, was that it encouraged small and inefficient (or even marginal) farmers to cling to their land as a source of income.

Dirt farmers who spent many long hours in the field earning a livelihood did not want to hear cold economic facts which contradicted their desires. They wanted government action to help them before they went broke. They simply voted for the party promising them the most assistance even though their farms were economically unsuited for modern circumstances. One Indiana farmer typical of this genre wrote the Agriculture Secretary, "As I have been a republican [sic] all my life, with two grandfathers who were Civil War vets and both Lincoln supporters untill [sic] now I feel myself slipping as we are headed for a Period [sic] equal to 1932 of which I well remember."[46]

Congressmen invariably intervened to secure special privileges for farmers of this type. Requests were made to allow them to exceed acreage allotments or to be exempt from various compliance regulations. This sort of special exemption tended to jeopardize the programs in their entirety but such practices were justified on the basis of political expediency. When Benson refused to risk ruining the effectiveness of various programs and to realistically advise small farmers of their predicament, he was accused of being opposed to the family farm. Benson found it extremely difficult to cope with the problem of the inefficient producer. For instance, a Minnesota farm wife, the mother of nine children, wrote directly to the President with her complaint. She pleaded for federal help. Her husband worked from fourteen to sixteen hours a day just to eke out a living. They had struggled for sixteen years to keep their 160 acre farm. "Is this inefficiency," she wrote sarcastically. "Shall we be the victims of having to loose [sic] our hard earned, hard worked place by clamping down on the farmer in order to level things off?"[47]

Close friend William I. Myers, who met with Benson often as head of the National Agricultural Advisory Commission, tactfully suggested the Agriculture Secretary place more public stress on his "desire to help promote the welfare of agriculture and the nation."[48] After hearing the same recommendation from other close acquaintances, Benson notified Don Paarlberg, who often helped him write speeches, that "many of our friends feel that we have talked enough about self-sufficiency and freedom, and that now is a good time to shift emphasis to safeguarding the farmers' interest and making farm policy effective in bringing the support and help which farmers need today and in the future."[49]

The dilemma confronting Benson resembled that of small manufacturers who plead for tariff protection when in

point of fact they are too inefficient to exist. Also the
small plant desires survival even when overall economic
needs dictate a policy favorable to the national economy.
So it was that Ezra Taft Benson, while favoring the retention of as many family farms as possible, had to play the
role of the hard-hearted administrator seeking the welfare
of all of agriculture. Political rhetoric might be com-
forting to small farmers, but their plight was one over
which he had no control. Agriculture had become big business with heavy investments and no amount of nostalgic day-
dreaming would reverse that trend. He was fully aware of
this economic fact when he began to formulate an agricultural policy commensurate with the needs of the 1950's.

Chapter V

Formulation of a New Farm Program

In mid-July of 1953 Ezra Taft Benson notified both
Senator George A. Aiken and Representative Clifford Hope,
each chairman of their respective agricultural committees,
that the USDA was engaged in a massive review of all aspects
of farm policy. Involved was a series of studies undertaken by special task forces, farm organizations, and the
interim National Agricultural Advisory Commission. Recommendations were being requested from a wide variety of
sources both from within and without his department. "In
accordance with well established tradition," he claimed re-
assuringly, "this review has been bipartisan in nature [and]
it has been undertaken without a preconception of what it
should reveal."[1]

Both Aiken and Hope were extremely zealous of congressional prerogatives and resented any suggestion of any
substantial consultation beyond the confines of Congress.

It was Aiken's personal opinion that the new Agriculture Secretary should have met exclusively with members of Congress to work out a compromise farm program suitable to all farm bloc factions. The Vermont Senator, by the way, had long championed more flexibility in price supports.[2] Representative Hope, on the other hand, staunchly supported the principle of 90 per cent of parity, but might have been approachable in terms of moderate reforms if certain concessions would have been granted. Hope represented the entrenched agricultural establishment which resisted any major departure from the 90 per cent parity formula.

Congressional fear over what Benson would propose led to a plethora of unfounded rumors that his dismissal was imminent. In June, for instance, Fred Seaton (Deputy Assistant to the President) was forced to inform Eisenhower, "Because of Drew Pearson's Merry Go Round column which erroneously charged I had advised you that Mr. Benson was a political liability, I would deeply appreciate your correction of the mis-statement."[3] Not only did Ike reassure his Agricultural Secretary that this gossip was untrue but he also utilized the occasion to prod members of his party to speak up and defend Benson. When certain cooperative Republicans issued press statements praising Benson, the President in turn sent them each personal notes of thanks for their assistance. In one such commendatory letter to Arthur V.

Watkins, Ike told the Utah Senator: "Benson is en route to becoming one of the nation's great Secretaries of Agriculture. Staunch support like yours is very heartening, I know to him and also to me."[4]

When columnist George Sokolsky made the unwarranted claim that Clifford Hope was leading the dump Benson movement, the Kansan vigorously denied it.[5] Thinking he had ended this pernicious gossip, Hope was utterly amazed when informed by presidential advisor Gabriel Hauge that Senator Wallace F. Bennett of Utah had publicly charged the Congressman from Kansas with seeking to engineer Benson's overthrow. "I don't know whether you have seen this speech," wrote Hauge sympathetically, "but I want you to know that I found his comments about you most implausible and I reject them completely."[6]

Hope did disagree with the Secretary of Agriculture, but had refused to join other Midwestern Republicans in their public criticisms of Benson. He was, therefore, astounded by the allegations made by Senator Bennett. Speaking before the Rotary Club of Salt Lake City, the Utah Senator had intimated that Hope's opposition to Benson was attributable to the fact that: "He wasn't selected. . . . Now he demands Ezra Benson's resignation, and his name is again being mentioned as Ezra Benson's successor. I think the implications there are obvious."[7]

Not wanting this in-fighting to continue, Clifford Hope notified Hauge of his intention to refute the allegation.[8] Writing directly to Senator Bennett the Kansas Congressman informed his Republican colleague: "You indicate that I have been attacking Secretary Benson," asserted Hope. "Nothing could be farther from the truth. . . . On the contrary I have been one of his strongest defenders."[9]

The junior Senator from Utah accepted this explanation. And for a time the politics of agriculture calmed down. Any movement, whether overt or covert, to build a backfire under the new Secretary had failed. Congressman Hope subsequently issued numerous press releases supporting Benson's efforts to review agricultural policy.[11]

On July 20, 1953 the President further strengthened Benson's hand by issuing Executive Order No. 10472 which established the permanent National Agricultural Advisory Commission. The eighteen-man commission was ostensibly balanced between Democrats and Republicans, and was to have regional representation from all rural areas in the nation. William I. Myers was designated chairman and Don Paarlberg served as its full-time secretary. Its specific function was to "review the policies and administration of farm programs within jurisdiction of the Department of Agriculture . . . and advise the Secretary of Agriculture in regard thereto."[12]

This advisory group was representative of a variety of commodity groups and various aspects of the agricultural industry. Members were chosen from the Farm Bureau, agricultural colleges, co-ops, and organizations generally friendly to the administration. This advisory commission was viewed by the more militant farm organizations with a jaundiced eye. These included the National Farmers Union and the National Farm Organization (which came into existence in 1955). Although Congress did not always accept its recommendations, the NAAC performed a useful function. It served well as a sounding board to test out new ideas. True D. Morse probably best summed up USDA feelings about the NAAC when he told the Secretary its "major contribution" would lie in "the prestige which this advisory group gives to back up and work on programs which have had their consideration."[13]

Whereas there was a general consensus among the members of the NAAC, occasionally a voice of dissent was heard. D. W. Brooks, General Manager of the Cotton Producers Association, once complained to True Morse that "there is somewhat of a feeling that the Commission is not getting a chance to look at the real policy problems of the Department of Agriculture."[14] On another occasion Brooks challenged the accuracy of the minutes, protesting that they did not correctly reflect the commission's favorable attitude on price supports for cotton.[15]

NAAC member, G. W. Wood of the School of Agriculture at Oregon State College, let True Morse know on one occasion he did not intend to be a mere puppet for the USDA. "The Commission should not be pressed for a decision on items listed on the agenda unless adequate time is given for analysis of the problem," he insisted. Pointing out that at the last meeting "pressure was put on the Commission to take a vote in favor on the particular piece of legislation" favored by Benson, he warned against "prostituting the position of the Commission."[16]

Understandably William I. Myers, chairman of the NAAC, worked hand in hand with Ezra Taft Benson. Dean Myers agreed in general with Benson's views on agricultural policy and did all that he could to advance them. Myers understood that the formulation of farm programs involved more than just making policy decisions. He understood the political ramifications and informed Ike in confidence that Senator Aiken would be a firm supporter of the administration's farm program, but not so with Representative Hope. The latter's reaction, according to Myers, was "friendly but completely negative since he seems to feel no responsibility of leadership in controversial matters that might affect his political future."[17]

It was discernible in an address to the American
Institute of Cooperation that Secretary Benson was trying to
establish a more positive image of his leadership. He did
not overtly blame Democrats for the failures of the current
programs but attempted to build a groundswell of bipartisan
support for future programs by calling for unity. The
problems to be faced were far too serious, he reasoned,
to play off Democrats against Republicans, rigid supports
against flexible supports, cattlemen against wheat growers,
or dairy farmers against cotton producers.[18]

Rendering an account of his stewardship, he listed
the following concrete achievements: reorganization of the
USDA was completed; a National Agricultural Advisory Commission had been established on a permanent basis; and farmers
in four hundred drought-stricken counties were able to receive special loans and/or purchase government stocks at
reduced prices. In addition: a reseal program was announced for the last year's corn and oats crop to provide
for on-the-farm storage; Commodity Credit Corporation loans
were being made available; one hundred twenty-five ships of
the reserve fleet now served as emergency storage bins;
Greece contracted to buy six million bushels of government-
owned wheat; and in addition Pakistan, through a special aid
program, was to be the recipient of thirty-seven million
bushels of wheat. Such action, boasted Benson, would help

remove the price-depressing effect of surpluses and thus
alleviate financial hardships all along the agricultural
front.[19]

Secretary Benson had long been an advocate of overall reductions in government spending. He all too soon discovered, however, that circumstances made it difficult to
effect economies. Budget Director Dodge informed Eisenhower
that Agriculture Department projections for fiscal 1955 exceeded expectations by some $35 million.[20] Benson had al-
ready been allowed an override of $15 million and now Dodge
complained that he was again seeking additional funds. When
the President inquired as to why an increase in expenditures
was taking place, Benson justified it in order to expand
utilization research. This decision was a "major policy
matter," the Agriculture Secretary argued, since heretofore
research in the agricultural field was primarily directed
toward increasing crop yields. By spending money on research
to find new uses for farm commodities, the government eventually would be able to cut agricultural appropriations.[21] By
increasing consumption or discovering more useable means to
divert farm-produced surpluses into industrial channels,
went his logic, future expenses for storage would decline
proportionately. Costs for federal storage programs were
soon to run over a million dollars a day, hence this was no
trifling matter.

Balancing the federal budget was a serious concern to Benson and he tried earnestly to effect savings for the fiscal year 1955 by forcing states to carry a larger share of the financial burden relative to USDA projects within their boundaries. He announced to the President that substantial reductions in a number of programs carried on cooperatively with the states was necessary. Projects involved in this budget cutback related to indemnities for destruction of livestock contaminated with tuberculosis and brucellosis; costs of maintaining quarantines; and paying for activities involving pest control. Knowing ahead of time that state officials would resist this, the Secretary of Agriculture confided to Eisenhower, "What we need is some means of obtaining an understanding and acceptance of the principle of greater reliance on local effort."[22]

Ike had made fiscal responsibility a major issue in the presidential campaign yet he could not deny outlays of federal funds needed to counteract the devastating effect of widespread drought in the Southwest. Benson reported to the President that as of October, 1953 the government had already spent $40 million to aid farmers in these states and that a supplemental appropriation of $150 million might well be needed for fiscal 1954.

Eisenhower raised no objections to this type of spending for several reasons. First, the cattlemen were in dire straits. They had suffered terrific losses and needed help. Secondly, political circumstances forced Ike to take action. Governor Allan Shivers of Texas, a Democrat, had supported Eisenhower over Stevenson for the presidency and this no doubt contributed to the GOP victory in the Lone Star state. Texas was plagued by adverse weather conditions and its farmers were seeking federal assistance. Also, Ike's close political ally, Governor Dan Thornton of Colorado, pushed for increasing amounts of federal aid to the ranchers of his state.

When the President attended a governors' conference at Amarillo, Texas he was met by Senator Lyndon Johnson (D-Tex.). The President needed the support of the minority leader on many other political matters and promised relief to Texas and other states hit by drought. President Eisenhower was politically astute enough to know when to trim his sails. He would keep the budget under control, but not at the expense of alienating political allies.[23]

Despite a myriad of special problems and political controversy, not to mention routine matters, the administration went about preparing a farm program so it could be presented to the 1954 session of Congress. Enactment at this time would then permit its implementation in 1955. While Benson was making his plans so were GOP leaders associated with the farm bloc. The majority of these

Republicans were pro-high price support men. Clifford Hope, Chairman of the House Agriculture Committee, and H. Carl Andersen, Chairman of the House Subcommittee on Agricultural Appropriations, were both in this category. So was Senator Milton Young who chaired the Senate Subcommittee on Agricultural Appropriations. It was going to take a considerable amount of White House leadership to secure legislative support for Benson's reforms.

Certain Congressmen from dairy states were already up in arms over Benson's drastic move in lowering price supports for butter from 90 to 75 per cent of parity in one swoop. Representative August H. Andresen (R-Minn.) transmitted his dissatisfaction about this sudden move by pointedly writing to the President. He told Eisenhower, "I am sorry that officials in the Department of Agriculture have not deemed it advisable to confer with members of Congress who have been working on the subject for many years."[24] Benson was forced to take this step because consumers were buying oleomargarine and the government became the recipient of huge amounts of unwanted surpluses.

Benson found it no easy task to prepare a major farm program. Not only was Congress involved but other departments and bureaus had to be consulted. He was unaccustomed to the ways of Washington and this soon got him into trouble. Budget Bureau Director Joseph M. Dodge let

Sherman Adams and Bernard M. Shanley know that certain aspects of USDA proposals relating to wool and the disposal of surpluses were in conflict with high-level administration discussions about these matters. Dodge complained: "Here again, apparently, the specific bill has been drawn without prior consultation or review by the White House staff or the Bureau of the Budget and without clearance with other departments at interest."[25]

To correct this recurrent situation Dodge and Shanley drew up a memorandum which Sherman Adams signed and sent to the Secretary of Agriculture. Marked "For Eyes Only of Ezra Taft Benson," the communication explained the difficulties in connection with the preparation and introduction of legislation related to the President's agricultural program. It explained the steps that were necessary to coordinate efforts. Hence Benson was advised by Adams, "I would be appreciative if you would have those in your Department cooperate more fully with the standard operating procedure."[26] Benson learned quickly and thereafter avoided such complications.

The administration farm program was formally unveiled on January 11, 1954, when the President presented a package proposal to Congress. It represented a carefully constructed compromise. Specific recommendations reflected Benson's desire for lower price supports. This was tempered by

Eisenhower's requirement that any proposed reductions be implemented slowly. The twin features of flexibility and gradualism were therefore incorporated into the measure as follows:

1. The new program should first be given an opportunity to start operating without the handicap of such large accumulated surpluses. This to be done by setting aside certain quantities . . . , [thus] eliminating them from price support computations.

2. The 1948 and 1949 Agricultural Acts were soundly conceived and received bipartisan supports. The principles on which they were based are particularly applicable . . . [with] improvements and modifications.

3. After the 1954 crops the level of price supports for the basic commodities will be gradually related to supply, promising farmers greater stability of income.

4. Modernized parity is to become effective for all commodities on January 1, 1956, as scheduled by law. Provisions should

be made for moving from the old to
modernized parity in steps of five
percentage points of the old parity
per year until the change from old to
modernized parity has been accomplished.

5. The key element of the new program is
a gradual adjustment to new circumstances and conditions.[27]

In his message to Congress Eisenhower insisted that
there be no further delay in treating the fundamental
causes which created an overproduction of farm commodities.
Lower price supports he argued would reduce production
while stimulating consumption. It would, among other
things, check the further loss of foreign markets due to
artificially induced price levels. Also the lowering
of cotton subsidies would allow competition with synthetics; and decreasing parity levels on cereal would
alleviate the cost-price squeeze on farmers who buy corn
or other grain feeds for the raising of livestock. The
only commodity for which increased support prices were
asked related to wool, of which two-thirds was still being
imported.

In addition Ike asked for broad discretionary powers to deal with the so-called set-aside of $2,500,000,000 worth of surplus food and fiber. These reserves, he assured Congress, would not be used to shrink acreage allotments (as the original 1938 formula prescribed) but would be channeled into domestic and foreign markets. The administration farm program, concluded Eisenhower, was "designed to achieve the stability and growth in income over the years to which our farmers are entitled and which the Nation must assure in the interest of all 160,000,000 of our people."[28]

The day after the President sent his message to Congress, Ezra Taft Benson addressed the delegates of the National Council of Farmer Cooperatives in Chicago. He took the opportunity to present the administration farm program as reflecting not just his ideas but one truly representative of Eisenhower's thinking. It was formulated in the "spirit of responsibility," maintained Benson.[29] Launching into a defense of the flexible features of the proposed measure, Benson reasoned that any long-range solution had to contend with ways and means of preventing the accumulation of price-depressing surpluses. This he observed would come about only when the old parity formula (based upon the years 1910-14) was reformed. A modernized formula would be computed on the basis of data relevant to the last decade. Gradual transition to this modern parity would provide an economic cushion, explained Benson, but it was necessary to adjust production to contemporary market demands. He insisted, however, that land diverted away from cultivation of corn, cotton, or wheat should not be used for planting other commercial crops. Wise land use and conservation projects, he predicted, would aid in maintaining a balance in overall agricultural output. And finally, Benson defended the set-aside procedure of not counting surpluses already accumulated in terms of acreage calculations as the only feasible manner in which to give the new program a chance to operate.

In order to generate grassroots support for the new farm program, Benson travelled about the country giving speeches to as many agricultural organizations as possible. He had to educate the agrarian sector to reform and revise the whole price support system much like Henry A. Wallace once had to educate them to accept it. Addressing a National Farmers Union convention in Denver, a group openly opposed to his views, the Agriculture Secretary stood by his program and announced confidently, "I am going to see it through just as long as the President of the United States wants me to remain in his Cabinet."[30]

At Ithaca, New York, Benson told a Farm and Home Week Conference that taxpayers would not continue to pay huge sums for programs that did not accomplish the job

for which they were intended. Using startlingly frank
language, he proclaimed, "I am unalterably opposed to programs that substitute government aid for reasonable self-
help."[31]

On his home ground in Logan, Utah, the Secretary
told members of the Cache Valley Breeding Association that
it was wrong to measure the success of farm programs by the
gyrations of a "political applause meter."[32] In trying to
modernize and update the farm program, Benson was aware that
in the short run some farmers might be hurt. His strategy
was to convince them by logic and moral suasion that the
administration's position was the best solution for the
long-range interests of agriculture.

Back in Washington Benson spoke to a group representing the frozen food industry. Pointing out how government research gave birth to the frozen food industry, he encouraged further efforts on their part. "I am thoroughly
convinced that most of agriculture's present problems can
be met through increased research and education and improved
marketing methods," he told them.[33]

In trying to reform agriculture, Benson placed
great emphasis on research, education, and implementation
of new marketing techniques. His background had been spent
working with co-ops where better merchandising, packaging,
and salesmanship did promote higher prices in quick fashion.

This had been proved by the citrus fruit industry, the walnut growers, and with processing potatoes. He wanted other producers to emulate these techniques. Hog raisers still produced lard and dairy farmers turned out huge quantities of butter. The public consumed neither in amounts equivalent to vegetable oils or margarine. He wondered why they did not seek to develop and merchandise new products (e.g. fancy hams, stuffed pork chops, non-fat milk, yogurt, etc.) or why they neglected to utilize advertising.

Benson's strategy when appearing before congressional committees was to predict dire consequences for the future unless administration proposals were adopted immediately and in their entirety. In testimony to the House Committee on Agriculture he cited statistics to back his prognostication. Quoting Commodity Credit Corporation figures, he revealed that between January, 1953 and January, 1954 there was an increase of more than $1.5 billion over a period of one year in the amount of commodities owned outright by CCC. Benson buttressed his argument further. There would be no surcease in surpluses with regard to wheat, cotton, and corn, he indicated, unless price supports were reduced. "At what point will the 140 million Americans who do not live on farms rise up . . . and demand not revision but outright elimination of all direct aid to agriculture?"[34] The need for reform was evident to him. The old, rigid price support system was obsolete and outmoded. Its continuance would, in his judgment, actually harm agriculture rather than assist it.

Testifying in like manner before the Senate Committee on Agriculture and Forestry, Benson again pointed out the shortcomings of the old and inflexible price support system. With surgical precision he dissected and displayed its patent failures. Overproduction, loss of markets, and high costs of storage were stressed over and over again to illustrate that the system needed reforming. To top it all off, he asserted, Congress had tinkered with the program so much that it no longer resembled a coherent plan. Acreage allotments were not strictly enforced, price support levels were set without any reference to actual market conditions, and cross compliance was ignored whenever enough constituents registered complaints.

To imprint indelibly upon the minds of the committee what this incongruous process had done, he referred to the President's request to increase the Commodity Credit Corporation's borrowing authority from $6.75 to $8.5 billion. "This is for the remainder of the 1953 crop and for the crop of 1954," noted the Agriculture Secretary. "I hope that it is enough."[35] The implication was obvious. Unless the new farm program were enacted, thus cutting

down on excess output of food and fiber, Congress was going
to have to dig up more money just to handle storage problems.

To say that members of the farm bloc who supported
high price supports were bedeviled by Benson's cold logic
would be an understatement. Many were in a state of chill-
fury. Both Democrats and Republicans in favor of established policy tried not so much to refute Benson as to ruin
his credibility. They portrayed the Agriculture Secretary
as an enemy of the farmer and one who opposed all efforts
to aid them. This tactic did much to create a false image
of Benson--a sort of straw man whom they could flail in
political speeches.

Called back before the Senate Committee, the Agriculture Secretary never relented in his marshalling of
facts to support his stand. Without being timorous he
once more pointed out the severity of the surplus problem.
Again he arrayed massive statistical evidence to hammer
home his point. If no wheat were harvested at all in 1954
(and expected yields were set at 900 million bushels),
Benson declared, the 875 million bushels carryover would
take care of all domestic needs for an entire year. Also
in storage were 9.6 billion bales of cotton and 900 million
bushels of corn (a new record). The danger he emphasized
was not from potential shortages but from a "program which

makes the government the principal owner of a farm commodity."[36]

When arguments were made to counter Benson's position, he fielded them with steadfast skill. Would not farmers plant more to offset lower price supports? His reply was simple. Long-range studies indicated that a 10 per cent reduction in the price of wheat on the average would result in a 2 per cent drop in acreage the following year. Could not the present acreage allotment-production control system be made to work? Yes, Benson affirmed, if Congress would authorize meaningful enforcement of acreage allotments, marketing quotas, and cross-compliance. All of these devices were being circumvented for political reasons, thus creating an economic monstrosity that no longer resembled the original 1938 program. Too many of its automatic adjustment features were circumscribed by political expediency. "I am fearful," concluded the Secretary of Agriculture, summarizing his presentation, "that if we do not heed the storm warnings now on the horizon many positive gains in the field of agricultural legislation will be swept away."[37]

By emphasizing the ill effects of the old farm program, Benson hoped to convert non-farm bloc members. This paid off to a considerable degree. For example, Senator John F. Kennedy and other urban liberals broke with fellow Democrats to render strong support for the policy advocated by Benson.[38] When it came to realistic facts Benson was in a strong position. But, as he would learn, irrefutable logic does not always win in the halls of Congress.

Because GOP farm bloc congressmen complained to Eisenhower about this tactic, the President did caution Benson about appealing too much to urban self-interest if it worked to the disadvantage of the rural sector. "We've got to think of the farmer and the consumer simultaneously," the Chief Executive advised his Agriculture Secretary in a cabinet meeting.[39]

Because Congress refused to lower price supports-- news from the House of Representatives indicated they de- sired another flat extension of the 90 per cent parity formula--Eisenhower decided to take his cause directly to the people. Choosing a friendly forum, Ike addressed the opening session of district chairmen of the National Citi- zens for Eisenhower Congressional Committee. Receiving national news coverage, President Eisenhower charged that farm bloc clamor had concealed from the nation the fact that a change from rigid supports to flexible supports would affect less than one-fourth of the income received by farmers. It was not going to bankrupt agriculture. In defense of his proposal to Congress, the President claimed his program proposed price supports with sufficient flexibility to encourage the production of needed supplies without flooding and depressing American markets. He argued that gradualism in its application would prevent an abrupt downward plunge of the price level of basic commodities. Implying that foes of his program were more interested in bribing farmers with subsidies to get reelected than correcting maladjustments, Eisenhower announced that as for himself, "I know that what is right for America is politically right."[40]

Ike's appeal drew a positive reaction from farm leader Herschel D. Newsom, Master of the National Grange. He sent his views to Presidential Assistant Sherman Adams. What impressed him was Eisenhower's recognition that while balance in production was being restored, it had to be accomplished slowly. He noted, furthermore, "I have not seen recognition by the Department of Agriculture of the President's own emphasis on gradualism." It also was his judgment that rival Allan Kline of the American Farm Bureau Federation was much too prone to want quick reductions in price supports with no concessions or compromise. This was tantamount, he contended, to implementing the old Agriculture Act of 1949 with no concern for a period of adjustment.[41]

As a follow-up to Eisenhower's speech, it was agreed that Secretary Benson and Vice-President Nixon would make a joint appearance on television. They publicized the fact that the administration's new farm program merely intended to implement legislation originally passed in 1949. They stressed the need of returning to flexibility as a realistic step in solving the problems of agriculture. "Actually, the administration's program is based on similar principles to the one which both Democrats and Republicans agreed upon six years ago," reasoned Richard Nixon, "I know because I was a member of Congress in 1948 and 1949."[42]

To this national audience, Benson accentuated the need for drastic reduction in price supports. At the end of World War II, he explained: "We stopped all-out production of munitions and ships. But we didn't put a stop to all-out production of surplus food."[43] Although Benson's position was stated candidly and possessed creditability, with an off-year election coming in the fall of 1954, Democrats were not eager to alter the established farm program. They were much more interested in making political capital out of the mess in agriculture than in setting up a sound system for shifting agricultural production away from surplus commodities.

A plethora of proposals gave members of Congress much to work with in putting together a vote-winning package. Not to be left out were many GOP members representing rural areas. They also got in on the legislative logrolling with gusto. The clear consensus was to support prices as high as possible and to go for two-price systems where, for instance, wheat would sell higher at home than abroad. Realizing what was going on Eisenhower used the prestige of his office to put considerable pressure on Congress to follow up on his program.

The brunt of Republican leadership in the House was delegated to Charles Halleck of Indiana. Speaker Joseph Martin allowed the majority leader, a Midwesterner, to maneuver the farm bill through the lower chamber. It was tough going because minority leader Sam Rayburn of Texas, a pivotal figure, found much support on both sides of the aisle for keeping 90 per cent of parity as the basic ingredient in any farm bill.

Halleck simply had to report to the White House that it was virtually impossible to get flexible price supports with a range as wide as from 75 to 90 per cent. Senate majority leader William Knowland of California concurred with this assessment of the situation. Even so Secretary Benson objected to any compromise and wished to hold the line. Eisenhower, however, was prone to take half a loaf rather than none and went along with Halleck's suggestion that they settle for a range of 82.5 to 90 per cent. This more modest reduction, it was felt, would have a better chance of passage.[44]

After prolonged debate the Agriculture Act of 1954 was finally enacted. The compromise promoted by Halleck provided the narrow margin for victory. It was signed by the President on August 28 with the statement that "this new law--the central core of a vigorous, progressive agricultural program--will bring substantial, lasting bene-fits to our farmers, our consumers, and our entire econ-omy."[45]

Title I of the new farm act authorized the setting aside of $2,500,000,000 worth of Commodity Credit Corpora-tion surplus holdings when it came to the computation of price support levels. Food and fiber involved were: wheat, upland cotton, cottonseed oil, butter, nonfat dry milk solids, and cheese. Disposition of these products was to take place as follows: (1) foreign relief, (2) development of new markets, (3) school lunch programs, (4) stockpiled for national emergencies, (5) used for research purposes, (6) domestic disaster relief, and (7) sales into the home market when shortages appeared. A companion law, the Agri-cultural Trade Development and Assistance Act (which will be discussed shortly), provided a mechanism for disposing of large amounts of excess farm commodities.

Title II dealt exclusively with flexible price supports and their implementation. The minimum level of the parity rate would be 82.5 per cent for basic crops in 1955 and thereafter it would range from 75 per cent to 90 per cent depending upon market conditions. Of the six so-called basic crops--which were wheat, corn, cotton, rice, peanuts, and tobacco--only the latter had a mandatory 90 per cent support level. Strict production and marketing controls were traditionally enforced by farmer committees in the tobacco industry, hence they had no surplus problem. Benson, by the way, did not object to this provision because he was satisfied that tobacco growers would continue to police themselves relative to compliance.

Title III provided that transitional parity would commence January 1, 1956 for basic commodities. A reduction of 5 per cent would take place annually until the switch over to modernized parity was completed. The latter formula took into account price-cost relationships during the most recent ten-year period.

The last four titles dealt with a variety of things. Title IV allowed the USDA to set regulations with regard to containers (size and shape) and established certain import restrictions on fruits and vegetables (to make sure they were up to U.S. standards). Title V extended federal administration of conservation for two years with provisions

for states to take over after that time period. Thereafter
federal funds would be allocated to the several states on
the basis of need with the stipulation no one state would
receive a reduction of more than 15 per cent any one year.
Title VI transferred jurisdiction of overseas agricultural
attachés from the State to Agriculture Department. Title
VII provided for continued price supports, ranging from 60
per cent to 110 per cent of parity, for wool and mohair.
Payments to producers were to be financed from import
duties. Incentive subsidies were to continue until attainment of an annual production of 360,000,000 pounds of wool.

In addition to the Agriculture Act of 1954 the rural
sector benefitted from other congressional measures such as
the St. Lawrence Seaway Act; amendments to the Social Security Act which enrolled farmers and farm labor for the first
time; and tax relief in the form of depreciation allowances
on mechanical equipment. A new Watershed Protection and
Flood Protection Act was enacted which provided funds for
joint federal-state programs. An amendment to the Water
Facilities Act also made loans to farmers available for
reforestation, construction of drainage facilities, and
other small-scale conservation projects.

Despite total budget cuts by the Eisenhower administration amounting to some $12 billion, agriculture fared
quite well. Congress appropriated $20 million more for

1955 than the USDA had received for 1954. Funds were provided for utilization research and expansion of farm-to-market roads. A $15 million credit program was approved for the Farmers Home Administration and amendments to the Farm Tenancy Act authorized federally insured loans to farmers wanting to purchase farmsteads. All in all rural America had been treated quite favorably by this legislation.

Although Representative Clifford Hope had capitulated to presidential pressure in going along with flexible price supports, he in no way repudiated his belief that high price supports were far more beneficial than low ones. In a report to accompany the House version of the 1954 farm bill, which had recommended a flat extension of 90 per cent of parity, the Kansan claimed Congress and the people now accepted the principle of price supports. Such policies had been in effect for more than twenty years. He did have to strain his argument somewhat by inferring that maintenance of rigid 90 per cent supports did not violate the flexible parity principle of the Agricultural Adjustment Act of 1938. To him the only question that existed revolved around "what is the best way to do the job, and the committee feels that under the conditions existing at this time, 90 per cent supports, with effective production control, will work better than a flexible price support program at lower levels."[46]

With a modicum of reform achieved and other important gains in farm legislation, Ezra Taft Benson could
honestly canvass for votes by telling farmers what the Republican administration had done for them. Eschewing
political cant Benson used electioneering as a means to
further educate farmers to the economic problems they faced.
This did not make for speeches with built-in emotion for
audience reaction. When Benson spoke at an election rally
his tone was more nearly that of a pedant. After a low-key
speech to a crowd at the Oregon State Fair, for example, he
felt compelled to announce: "The problems of agriculture
cannot be solved through political hocus-pocus--through a
government handout here and there--through this or that
pressure group."[47] This type of impolitic rhetoric did not
make him popular with special interest audiences.

In the Midwest, where Benson spoke to his state
counterparts (commissioners, directors, and secretaries of
agriculture), he revealed what he undoubtedly believed to
be the most important accomplishment thus far. To him it
was the fundamental fact that the 83rd Congress had turned
the corner toward basic reform and was at last reversing
the trend of the postwar period. "The rapid drift toward a
regimented agriculture has been checked," he announced, "a
new direction has been set toward greater responsibility and

freedom for agriculture."[48]

In general farmer reaction to the Agriculture Act of 1954 tended to fall into two patterns. Large commercial operators liked the relaxation of restrictions while small-scale farmers did not approve of the flexible features. Some, however, took the point of view as expressed by a manager of an Oklahoma accounting firm who owned a large wheat farm. He complained to Benson that he was still subject to acreage allotments even though he did not want government doles or subsidies. Impatient over the slowness of a shift in policy and making obvious his disgust, he wrote: "I am deeply disappointed in the law just passed by a so-called Republican Congress, that is nothing more than an extension of the old New Deal and Fair Deal program."[49]

On the other side of the fence came a typical complaint from a farm editor who owned a small, less efficient dairy farm. He viewed flexible price supports as an economic threat to his income. When parity was lowered, and he got less for his milk, three options were open to him: (1) quit farming, (2) take a loss, (3) increase his risk. Taking the last alternative, he built another silo and added ten more cows to his herd. Here was an example of a marginal operator who, unable to compete on his own, depended upon government assistance for survival. A further lowering of parity might well have caused him to sell out. The protesting editor, who thought he knew something about farmers' habits, closed by warning Under-Secretary Morse: "Maybe that's okay for us but nationally it further impairs the price of milk and adds to the production without in any way changing or helping to change the consumption. . . . That is the farmer's traditional way."[50]

A news director of a Florida radio station (WTRR of Stanford), baited a nice political trap for Ezra Taft Benson by sending him a loaded question. The Agriculture Secretary was asked to comment on how small farmers were expected to make a living without the boost their income derived from high price support payments. In what was meant to be a helpful reply, but when later quoted out of context sounded rather callous, Benson answered: "You ask about my advice to farmers who face losing their homes, equipment, and life savings. If I were in that condition, I would check closely to see if I was operating as efficiently as possible. If I needed credit and could get it locally, I would investigate to see if I were eligible for credit under a federal assistance program. If this still did not prove satisfactory and I had a small farm that did not require my full attention, I would attempt to supplement my income through outside work."[51] It was this sort of candid expression which had adverse political repercussions. Realistically many inordinately small farmsteads were incapable of

supporting those who lived upon them. Either they had to
seek outside income or move from the land. The third course
was to seek more federal money in the form of price supports.
The last alternative, Benson reasoned, was self-defeating in
the long run since it only aggravated the surplus problem.
And that in turn invariably lowered commodity prices.

To convince farmers that the provisions of the Agriculture Act of 1954 were really in their best interest, the
timing employed by USDA for its implementation was all-
important. Senator Everett M. Dirksen (R-Ill.) was a
staunch supporter of Benson's policies, but he was also a
consummate politician. He wired Ross Rizley, an Assistant
Secretary of Agriculture, that some of "our friends on the
ballot" in the fall were deeply desirous that some finesse
be used concerning the issuance of compliance regulations.
Broadly hinting that they wait until after the election, he
said, "There are some areas in which premature regulations
could be damaging. I suggest a conference discussion before
action is taken."[52]

Cross-compliance was a headache for the USDA since
farmers habitually tried to take advantage of loopholes by
avoiding restrictions. If at all possible acreage was
diverted from one crop to another. Mid-term elections or
no, Benson ignored Dirksen's suggestion and proceeded to
announce that the 55 million acreage allotment in effect for

wheat would be strictly enforced with penalties for all
violations. The first priority as the Secretary saw it was
to keep production down because a huge carryover of more
than 900 million bushels already filled storage bins. Actual consumer needs would have necessitated the planting of
only 19 million acres in wheat but Congress had arbitrarily
maintained the existing quota for the benefit of wheat
farmers. Defying market outlooks farm politics in the wheat
belt influenced agricultural legislation in a detrimental
way. It was this practice which Benson tried to halt.

Once announced it was inevitable that the Solons on
Capitol Hill would seek relief for their constituents regarding USDA compliance regulations. Senator Lyndon Johnson
made a strong request that exceptions be made in the case of
Texas farmers hurt by the drought and Arthur V. Watkins
pleaded for an easement relative to farmers in Utah.
Johnson's appeal was taken under advisement[53] while the
latter was told by Assistant Secretary Ross Rizley that the
"present large surplus of wheat does not justify wheat
acreage allotments being relaxed for the nation as a
whole."[54] Again the objectives of the total program con-
flicted with short run needs of specific farmers.

To a farmer's way of thinking, if he ignored the
larger picture, the more land under cultivation the more
money he would make. While this oversimplified things by

ignoring the surplus problem or market conditions, any move
by the USDA to keep acreage within limits or to enforce
cross-compliance usually brought with it resentment from
that part of the farming community represented by smaller
operators. Worried Congressman Carl T. Curtis of Nebraska
pushed the panic button after a visit to his home constitu-
ency. This conservative GOP Representative was appalled at
the hostile reaction of some farmers in the cornhusker
state. He took it upon himself to tell the Agriculture Secretary of his discontent. "I think we have a real problem
on our hands," wrote Curtis, adding the warning: "some
careful observers liken it to 1948."[55] The traumatic experience of losing the farm vote to Harry Truman still lingered
in the memory of Midwest Republicans.

Perturbed by what Carl Curtis said, Benson reminded
the Nebraskan of the responsibilities of both of their
respective offices. Curtis was told that acreage reduction
and enforcement of cross-compliance regulations were
corollaries of high price supports. Certain congressmen had
claimed farmers would accept limitations on production in
exchange for federal assistance. "You may have noticed, as
I have," Benson pointed out, "that when it becomes necessary
to apply the controls under the law, these same people
steadfastly refuse to become in any way identified with such
restrictions."[56] On this point the Agriculture Secretary

was correct. Members of Congress were happy to take credit for USDA funds going into their district but were quick to disassociate themselves from government-imposed restraints.

What was happening was this. As acreage allotments got smaller, it became increasingly difficult for the owner of a small family farm to make a living. He naturally pressed for permission to exceed his quota or divert to another crop. But to allow this, which individual congressmen urged on frequent occasions, meant that other problems were created. When, for instance, farmers were permitted to use otherwise idle acres for the growing of vegetables for commercial use, it raised havoc with those already in this field by lowering the prices. Carlos Campbell, Executive Secretary of the National Canners Association, reminded Secretary Benson that "crops grown on acreage under contract to a processor . . . [are] irretrievably committed to sale in the form of the canned product."[57]

Another complaint about the influx of new entrants using diverted acres came from George Goddard, Secretary of the Dried Bean Council. He petitioned Benson to expand quotas for prime producers before allowing outsiders to grow beans.[58]

The logical direction of strict compliance to federal regulations was obvious. It would have been tantamount to freezing each farmer permanently into the production area of his basic commodity. This would in reality curtail freedom to plant any other crops. Also for all intent and purposes it would prevent a beginner from entering into a well established commercial field unless he purchased both the land and the acreage allotment permit (referred to as the history of the farm). It was this situation which Benson wanted to head off and for that reason he looked askance at all federal controls related to agriculture.

The White House succumbed to the intense political pressure of the moment and overruled Benson. Eisenhower ordered him to rescind his announcement about stringent enforcement of cross-compliance. Justification for the Agriculture Secretary's sudden about-face was rationalized with the USDA statement that "removal of previously proposed special controls on the production of some crops in 1955" constituted a move toward "greater freedom of operation for farmers."[59] Additional excuses as to why controls were being modified included widespread drought, a substantial reduction in the corn crop, the Department's desire to eliminate expensive controls wherever possible, and "other developments."[60]

The Republican party was more intent on retaining control of both houses of Congress (thus the need to hold the farm vote) than in implementation of a consistent and comprehensive program in agriculture. Their majority was

slim in the lower chamber and almost nonexistent in the
upper. Many issues other than those dealing with agriculture
were involved in the campaign but congressmen with rural
constituencies succumbed to the pressures of the moment.
In American politics each elected official is ultimately on
his own. Survival is the first law in politics and this
made for much confusion when it came to party discipline in
the realm of agricultural legislation.

Chapter VI
The Problem of Plenty

Certainly no Secretary of Agriculture exceeded Ezra
Taft Benson in energy or ingenuity when it came to finding
ways to dispose of surplus farm commodities. His record
here was truly remarkable. Also, no predecessor outdid him
in fostering utilization research or in improving marketing
techniques. The primary goals of Benson's efforts were to
channel excess food and fiber into either domestic markets
or overseas outlets. This was to be a basic attack on the
price glutting existence of farm products with no saleable
outlet at home. In addition to striving to regain or expand foreign markets an effort was made to promote research
programs as a means for finding new uses for surpluses.
This, along with flexible price supports, would ostensibly
cap the cornucopia of overproduction. Therefore the overall
solution devised by Benson was practical and looked toward a
permanent solution of the predicament confronting agriculture.

Congress passed the Agricultural Trade Development and Assistance Act on July 10, 1954. This notable piece of legislation, known as Public Law 480, was originally sponsored by Senator Andrew F. Schoeppel (R-Kans.) and Representative Robert D. Harrison (R-Nebr.). As finally passed PL 480 had three titles. The first authorized sale of surplus agricultural commodities for foreign currencies with a provision allowing for an annual financial loss of $700 million to the Commodity Credit Corporation on such transactions. Title II empowered the President to send excess agricultural output to needy nations considered friendly to the United States at a cost not to exceed $300 million in a three-year period. And last, Title III permitted the use of surpluses for domestic distribution to distressed or disaster areas when such disposition did not interfere with normal marketing. Another provision allowed for barter to acquire products deemed necessary for national security. "Friendly nations" as defined by Congress specifically excluded the Communist bloc. One other stipulation provided that overseas shipments had to be carried in American vessels.[1]

On August 28, 1954 the President notified Ezra Taft Benson that he would have the major responsibility for disposing of the set-asides, a provision of the Agriculture Act of 1954, and on September 9th Eisenhower also delegated to the Agriculture Secretary authority to carry out Title I of

PL 480. At the same time Harold Stassen, Director of Foreign Operations, was given power to implement Title II.

Because disposition of surpluses overseas involved matters of foreign policy, President Eisenhower elevated special consultant Clarence Francis to the chairmanship of the Interagency Committee for Agricultural Surplus Disposal. ICASD, or the Francis Committee as it was commonly called, served as a policy-making agency. Its members included representatives from the USDA, State, Treasury, Commerce, Budget Bureau, Council of Foreign Economic Policy, International Cooperation Administration, and Operating Coordinating Board. Special White House assistant James B. Lambie, Jr. was designated by Ike to be Deputy Chairman of this coordinating group.[2]

The task of getting rid of surpluses, as we shall see, was a very involved and complicated process. Commodities sold on a straight dollar basis posed no special problems other than the seeking of primary markets. Confusion set in when sales were made for foreign currency since such money had to be spent within the country making the purchase. Also when food or fiber was traded or bartered in huge quantities, sold at preferential prices, or given away, such actions tended to disrupt the normal channels of international trade. Likewise selling below the world market price or invading territory traditionally

belonging to another country was explicitly prohibited in
the General Agreements on Trade and Tariffs (of which the
U.S. was a signatory).

Because American agriculture had been subsidized for
several decades, many U.S. farm products were priced so high
as to discourage foreign buying. Egyptian cotton, Canadian
wheat, or Australian butter undersold American-produced
counterparts. Thus the USDA and those on the Francis Committee were faced with monumental problems in trying to dispose of surpluses which were in general too costly for the
world market.

To promote overseas sales of American agricultural
commodities Ezra Taft Benson took extraordinary measures.
In 1955 he decided to visit Latin America, Canada, and
Europe on a special trade mission. His trip in the Western
Hemisphere included stops at Puerto Rico, Cuba, Trinidad,
Costa Rica, Nicaragua, Guatemala, Virgin Islands, Panama,
Mexico, Colombia, and Venezuela. While touring the Central
American republics Benson used every means to open markets
for U.S. grain and whole milk.

Not unexpectedly the Secretary often had to deal
with Latin complaints. Cuba was concerned about the
American sugar quota and South American countries wanted
good prices for coffee. While seeking privileges and
preferential treatment for their own commodities, each

nation on the other hand wanted the United States to promise it would not engage in dumping. Benson became convinced that he was simply going to have to fight for markets and not be intimidated by retaliatory threats of import quotas.[3]

Within the administration there were those who feared that Secretary Benson's aggressive trade expansion program would harm U.S. foreign policy. As the leader of the free world, the United States had tried for years to bolster the economies of friendly, non-Communist countries. John Foster Dulles consistently argued against either dumping or pursuing any type of trade policy which would in any way weaken the economic strength of America's free world allies. A cleavage arose within administration ranks over this point. Benson espoused an aggressive policy of regaining and enlarging our overseas outlets while Dulles, backed by Clarence Randall (chairman of the Council of Foreign Economic Policy), pressed for a lenient trade policy which yielded if not outright forfeited markets to our allies and the non-aligned nations. Obviously the latter line of action meant an imbalance in trade and financial sacrifices on the part of the United States.[4]

Addressing the Canadian Federation of Agriculture at Regina in Saskatchewan on June 14, 1955, Ezra Taft Benson sought to justify the U.S. trade expansion program. He told his Canadian audiences point-blank that "we are not engaging in any cut-throat race for markets." The United States, he insisted, would abide by the International Wheat Agreement, "but there is no reason why we should not set an example for the world of friendly competition--of fair competition."[5] Benson emphasized that Canada already had a favorable balance of trade with the United States. He contended therefore it could easily stand minor dislocations of its markets. Reassuring Canadians, while speaking in the neighboring province of Alberta, the U.S. Secretary of Agriculture declared emphatically that PL 480 would not cause them to lose their share of world trade.[6] Canadian officials remained apprehensive nevertheless. They did not relish any renewed competition from their neighbor to the south and interpreted Benson's words as a warning the United States was about to launch a vigorous offensive to recapture its lost markets.

Indefatigable in his efforts, Benson again went on a trade mission from August 28 to September 14; this time to Europe. His tour included England, Scotland, Denmark, France, Italy, and Switzerland. Meeting with U.S. agricultural attachés from some twenty countries in Paris, the Agriculture Secretary briefed them on America's new trade policy. He announced, "We are employing Congressional authority, as given in Public Law 480, Public Law 665

[Mutual Security Act of 1954], and others, for liquidation of excess stores of farm products."[7]   U.S. trade policy would be guided by three principles, he declared, and enumerated the following points: (1) we will compete fairly; (2) we will stress quality; and (3) we will seek mutually profitable deals. Attachés were instructed to use all the promotional techniques at their command to gain new markets on the continent.

Just before concluding his six-nation trade trip, Benson was asked to address the International Federation of Agricultural Producers then meeting in Rome. Using this important forum to explain U.S. policy he told the delegates attending this convention that while his country was determined to broaden its markets, it had "no intention of dumping." To a considerable degree, the Secretary of Agriculture reasoned, American farm surpluses existed because the United States had refrained from unloading them upon the world markets despite loss of legitimate outlets. He decried conditions that kept American farm products out of some countries because of quantitative import controls and currency exchange restrictions. His final plea stressed the need for multilateral removal of trade barriers so that private commerce might replace state trading.[8]

Perceiving the value of Benson's overseas contacts, Clarence Francis also went abroad in quest of new markets.

Traveling to France, Spain, Greece, Turkey, and Italy from
May 5 to July 7, 1955, Francis personally expedited many
aspects of surplus disposal. He completed his trade junket
with a first-hand inspection of the U.S. exhibit at the Rome
Trade Fair. The Foreign Agricultural Service of the USDA,
with the assistance of its agricultural attachés, sponsored
such displays all over the world. These promotional projects, the first of which was held in Cologne, Germany in
1955, were effective ways to interest foreign buyers in
American farm products.

Before entering government, Clarence Francis had
been in the milling business. As head of the Interagency
Committee for Agricultural Surplus Disposal he was fast
becoming aware of the complex nature of the problems caused
by surpluses. Both he and his deputy, James M. Lambie,
used great ingenuity to contrive new ways and means to get
rid of excess farm commodities. Despite these efforts,
surpluses still mounted. Wheat, cotton, corn, and dairy
products constituted 80 per cent of the surplus on hand.
"In sheer magnitude," stated an ICASD report, "wheat over-
shadows all other commodities." In addition to the cost of
the commodity subsidy, the storage costs were enormous.
The Commodity Credit Corporation was paying $700,000 per
day and on top of that inventories held over from previous
years became subject to losses due to deterioration.

Reflecting extreme pessimism the report predicted, "Under the laws and politics now in effect we will continue to add to these surpluses."[9]

Drastic new steps were needed, as well as those already taken, to speed up disposal of surpluses. Both Francis and Lambie set forth a simple solution which met with immediate State Department opposition--namely, sell surplus commodities at bargain prices. They maintained "lower prices should be expected to expand both domestic and export sales." Despite this the State Department held firm to its contention that this constituted dumping.

Francis and Lambie also drew attention to another roadblock. Refusal on the part of the United States to engage in trade with the Communist bloc needlessly eliminated a prospective outlet of enormous potentiality.[10] A request by the Soviet Union to buy huge quantities of butter, for instance, had to be turned down because of the PL 480 prohibition about selling to Communist nations. The intent of congressional thinking, fully supported by John Foster Dulles and the State Department, presumed the withholding of U.S. goods from Soviet bloc countries would weaken their economic strength. But needless to say it also deprived the United States of a potential market for agricultural commodities. Not only was reform in agriculture necessary, but also needed was a change in Cold War attitudes.

Aside from foreign policy obstacles still another problem hampered extrication from the surplus morass. Foreign buyers often complained that U.S. commodities which had been stored for a considerable period of time were not equal in quality to fresh commodities. Consequently they protested any receipt of damaged or dirty goods. Because American agriculture was so highly mechanized, crops were often blemished in the process of being harvested. Cotton picking machines did the job faster and more cheaply than hand labor but added refuse, such as leaves, to the final product. The same thing occurred with wheat and other cereals. In addition corn kernels were oftimes broken or crushed by mechanical pickers.

Once ready for export another hurdle erected by Congress was the requisite that surpluses had to be shipped in American bottoms. Not only did other nations resent this practice but much to the dismay of Francis and Lambie they soon discovered there was an acute shortage of U.S. merchant vessels. Many delays were directly attributable to lack of cargo space and yet available shipping by foreign companies could not be used.

In an effort to find unexplored avenues for disposing of surpluses, Clarence Francis brought in Ernest T. Baughman as a special consultant. Baughman was assistant vice-president of the Chicago Federal Reserve Bank and an expert in international trade. Methodically he reviewed the entire trade picture.

First of all he called for a consolidation of all programs dealing with export of surpluses. By combining PL 480 with PL 665, along with foreign aid projects of other agencies, a clear set of guidelines could be established. Secondly, he warned against selling agricultural commodities at cut-rate prices since such dumping would prompt retaliatory action if done in large volume. Thirdly, Baughman suggested that flexible supports in the short run would not significantly reduce production or increase consumption of surplus basics.[11]

The scenario drawn was anything but optimistic. Baughman's prognostication included the following forecast: "(1) It is doubtful that the volume of transaction can be materially increased without doing the United States more harm than benefit . . . ; (2) Prospects for a further substantial increase in special exports, therefore, do not appear bright except as we may develop programs which open up new types of outlets. . . . Another possibility is an increase in volume of East-West trade; and (3) Barter probably will continue to move about the current volume of commodities if it is desired as a matter of policy to maintain a vigorous barter program."[12]

The State Department had a mixed reaction. They liked what Baughman said about the dangers of dumping but had strong reservations about seriously considering the subject of entering into trade with the Soviet bloc.

Assistant Secretary Earl L. Butz expressed USDA's strong reservations about the report. He did not relish publishing information indicating the U.S. was in any way considering dumping or intended to trade with Russia and her satellites. The latter subject was laden with political dynamite. Butz likewise felt any references to the improbability of reducing surpluses quickly would be harmful to future prospects of reducing still further the parity ratio. "If the prospects for disposals are so dim in the next few years," he asked Gwynn Garnett (head of the Foreign Agricultural Service), "will this not mean that any benefits from the flexible price support program will be delayed indefinitely?"[13] That was exactly what the Baughman report inferred and thus the USDA wanted it kept confidential.

Contrary to Department of Agriculture reservations Assistant Budget Director Ralph W. E. Reid advised Clarence Francis neither to conceal nor to alter it. "In each case," he insisted, referring to sections the USDA wanted to rewrite or soften, "it is to delete reasonable but controversial statements of individual judgment because they do not conform to present government policies or actions."[14] Reid warned against political repercussions lest results of this study leak out and give rise to misconceptions and false rumors.

Clarence Francis agreed that it should be released for public consumption but advised some revisions. He informed Budget Director Dodge, "I believe it should be corrected where factually incorrect and where extreme rather than moderate verbiage has been used to express a viewpoint, and declassified with only those changes."[15] When the Baughman report was eventually released it was without fanfare. Few outside the administration took any notice of it.[16]

A spirited cabinet discussion was stimulated, however, as they discussed anew the problems raised by this study. John Foster Dulles restated his opposition to any trade activity even remotely resembling dumping while Ezra Taft Benson defended his aggressive program of fighting for foreign markets. Both Dulles and Benson, however, were leary of selling to Communist nations while Harold Stassen spoke out in favor of it.

Two recent examples lent a hand to those arguing for trade with the Soviet bloc. When Poland tried to buy U.S. wheat and was turned down, they simply purchased it from Canada. After Yugoslavia was denied surplus wheat from American stocks they had to acquire it from the Soviet Union even though it was U.S. policy to win Marshal Tito over to the side of the West.

Taking the initiative at this point, President Eisenhower then introduced the principle of "net advantage."[17] He was convinced that the United States would gain more by selling to Communist nations than by refusing to, and his position carried the day.

The change in administration policy toward the Iron Curtain countries was a significant shift of U.S. foreign policy. Although opposed to the sale of farm commodities to Communist countries on credit and not in sympathy about selling to the Communist bloc if it strengthened them economically, Secretary Benson voiced no major opposition at this time to a volte-face. The Agriculture Secretary did after all want desperately to get rid of domestic surpluses and this turn-about in policy would soon open up new markets heretofore sealed off from American farmers.

America's significant role as leader of the free world alliance had for quite some time adversely affected the prosperity of agriculture. Often the nation's self-interest was sacrificed for the common good of its friends. Not selling surpluses to Communist nations, for instance, might have had strategic value but it hurt the farmer. Concern for the economic strength of Cold War allies or non-aligned nations proved to be an expensive proposition. It meant the United States either had to yield markets to other countries or support them with direct foreign aid grants. Likewise the U.S. frequently imported farm products to bolster foreign economies. Thus while trying to increase U.S. exports USDA often found itself at odds with an entrenched mode of thinking within the Department of State.

Gwynn Garnett, whose Foreign Agriculture Service was vainly trying to expand overseas outlets, complained constantly about the inexcusable delays imposed by the State Department. He thought it undercut his own efforts when Dulles insisted "that as a condition of a Title I program [of PL 480], foreign countries must agree to take fixed quantities of the commodities offered from competing exporting countries."[18] This practice of course reflected American idealism in its concern for other nations but definitely harmed the nation's trade promotional program by ignoring economic self-interest.

Those countries competing with the United States were not reticent about remonstrating to the State Department over alleged USDA dumping practices. Nations registering formal protests included Canada, Australia, New Zealand, Thailand, Uruguay, Burma, Egypt, Denmark, and the Netherlands. Typical of the complaints lodged were those

of New Zealand. In an Aide Memoir from the New Zealand
embassy on January 11, 1954, the Department of State was
politely informed that sales made under PL 480 violated the
General Agreement on Trade and Tariffs because they constituted dumping.

A second note rather firmly reminded the Secretary
of State that New Zealand was among the largest exporters
of cheese, non-fat dry milk solids, and butter in the
world. Displeasure was solemnly albeit forcefully indicated
over U.S. practices. If prices were depressed by such
moves, the communication admonished, "New Zealand might be
forced to sell its dairy products under distress conditions."[19]

Still a third diplomatic note from the New Zealand
ambassador argued more vehemently that recent sales of U.S.
butter to Venezuela and Peru for 41 cents per pound had
jeopardized their entire national economy. New Zealand had
been selling butter to Panama, its traditional customer,
for 50 cents a pound but now the Panamanians were demanding
that they match the U.S. price. Even worse, claimed the
ambassador, when New Zealand was finally forced to reduce
its price to 45 cents per pound, the U.S. Department of
Agriculture made another sale to Panama of 29,952 pounds
of butter at 41 cents per pound. This practice, it was
charged, constituted dumping under the GATT provisions to

which the United States was a signatory. "It would be deeply regrettable," warned the New Zealand ambassador, "if the United States export programs . . . caused a general weakening or depression of the world butter market."[20] New Zealand lodged protests like this even though the United States was quite generous in allowing that nation's products to enter the American market.

Not only foreign countries but American congressmen found fault with the Department of Agriculture's implementation of America's new trade policy. Representative Walter Judd (R-Minn.) wrote Ezra Taft Benson in 1954 of his dissatisfaction over the manner in which the PL 480 program was being carried out. The Minnesota congressman, a former missionary to China, was greatly interested in preventing Communism from spreading throughout Asia. Since mainland China had already gone Communist, his concern now was in preventing the new and emerging nations from identifying their nationalist movements with Communism. Having introduced the original measure (H.R. 5954) in 1953, which later evolved into PL 480, he wanted its major emphasis to be on foreign aid rather than mere expansion of markets. Since the bill was sent to the House Committee on Agriculture, instead of the Committee on Foreign Affairs (Judd was chairman at the time), a specific provision dealing with foreign aid was deleted. Judd's aim was "to use our agricultural surpluses to implement our foreign policy objectives--such as giving newly independent countries or countries threatened by Communist pressure, from without or within, a greater will and capacity to defend their independence by helping with their food deficits and strengthening their economies so that they would become better able to feed themselves, increase their production and expand trade."[21]

After getting no satisfaction from the House Agriculture Committee, Judd got an amendment (Section 550) tacked on the Mutual Security Act, which was PL 665, to allow surplus agricultural commodities to be used to bolster the economies of underdeveloped countries. Harold Stassen, who administered the Mutual Security Program, used some $240,000,000 worth of excess farm food and fiber in one year for that purpose. After taking note of this unexpected utilization of surpluses, Titles II and III were added on the Agriculture Committee's bill and it was passed as PL 480. Because of that action the disposition of surpluses as an aspect of foreign aid was taken away from Stassen and given to Ezra Taft Benson. Judd's apprehension increased because the Agriculture Secretary tended to stress the selling of farm products rather than purely administering a foreign assistance program.

After a deal was made with Japan for the sale of
U.S. farm surpluses there, Walter Judd wanted Benson to
remember that an important consideration in the negotia-
tions with Japan was the use of yen accruing to the United
States from the sale of farm products. The Minnesota congressman insisted the "currency should be used in a manner
to come to grips with the basic problem of facilitating
Japan's economic life without increasing dependence on Communist areas."[22]

Believing that the USDA was more interested in bet-
tering the lot of American farmers than in fighting Communism, Judd was somewhat anxious about the way Benson administered the program. As Judd stated it: "I was unhappy
about the misuse of the Act by the Department of Agriculture under the pressures to reduce our farm surpluses at
almost any cost to our foreign policy relations or our
regular marketings or world prices. Sometimes I felt my
'baby' had been converted into a monster."[23]

While Walter Judd wanted sale of surpluses for foreign currency to be used to aid the recipient nations,
Clarence Randall wanted to terminate the entire practice as
soon as possible. The chairman of the Council on Foreign
Economic Policy informed Clarence Francis of his belief the
"President should advise the Congress of his conviction that
local currency sales and barter should be regarded as

temporary expedients, and of his opposition to permanent
status for the legislation because of its conflict both
with the administration's foreign trade policy and the administration's desire to further the removal of government
from business."[24] When the USDA carried out provisions of
PL 480 it was for all intent and purposes engaged in state
trading. Albeit the U.S. government was the only agency
capable of handling such vast amounts of commodities,
Randall still did not like this federal involvement and in
many ways Benson also found it distasteful.

In his criticism of PL 480 activities, Clarence
Randall used a transaction with a Latin American country
to make his point. The Commodity Credit Corporation had
sold $24 million worth of stored stocks to Colombia for
the equivalent of $17 million, but payment was taken in
pesos. Each peso was valued at 40 cents American money.
Since local currency had to be spent within the buyer
country, the U.S. Treasury Department offered these pesos
at a discount price of 20 cents to any government agency
capable of using them. In this instance foreign aid was
not very well correlated with surplus disposal and there
was no planned way to use the money for the best advantage
of the Colombian economy. The foreign aid muddle was all
too frequently the result of ideological rigidity rather
than rational planning.

Randall's 1956 report also scored the performance of
the USDA on the following account. If the United States was
on the one hand officially opposed to export subsidies,
dumping, or state interference in international trade, then
should not this country set an example by not engaging in
similar practices? Also, the U.S. was committed to encouraging multilateral trade, but had concluded bilateral trade
agreements with thirty foreign governments. American trade
policy was in many ways fostering exactly what it had formerly opposed.[25] Here Randall was again insisting on a type
of ideological purity (i.e. extension of the free enterprise
system in international trade) before the problem of surpluses and lost markets had been solved.

From Ezra Taft Benson's point of view he believed
the time had come for the United States to break the self-
imposed bonds on its trading practices or even more overseas
markets would be lost in the near future. The U.S. was by
no means the only nation looking out for its own economic
interests. In a report on the work of USDA trade missions,
Assistant Agriculture Secretary John H. Davis focused on the
fact that virtually all nations placed roadblocks of their
own in the way of free trade yet complained about U.S.
practices. In trying to implement PL 480 USDA officials
repeatedly ran up against state-trading, subsidies, bilateral
trading, protectionism, import restrictions, and dumping by

other nations. Inconvertibility of currencies added to the
burden of widening world trade. Comparatively speaking the
United States showed considerable restraint at a period when
it could no longer ignore the plight of its own domestic
agriculture.[26]

The National Agricultural Advisory Commission discussed the possibility of reestablishing a food stamp program and Senator Aiken prepared such a bill for the legislative hopper. A USDA report prepared for the cabinet did
not consider this proposal feasible and therefore declined
to support it. The position paper claimed: "According to
the Department's records the previous program of this type
presented difficult operating problems, was both complex and
costly to administer, and proved to be more effective for
some commodities than for others."[27]

When a domestic relief bill was co-sponsored by
Dirksen (R-Ill.) and Capehart (R-Ind.), which would have
authorized the milling of surplus wheat and corn into flour
for free distribution to the poor, the Agriculture Department's objections were stated as follows:

> (1) It will be relatively ineffective from
>   a surplus disposal standpoint, since
>   it is believed that relief distribu-
>   tion of flour and cornmeal from CCC

> stocks will largely displace other
> usage of these items, and will not re-
> sult in any substantial decrease in
> CCC stocks of wheat and corn.
>
> (2) It would have the effect of increasing
> the needy family program both in the
> number of states and individual re-
> cipients . . . [and] the donation of
> flour and cornmeal would prolong this
> program beyond the point where it is
> necessary.[28]

Government research, however, was given a high
priority by Benson. The Secretary had gotten Congress to
pass PL 540 which provided increased funds for agricultural
research. To help implement this program the President
appointed J. Leroy Welsh to head a Commission on Increased
Industrial Use of Agricultural Products. The Welsh Commission discovered that industrial outlets for agricultural
products amounted to only 7 per cent of the total volume
produced. Recommended was a crash program in utilization
research not only in USDA facilities but in land-grant institutions, experiment stations, non-profit organizations, contracts to private corporations, and projects in foreign
countries where local currency could be used by government
agencies.[29]

An accelerated program of basic research was also
advanced in order to discover new ways to use farm commodities as substitutes for synthetics. It was hoped, for
instance, that chemicals normally obtained from coal or
petroleum might be extracted from farm products. Since
principal components of many agricultural crops were in
essence such basic substances as: cellulose, starch, sugar,
oils, and protein, the aim was to find ways in converting
these basic ingredients into commercially useable products.
After considerable study, the Welsh Commission urged research be done to find ways of making adhesives from wheat;
paper from corn; chemicals from grain; and emulsifiers from
cotton seeds. Other possibilities involved treating cotton
to replace synthetic fiber; using crop residues (e.g. corn-
stalks) for composition in construction material; or the
manufacture of plastics from the whey, lactose, and casein
contained in milk.[30]

Ezra Taft Benson placed a premium on finding new
uses for farm products. He pushed exploratory programs on
all fronts by authorizing research contracts with private
firms for the following projects: (1) developing commercial
uses for dialdehyde starches; (2) manufacturing paper
products from cereal starches; (3) finding uses for wheat
glutens; and (4) extracting substances from grain for the
making of resins, plasticizers, and chemicals. In those

cases where feasibility studies warranted action--pilot plants would be constructed to demonstrate practicability of production for commercial use.[31]

Another series of grants were let to individual scientists, universities, and non-profit research organizations for "fundamental and applied research on the major constituents of surplus agricultural commodities."[32] Regional USDA laboratories, located in California, Louisiana, Illinois, and Pennsylvania were assigned the task of seeking new uses for carbohydrates, dried whole milk, and cotton. And finally the Agricultural Research Center at Beltsville, Maryland received the job of finding new plants for commercial farming. They were to test the feasibility of raising such new and exotic crops as bamboo, kenaf (for twine), jojoba (for wax), safflower (for oil), sesame, pistachio nuts, sunflowers, and high amylose corn for starch.

Harboring some reservations about Benson's ambitious research program, Clarence Francis unburdened himself to presidential advisor Gabriel Hauge. "I think I would change the emphasis in the program," he maintained, "and devote more . . . [effort] to fundamental research, relying upon industry to apply the findings for practical results just as they have always done." He did not like the idea of federally built pilot plants when private industry would

have constructed them on a contract basis. If the USDA
insisted on doing research in its own laboratories, he felt
outside scientists should then be brought into the department. Finally, with an air of futility, he predicted, "My
guess is that [in] starting research from scratch, it may
take five years before . . . [results are] developed into
commercial operations of any size."[33]

After four years of relatively high expenditures
for agricultural research White House staffer John Hamlin
complained to Sherman Adams that Benson was once again
exceeding his budget. What really perturbed Hamlin was
that too much emphasis was still being placed on production
research and not that geared for finding new uses for farm
products. Even though utilization research had been greatly expanded by Benson, he found it constituted only one-
third of all research activity. The USDA continued to
spend money on developing more productive varieties of
seeds, finding better fertilizers, discovering new pesticides, and improving cultivation techniques. While successful, these efforts helped create more surpluses--not to
find ways to dispose of them. Blaming outmoded attitudes
and congressional pressure, not Secretary Benson, Hamlin
confided to Adams: "Ill-advised public pressures operating
through the legislative branch are chiefly responsible for
our departure from a free agricultural economy into one of

increasing complexity. Similar pressures operating through the same channel are further aggravating the problem by opposing any real shift in emphasis from production to utilization research."[34]

The impasse confronting Benson was compounded by intransigence on the one hand and impatience on the other. The bureaucratic establishment within the USDA still pursued its traditional ways, which meant emphasis on production instead of concentrating upon solving problems related to consumption and marketing. Congressmen belonging to the farm bloc continued to regard short-run gains as preferable to the long run. The White House in turn was influenced by the political considerations of the legislative branch; therefore Ezra Taft Benson found himself unable to satisfy everyone. His approach was to concentrate on real solutions which by their very nature involved time to consummate. Because of mid-term losses in Congress Republican party officials were desirous of some new farm program for 1956. They wanted quick results for immediate political gain. Within this context and under heavy pressure to deliver something tangible the Secretary of Agriculture began to devise a new farm program to supplement his overall goals. He was now fully aware that no administrator in government could function without taking cognizance of political cross-currents. What he would seek to do was enormously difficult. Benson desired a program consistent with comprehensive objectives while coming up with one satisfactory for those seeking to placate certain segments of the farm population.

Chapter VII

The Soil Bank

Appearing before the Senate Agriculture Committee on January 19, 1955, Ezra Taft Benson expressed the view that the post-Korean decline in U.S. farm income had at least been checked. He predicted a prosperous decade once the administration's farm program began to operate without past encumbrances. This hopefulness was based on an expectation that the "basic philosophy underlying the Agriculture Act of 1954 will encourage individual farmers who are efficient and ambitious to participate profitably in the thrilling opportunities ahead of us in the growing science of agriculture."[1]

The tangled skein of politics had its way of hamstringing all attempts by Benson to work out a lasting solution on economically feasible lines. Congressional critics such as Wisconsin's Senator Joseph R. McCarthy took advantage of a momentary fall in farm prices to publicly upbraid the Eisenhower administration. McCarthy, still smarting from his censure by the Senate and feeling bitter about being repudiated by fellow Republicans, castigated the Chief Executive for failing to help farmers. He blamed depression-like conditions on Benson's policies, which were portrayed as a veritable persecution of rural people. Following this vicious volley, McCarthy chided, "Although I cannot imagine why this should be the case, it seems to me that your administration is engaged in open war against the farm community."[2]

By late fall in 1955 it was apparent that sliding farm income, even though temporary, would have adverse political consequences in the 1956 presidential election unless something was done to halt the decline. To compound GOP woes, President Eisenhower suffered a heart attack on September 23 and his future status as a candidate for re-election was very much in doubt. In cooperation with De-partment of Agriculture officials, key White House personnel prepared a realistic assessment of farm problems and what could be done to remedy them prior to the 1956 election. Maxwell Rabb (a lawyer who served as secretary to the cabinet from 1954-58) sent each cabinet member a personal copy of this report on October 5, 1955.

Without any excuses for its political orientation the report started right off by conceding that "the farm

situation has worsened while we have been in office." Since
farm income had dropped 20 per cent since the peak of the
Korean War, they realized they were vulnerable. To make
things worse there was no prospect of a quick upturn in
1956. In politics the incumbent inherits the blame regard-
less of mitigating circumstances, so the recommendations
made were for action, not rebuttals. Suggestions for immediate consideration included raising price supports, pursuing an even more vigorous program of surplus disposal, and
expanding relief programs. Long-range proposals contained
the following:

1. Appropriations to use perhaps $200
   million additional of Agricultural
   Conservation Program funds to help
   farmers shift crops to grass or
   forest on those lands not well
   adapted to cultivation.

2. A package program for wheat.

3. Legislation to make cotton more competitive, pricewise, so as to increase
   exports and domestic use.

4. Rural Development Program for low income farmers, including legislation
   and appropriations.

5. Great Plains Program, including needed
modification of existing federal program.

6. Perfecting legislation within the general framework of existing law.[3]

This briefing of the cabinet on various alternatives for concrete action was but a prelude to a full-scale
discussion at the next scheduled meeting. Unlike those of
his predecessors, Eisenhower's cabinet often held sub-
stantive talks on major issues where each member received an
opportunity to offer suggestions. Frequently formal position papers were presented to explore fully any given
policy. Minutes were kept by a secretary and periodic action reports were issued to keep everyone posted on legislative progress or how a specific program was faring after
being implemented.

The October 7th cabinet meeting was devoted almost
entirely to a discussion of agricultural problems in their
relationship to the coming election. Absent was Dwight D.
Eisenhower, who had not yet fully recovered from his heart
attack. Secretary Benson tried to explain the overall
economic adjustment of agricultural prices by attributing
some of the difficulty to a "cost-price squeeze" over which
he had no control. Benson did not deny that farmers were

experiencing difficulties from not receiving subsidies for commodities supported at artificially high prices, but he wanted to establish as a matter of record that his department was seeking to rectify these past mistakes.[4]

Harold Stassen made the pointed statement that it appeared absolutely necessary to prepare a farm program which would have the dual purpose of gaining rural support while possessing true merit. This also was the feeling expressed by Richard Nixon, then Vice-President, who presided over this cabinet conference.

The Secretary of Agriculture would normally have resisted any thought of allowing pure politics to enter into his decision-making except for the fact that he had just received a communication from the President. Prompted by top echelon White House staffers and other members of the cabinet, Ike's note contained clear-cut instructions to take positive steps to alleviate the present situation. Benson was told by the President to take some "temporary or specific action as in your judgment will meet any current emergency with which the American farmer and his family are faced."[5]

Consequently at the December 9th meeting of the cabinet Benson had ready in rough form a proposal to serve both short- and long-term needs of agriculture. To supplement the flexible price support system and surplus disposal

programs, a land retirement plan was offered as a bold
solution to the farm problem. By taking land out of cultivation and placing this acreage into what Benson called a
Soil Bank, surpluses could be prevented by bringing commodity
production into adjustment with market demands.[6]

Variations of this concept had been in existence and
in some instances older programs came close to this plan.
The original idea for the Soil Bank as such was implanted by
Martin P. Gehlbach of Lincoln, Illinois. It took several
years to germinate before it grew into a full-scale plan.
When the House Agriculture Committee held a public hearing
at nearby Bloomington, Gehlbach presented his plan way back
on October 17, 1953. Having served as an agent for the
Sangamon Valley Farm Bureau for many years, Gehlbach had
considerable knowledge of problems facing agriculture. He
presented to the committee his own ideas on what should be
included in a farm program. They were:

> 1. If the money spent on grain storage,
>   support prices, acreage allotments, and
>   other measures of our present program
>   were paid directly for the acres of
>   soil building legumes that farmers grow
>   on their farms, we could eliminate the
>   acreage controls.

2. The incentive payments paid on soil-
   building crops will not only serve to
   regulate the production of soil-
   depleting crops but will also provide
   the differential earnings to put agriculture on a par with industry and
   labor.

3. In the proposed agriculture program the
   farmer on a farm with a low yield per
   acre will be the first to recognize
   that an acre of legume with an incentive
   payment is more desirable than trying to
   secure a profit from the production of a
   depleting crop having a low yield, especially in a period of high farm operation
   costs.[7]

Studied and laid aside in 1954, the Soil Bank Plan
was reevaluated in 1956. Operational details were now
worked out by USDA technicians for presentation to Congress
early in 1956. Their work was reviewed and approved by the
National Agricultural Advisory Commission.

As a result of this intensive work, the land retirement program was organized around the twin concepts of
Acreage and Conservation Reserves. Highly productive land

would be eligible for the Acreage Reserve. Payment to the farmer for acres taken out of cultivation would be calculated on a rate of one-half the loan level of the commodity normally grown on the land. This had reference to the non-recourse loans offered by the Commodity Credit Corporation, which constituted the usual means whereby the government established a price support for any given product. Preliminary estimates revealed an acre of cotton-producing land placed in the Acreage Reserve would cost the USDA $45. For wheat it would run $15, corn $31, and rice at least $50 per acre. Figuring some two to five million acres of cotton acreage would be taken out of production, the total expense to the government would be at least $135 million and might go as high as $225 million. For retirement of 12 to 15 million acres of wheat acreage the cost would be from $180 to $225 million; for 4 to 6 million acres of corn--$125 to $185 million; and the three-tenths of a million acres of rice-producing land would total $15 million.[8]

Land with a low yield record could be placed in the Soil Bank Conservation Reserve. Payment to farmers for taking marginal acres out of production was projected to be in the neighborhood of $19 per acre with additional payments, not to exceed $25 an acre, for encouragement of forage or tree planting. No one quite knew for sure how much land might qualify for this aspect of land retirement. But even with only a superficial examination of the whole Soil Bank program it was obvious that this type of program would cost substantial sums of money.[9]

There were those both within and without the Department of Agriculture who at an early stage looked skeptically at the Soil Bank program. Assistant Secretary for Agricultural Stabilization, James A. McConnell, had grave doubts about the merits of the proposed plan. Perhaps he felt free to offer criticisms since his voluntary resignation was set to go into effect late in December of 1955. He wrote W. E. Hamilton, Research Director for the American Farm Bureau Federation, "I might say that so far I have not been able to see personally where any soil bank plan that I have looked at could be effective in controlling total agricultural production."[10]

Hamilton agreed with his friend, telling him, "I must say that I share your misgivings with regard to total agriculture production."[11] The official Farm Bureau position had been made abundantly clear when its national president, Charles B. Shuman, told the House Committee on Agriculture: "High price supports, fixed by government without adequate regard to supply and demand, result in lower farm income." Testifying on February 23, 1955, the AFBF head

explained why government subsidies were detrimental to the
long-range prosperity of agriculture:

1. Farmers who might go out of production
   of a particular crop stay in. New
   farmers who otherwise might not have
   gone into the production of a particular crop are encouraged to do so.
2. The amount of consumers . . . declines
   as the price goes up . . . substitutes
   . . . are encouraged and indirectly
   subsidized.
3. It is difficult or impossible to maintain exports when the U.S. price of a
   commodity is held above the world
   price.[12]

Secretary Benson could not have agreed more with
Charles Shuman but the leader of a farm organization did
not have to consider the political repercussions of his
pronouncements. Benson was under White House pressure to
find a way to help farmers financially while simultaneously
solving the dilemma of overproduction.

Circulated among top USDA officials was a document
titled, "An Appraisal of the Political Situation That Faces
Agriculture by Area and by Commodity." Vulnerable were

eleven Senators and sixty-three Representatives from the
Farm Belt who had won their respective seats by less than
5 per cent of the total vote in their state or district.
Laying it on the line, this White House-prepared memorandum
succinctly stated the basic fact of politics, "The farmer
votes his pocket book just as much as the businessman or
the laborer and his welfare will have a lot to do with
Republican results in predominately agricultural states."[13]
It was pointed out that in rural areas the farmer was the
key to GOP chances of victory. Politically speaking the
upshot was therefore manifestly clear. Something concrete
had to be done to convince each farmer that the Republican
farm program benefitted him economically.

Soon after Benson presented his outline of the Soil
Bank to the cabinet, Senator Karl Mundt proffered some free
advice to the Secretary of Agriculture. Referring to the
"fiasco" of 1954 where "the Republican members of the
Agriculture Committee of the House and Senate were treated
like orphans and ignored like lepers," he wrote, "I
implore you to call in the Republican members of the Senate
Committee on Agriculture to go over with us the presentation which is proposed to being made in January both as to
content and as to wording."[14] He was in effect calling
for Benson to yield to congressional demands for a farm
program that was politically expedient. This meant, of

course, an outright return to the old 90 per cent of parity scheme.

Also addressing a letter to Sherman Adams, the persistent Senator from South Dakota told Ike's top assistant it was absolutely vital to work as a team in the preparation of agricultural legislation. Mundt acknowledged that there was much merit in the Department's draft of a Soil Bank which would have political pulling power and in addition would make good economic sense. But he closed with a final reminder for Adams to "talk like a Dutch uncle to Ezra."[15]

To make the most of the situation Senator Mundt issued a press release claiming the USDA's preparation of a land retirement program was a "frank recognition of the fact that neither its flexible price support program nor the high rigid support program is adequate alone to meet the farm problems of this postwar era and the cost-price squeeze which this peacetime era has brought to the farmer."[16] Interpreting the decision to innovate a new plan which would withdraw surplus producing acreage from cultivation in the best political light, Mundt said it proved both President Eisenhower and the Department of Agriculture were determined to take necessary steps in order to step up the net income of the farmer and to cut him in on an equitable share of America's great prosperity.

Sherman Adams did request Benson to meet with GOP
members of both the Senate and House Agricultural Committees. After having conferred with the Agriculture Secretary, Senator Mundt felt quite optimistic over the possibilities of a Soil Bank. In his "Weekly Report from Karl
Mundt," sent to home town newspapers in his state, the South
Dakotan asserted, "There is much that is exciting and new
and constructive in the President's new farm proposals."[17]
The goal, he explained, was to insure a farm family sufficient net income to place it on a par with those of
unionized labor, industrial, or professional groups.

Describing how the Soil Bank should be used to win
farm votes, Senator Mundt again wrote Sherman Adams, with
copies to other White House staffers and to Republican
National Chairman Leonard Hall, advising that future
publicity should be geared to build up the image of the
GOP as the real friends of the small dirt farmer. He
called for a cessation of talk about flexibility and a
"shift of emphasis from parity on the farm product to the
family type farmer." If the Eisenhower administration
would assume a political stance as the defender of small
farmers the Senator claimed, it would be far easier to dis-
arm and defeat those critics trying to return the farm
argument to a basic contest over price supports.

137

To help Republicans achieve a new posture Mundt and
Senator Edward Thye (R-Minn.) introduced a bill with the
prime aim of checking the "growth of the corporate type
farm and to protect taxpayers against the continued payment
of six- and seven-figure checks in huge amounts to corporation farmers for products already in surplus."[18] There was
political merit in Mundt's proposed strategy because it
switched attention from the debate over price supports to
a strong, vote-getting position as champion of the family-
sized farm.

After a brief period of convalescence, President
Eisenhower was soon back on a fairly full schedule by the
first of the year. Incorporating the material prepared
during his absence, his farm message was sent to Congress
on January 9, 1956. In it the economic plight of farmers
was attributed to three causes: (1) production and market
distortions, the result of wartime production incentives
too long continued; (2) current record livestock production
and near-record crop harvests piled on previously accumulated holdovers; and (3) rising costs and high capital
requirements. Singled out as the main problem was that of
overproduction. "A government warehouse is not a market,"
the President reasoned. "Even the most storable commodities
cannot be added forever to government granaries, nor can
they be indefinitely held."[19]

This critique set the stage for presenting the Soil Bank as a means for retiring certain types of land from active production. This removal, he promised, would prevent accretion of more surpluses. Taking up the Acreage Reserve first, Eisenhower explained how participating farmers would be given certificates for commodities whose value would be based on the normal yields of those acres withheld in this Reserve. They would in turn be redeemed by the Commodity Credit Corporation in cash or kind at specified rates. This, the President predicated, "uses the surplus to reduce the surplus."[20]

Eisenhower described the Soil Bank's Conservation Reserve as a measure to safeguard America's "precious heritage of food-producing resources so we may hand on an enriched legacy to future generations."[21] He did not stress the value of rental rates to farmers as a supplement to their income, but rather emphasized the value of placing some 20 million acres of marginal land into legume cover crops, forests, or wild areas for fostering water conservation.

Although the President announced that surplus commodities valued at $4½ billion had already been disposed of, he nonetheless asked for increased authority for the Commodity Credit Corporation. Eisenhower requested legislation making it possible to sell CCC stocks domestically at below

regular market prices; to expand provisions for barter
arrangements; and to repeal Section 305 of PL 480 so as to
permit commercial transactions with nations of the Communist bloc. To facilitate greater home consumption of
surplus dairy products, he also sought an extension of the
Special School Milk Program for two more years with an
increase in appropriated funds from $50 to $75 million
per year.

 While not naming any maximum figure, the President
asked for a definite dollar limit on the amount of price
support loans to any one individual or farming unit. The
rationale for this request was a defense of the small
farmer. Eisenhower declared, "It is not sound government
policy to underwrite at public expense such formidable
competition with family operated farms, which are the bulwark of our agriculture."[22]

 Other proposals in the presidential message to
Congress included recommendations for increasing the
effectiveness of the Great Plains Program; a request to
increase by one-fourth (amounting to $103 million) the
budget for agricultural research projects; authorization
for refunding the tax on gasoline used on the farm; and
enactment of a comprehensive Rural Development Program.
After reiterating the principle that the government was
merely a "partner with the farmer--never his master,"

President Eisenhower maintained: "By every possible means we must develop and promote that partnership--to the end that agriculture may continue to be a sound, enduring foundation for our economy and that farm living may be a profitable and satisfying experience."[23]

Only one day after the farm program had been sent to Capitol Hill, Ezra Taft Benson was stoutly defending it before the National Cattlemen's Association. Addressing this gathering in New Orleans, the Agriculture Secretary painted a bright picture of the Soil Bank's potentialities. It would, he said, "meet the twin problems of surpluses and diverted acres."[24] To make flexible price supports work, Benson stressed, stocks of excess products had to be both eliminated and prevented. If enacted, he predicted, those goals could be achieved.

A few days later Benson spoke to the National Council of Farmer Cooperatives and forecast a new buoyancy in the market place would occur as soon as the Soil Bank became law. Once the depressing effect of surpluses had been removed, and he blamed the current 10 per cent drop in farm prices on this, he foresaw a long-range prosperity for farmers. The Agriculture Secretary let it be known that the asked-for refund of gasoline tax to farmers would add $60 million to rural income. Feeling confident this would be a popular set of farm proposals, Benson contended, "This is the administration's program--it is my program--and it is your program because it came from the grass roots."[25]

Included in the President's farm message was a request for major expansion of the Rural Development Program. This action was indicative of a desire on the part of the administration to do more to help small, less prosperous farmers. Congress had been remiss in providing funds for effective implementation. Based upon a USDA study titled, "Development of Agriculture's Human Resources," the initial recommendation for its enactment by Congress was made on April 27, 1955.

It was noted at the time that rural poverty was a widespread malady. Some 2,849,000 farmers, out of a total of 5,370,000 were found to have annual incomes under $1,000. The USDA report, which the National Agricultural Advisory Commission helped prepare, identified specific geographic regions which were in desperate need of some kind of special assistance. Primary areas so designated were: the Southern Piedmont, Appalachian Mountains, Southeastern Hilly, Mississippi Delta, Sandy Coastal Plain, Ozark Ouachita, Northern Lake States, and Northwestern New Mexico.[26]

The legislative proposal drawn up by the USDA was essentially meant to be a program of encouraging local

communities to help themselves. When, through the
initiative of some local group, a project was set up, then
the federal government would render assistance. This aid
was contemplated in terms of making the services of
existing agencies available rather than extension of
government grants. Technical advice could be received from
the Soil Conservation Service; vocational facilities would
be supplied by the Department of Health, Education, and
Welfare; credit would be made available through the
Farmers Home Administration; farm management counsel would
be provided by the Extension Service; job placement by the
Employment Service of the Department of Labor; and
assistance for relocation of industry to depressed areas
would be given by both the Department of Commerce and the
Office of Defense Mobilization. In addition, seminars and
training sessions were to be held to prepare community
leaders for the tasks of planning and carrying out their
own local projects.

The rural development concept possessed unrealized
value and might have been the first major step toward a
full-scale anti-poverty program. Likewise it would have
helped check rural migration to the urban ghettoes, thus
preventing future problems in that sector. But because
Congress seemed apathetic, the tremendous potentiality of
the project was never fully realized. It might well have

served as a major vehicle for aiding the noncommercial farmers to remain on the land or to retrain them for nonagricultural jobs. Had this been done during the 1950's many urban problems of the 1960's would have been abated and the ecological balance of man and nature could have been sustained. In 1955 legislation was sought to start fifty pilot projects in the one thousand counties most in need of help. The House approved a bill for $2,620,000 for research education, and administrative assistance to low-income families in rural regions but the Senate did not concur. Lending ability of the Farmers Home Administration was increased by the Upper Chamber and $350,000 was appropriated for administrative expenses. This too was approved by the House and that constituted the extent of Congress's interest in alleviating rural poverty.[27]

Even though no major appropriations were forthcoming—a small request for $1,350,000 by the Department of Labor was also denied—Ezra Taft Benson subsequently named Under Secretary True D. Morse as head of an interdepartmental committee to see what could be done despite lack of substantial support or funding from Congress.

The Secretary of Agriculture's first annual report on the status of the Rural Development Program did reveal some modest progress. Ten states had started community improvement projects under the guidance of Rural Development

Committees (broadly representative of agriculture and nonagricultural interests). The report indicated "other leaders in twenty-four states have now named fifty-four pilot rural communities and areas where the program will be focused in 1956-57."[28] Objectives listed included the encouragement of: more efficient farming; greater industrial and business development; improved levels of health, education, and family welfare; and increased participation in religion and civic life. The RDP report called for full participation by such individuals as farmers, businessmen, civic leaders, and church leaders in the planning and action phases of the program. All in all it represented a potential blueprint for local communities to control their own anti-poverty programs but congressional disinterest allowed it to go undeveloped.

Congress paid so little attention to the Rural Development Program that even by the end of the Eisenhower administration it was still a small-scale effort. By 1960 RDP had its own Coordinator, Harry J. Reed, and an Executive Secretary, Garland Marshall. Scattered projects in thirty-eight states and Puerto Rico were in existence. Specific examples of RDP endeavors indicate the nature of its work. A small industrial plant, hiring thirty employees, was acquired for Washington County, Florida; a parish in Louisiana passed a bond issue to purchase a $200,000 canning plant;

arrangements were made to build a meat packaging plant in
Georgia; a woodchip mill, to employ six people, was erected
in Illinois; in Minnesota a Christmas Tree Grower's Association was formed; strawberry production was increased in
Michigan; a co-op elevator and grain storage project was
constructed in Nebraska; and eligible farmers in Maryland
were given Social Security benefits.[29]

Since commercial farming was rapidly becoming an
agribusiness, this transition changed the very nature of
living on the land. Huge outlays of capital, much technical know-how, and large farmsteads were imperative for
making this type of commercial venture profitable. For
those with small land units who could not compete, only a
massive federal program of rural renewal, retraining, and
relocation would have sufficed to alleviate the dire
effects of poverty level farming. Unfortunately, neither
Congress, big farm organizations, nor the American public
in general really grasped the significance of the Rural
Development Program.

Since economic conditions were putting the squeeze
on smaller operators, a new farm movement came into being
in 1955. Two Corning, Iowa residents, Oren Lee Staley and
former Governor Dan Turner, provided leadership which led
to the founding of the National Farm Organization. Having
grown rapidly, the NFO had eighteen county locals in Iowa

and eight in Missouri by October 20, 1966. At its first regional meeting the following resolutions were passed:

1. We hereby petition our government for
   100 per cent of parity for our farm
   products.

2. In the event of farm surpluses we hereby state our willingness to accept
   reasonable controls.

3. In view of the fact that hogs and cattle are now being marketed for less
   than the cost of production, and as an
   emergency measure, we petition the Department of Agriculture to establish an
   immediate floor of approximately $20.00
   per hundredweight on butcher hogs and
   approximately $30.00 per hundredweight
   on good to choice cattle.

4. We pledge our cooperation with the
   United States Department of Agriculture
   in a reasonable long-range program.

5. We are a non-partisan and non-political
   organization.

6. We do not approve of any type of
   violence.[30]

When rumors about the militancy of this organization
reached the USDA, Assistant Secretary for Marketing and
Foreign Agriculture, Earl L. Butz, went to investigate the
NFO. Comparing NFO to the radical Farm Holiday Association
of the 1930's, Butz informed Benson, "I get the impression
that this new protest movement in Western and Southwestern
Iowa is not to be ignored, but it is not as serious as the
press makes it out to be."[31]

Developing the idea of collective bargaining the NFO
continued to grow. After its first national convention in
1955 the NFO expanded during the winter months to a membership of 180,000 in thirteen states. It proved to be a
tangible political force in the 1956 election and in 1958
NFO pushed negotiated contracts for farmers to raise the
prices of their commodities. It accepted only bona fide
farmers as members and drew clientele especially well in
areas where small farms were the rule rather than the
exception.

None of the national farm organizations were too
keen about land retirement, but for other reasons than
those registered by the NFO. Representing the conservative
viewpoint, Charles Shuman of the Farm Bureau opposed withdrawing acreage from cultivation because he thought it would
be ineffectual in checking overproduction. He favored
abolition of price supports and total freedom for commercial

agriculture.

Herschel Newsom of the Grange, who was pushing a permanent two-price system for wheat, regarded the Soil Bank as a useful "temporary stop-gap."[32] Leaders of the National Milk Producers Federation grumbled that it did nothing to raise the income of dairy farmers. National Farmers Union head James Patton claimed nothing the Eisenhower administration did ever really worked to the economic advantage of the nation's farmers.

Farm journal reactions were mixed although less critical than the views expressed by farm organization executives. The Farm Journal, with headquarters in Philadelphia and usually pro-Eisenhower in tone, claimed editorially: "Benson and Ike have really stolen the march on the Democratic party. . . . [It] is a real flip-flop for Secretary Benson. . . . You see, they had pretty much stuck their hopes on the flexible price support system."[33]

Capper's Farmer of Kansas made the rueful comment, "The Soil Bank is a sound idea and will be good for soil conservation, but it doesn't provide anything for farm income this year."[34]

And finally the editor of the Progressive Farmer, published in Birmingham, Alabama, observed, "I have heard indirectly that the Delta cotton growers are worried about where the tenant cotton farmer is going to wind up."[35]

The White House staff, GOP congressional leaders, and the Republican National Committee were becoming increasingly uneasy about rural unrest. They were relying on the Soil Bank to stem the tide of farmer dissatisfaction, but were not sure whether it would do the job. To gauge farm opinion in the fall of 1955, three GOP National Committeemen went as observers to a rural gathering at Pecatonica, Illinois. Sponsored by the National Grange, Under Secretary of Agriculture True D. Morse was to be the featured speaker. When the evaluations of crowd reaction were sent to Gabriel Hauge, he felt anything but happy when he notified General Persons: "I enclose the results of that little inquiry. This is just one more bit of evidence that I think we must gather in order to persuade Benson that things are serious."[36]

The account of the three GOP National Committee observers was bad news for political ears. With voter appeal as the only criterion the first evaluation noted: "Audience was respectful, but noticeably unenthusiastic" and "Listeners gave Morse courteous response, more to him as a decent, likeable person than to what he said."[37] Observer number two ventured these opinions: "Morse offered farmers nothing they would buy, merely advising them to suffer in patience until better times came"; "This observer found most of them displeased and some of

150

them outright angry"; "Farmers appeared to be strong for Eisenhower, but against his farm policy"; and "Benson is respected, but his policies are disliked."[38] A third assessment included such caustic comments as: "Morse did the best he could in putting out the Department of Agriculture's line, which is not going over any better today than it did two and a half years ago"; "This observer was shocked by [Herschel] Newsom's thinly-veiled criticism of the administration in certain fields" and "Republicans are in real trouble among farmers by 1956. . . . If something isn't done, the dissatisfaction could reach to Eisenhower personally."[39]

Alarming feedback on farm conditions came in from other sources as well. One of Ike's economic advisors, Gabriel Hauge, received one such communication from National Committeeman Val Washington. As a member of the Christian County Farm Bureau of Kentucky and therefore one acquainted with farm sentiment, he reported that Democrat Senator Happy Chandler had made political hay throughout the countryside by attacking Mr. Benson. The reason this strategem worked, he disclosed, was that "farmers are unhappy because of increased prices for what they buy and decreased prices for what they sell."[40]

Val Washington later wrote Hauge another critique on what he deemed to be bad policy decisions on the part of

USDA personnel. It was the Kentuckian's judgment that Commodity Credit Corporation practices relative to sales of surpluses had repeatedly disrupted domestic markets. He also ventured the opinion that stored stocks would be less likely to depress futures if they were not overly advertised. It was his judgment that Agriculture Department officials talked far too much about surpluses, thus drawing an inordinate amount of attention to them.

When his caustic comments on the CCC's selling practices were forwarded to the USDA, they were rejected with the notation: "Frankly, we find little merit to the suggestions, which if followed would constitute reversal of the administration's farm policy. . . ."[41]

The Commodity Credit Corporation did take the precaution of announcing temporary suspension of all sales of CCC-owned corn to domestic exporters. The reason given for this action was that it would help strengthen producer prices by reducing the amount of stored corn available for sale during the period of harvest and heaviest marketing.[42]

Val Washington was not satisfied with the response given to his suggestions nor with the subsequent actions of the CCC. He wrote Hauge once more citing published figures to prove the CCC had in fact stepped up its overseas sales. Consequently export firms were not buying the current crop for shipment. From October 5 to November 23

152

disposition of surplus stocks of corn actually went up from 2,111,000 bushels to 2,409,000 bushels. Likewise domestic sales to millers and processors had risen from 1,820,000 bushels to a total of 2,111,000.[43]

Not only did the policy of the CCC bother him, but Washington complained to Sherman Adams about the USDA's attempts to get congressional approval for selling surplus cotton at going market prices. Previously such cotton stocks had to be sold at a level of 105 per cent parity. Release of the huge inventories which CCC holds would completely demoralize the market price, argued Washington. The mere announcement of seeking to repeal the restrictive provision, he claimed, caused a price drop of cotton from $5 to $4 a bale. Such actions, he averred, aggravate the farm problem. His final monition noted the formation of a bipartisan coalition in the Senate to thwart Benson's proposal. "I have never seen a time when [Hubert] Humphrey, on the extreme left, was in agreement with [Karl] Mundt, [Allen J.] Ellender, [Milton] Young, and [Farm Bureau president] Charles Shuman on the extreme right."[44]

The White House staff was extremely sensitive to any and all indications of political unrest. What worried Benson was the prospect of not being able to remedy the situation because of overconcern with the political maneuverings of electioneering. Conceding at the outset that farmers were passing through a cost-price squeeze stemming from the inflationary period of 1941-51, he nevertheless claimed the "pessimists, of course, can always see trouble ahead." The solution was simple enough as he saw it. Farm income would increase at such time when markets were expanded. "I am confident . . . ," posited the Secretary, "that in all of our agriculture each commodity must be competitive price-wise, quality-wise, and promotion-wise."[45]

Under the leadership of Sherman Adams, the White House staff initiated an action-oriented plan to identify, isolate, and resolve immediately problems that might have an adverse effect on the 1956 presidential election. Dubbed "Operation Arrowhead," this political offensive was inaugurated in late summer of 1955. Gabriel Hauge led the way by listing eight trouble spots needing quick attention. The very first one dealt with serious farm problems. Enumerated were price supports on upcoming crops, the wheat referendum, sugar legislation, and addition of a new element to the next year's farm program.[46]

To get things coordinated with the Department of Agriculture, Hauge suggested to Sherman Adams that a council of war be scheduled. It was proposed that Benson, Morse, McConnell, and Butz be invited to sit down with "our side," Hauge's designation of the White House staff, which would include himself, Sherman Adams, and someone from General

Person's office. Topics to be discussed included: raising price support levels; lowering interest rates on disaster loans; expanding soil conservation programs; a land purchase program; two-price plans; expanding mechanism for disposing of surpluses; and "agricultural policy decisions with respect to E-day."[47] The latter reference of course being to election day.

A meeting of minds was reached at this important conference and Secretary Benson ordered his own staff to work on various ways to alleviate the farm situation without undermining the basic policy of implementing flexible price supports. The discussions relating to expansion of soil conservation programs or buying land from farmers gave impetus to the idea of land retirement. Thus evolved the Soil Bank Program as the principal attack on the farm problem.

An avalanche of unsolicited advice came in from Republican officeholders fearing defeat. Worried about election possibilities Governor Dan Thornton of Colorado forwarded some ideas of his own for incorporation into the new farm program. He suggested the establishment of a "world food bank" as a counterpart to the domestic program to spur disposition of surplus agricultural commodities. Other of his recommendations included possible government purchase and slaughter of cows to reduce herds and increase income quickly; excess grain to be sold to cattlemen at reduced prices; foodstuffs to be dumped into the ocean after prolonged storage had ruined their quality for human consumption; and a thorough study to be made to determine why "steak costs more today than it did three years ago when the cattle producer is getting about one half as much."[48]

Not only were Colorado cattlemen grumbling, so were corn and hog producers of Iowa. The rapid growth of the National Farm Organization was symptomatic of a political storm. For decades the Tall Corn State had been rock-ribbed Republican territory and now stalwart GOP congressmen were running scared. Led by conservative Ben Jensen, representing Southwest Iowa, a Hawkeye delegation consisting of H. R. Gross, Henry O. Talle, James I. Dolliver, and Karl M. LeCompte descended upon the White House to vent their displeasure over the administration's policy of reducing price supports. After a stormy meeting with Sherman Adams, Gabriel Hauge, Howard Pyle, Bruce Harlow, Gerald Persons, and Jack Martin, the Iowans left feeling something drastic had to be done fast to salvage their congressional seats.[49]

Trying to maintain some semblance of perspective, Secretary Benson refused to be stampeded by the panicky behavior of Midwest Republicans. He did not ever really consider repudiating his fundamental position on price

156

supports. But he did react positively to the pressure applied by Eisenhower. The Soil Bank as it was presented to Congress early in 1956 was the extent to which he would yield. Since the Soil Bank complemented his policy, it was supported. When it became evident that the House of Representatives intended to add debilitating amendments to the administration's farm bill, Benson would not countenance compromise.

Appearing before the House Agriculture Committee to testify on H.R. 12, he first scolded them for not recommending immediate passage of the Soil Bank program. They were thus responsible for an uncalled-for delay. He then proceeded to condemn all additions made to Eisenhower's original recommendations. "Changing the name or calling a surplus a 'set-aside' does not wish it out of existence," he reasoned.[50]

Also unacceptable to Benson was the House proviso for dual parity. He rejected outright any idea of allowing price supports to be based upon either the new or the old parity formula, depending upon which was more advantageous to farmers. Such a palliative would have negated the original intent of what was supposed to have been a rational and methodical means of transition. Nothing was acceptable to him except the continuation of the principle of flexibility based on a gradual transfer to the new parity. Only this constituted a real solution to overproduction and the accumulation of massive surpluses in government warehouses.

Benson also stated his firm opposition against an attempt to raise dairy price supports, contending such legislative action would "discourage the dairy industry from its valiant effort to promote consumption."[51] Likewise he came out against any two-price systems for wheat or rice. The Agriculture Secretary argued that such a program would have serious economic, administrative, and international repercussions that would be detrimental to farmers in the long run. He reminded the House Agriculture Committee that such a move on the part of the United States would violate Article I of the General Agreement of Tariffs and Trade. Benson favored competitive selling abroad, not an overt policy of dumping. What the Secretary of Agriculture wanted from Congress was passage of a Soil Bank without any encumbrances and no expedient tampering with the process of implementing flexible price supports.

The Democrats were skillfully trying to posture themselves for the upcoming election. And it must be said so were certain GOP members of Congress who had rural constituencies. This state of affairs openly invited political machinations involving all aspects of the bill. The result was not a carefully thought out Soil Bank Program but an omnibus measure with many attractive but costly vote-getting

features.   The Democrats thought they had cleverly maneu-
vered Eisenhower into a political corner.   If he vetoed the
measure they could criticize him for killing all farm legislation.   GOP leaders were aware of this and thus President
Eisenhower would shortly find himself caught squarely in
the middle of a political row revolving around his Agriculture Secretary and rural Republicans.

Chapter VIII

Farm Politics and the 1956 Election

Out of the Kansas prairie came the voice of William
Allen White, the editor of the famed Emporia Gazette. He
advised President Eisenhower to continue the farm policies
established by his Secretary of Agriculture. "Benson's
approach," White asserted, "is the only sane one--the only
healthy one--from the standpoint of the actual farmer, not
the politicians who by distortions and lies are trying to
squeeze votes out of the farmer."[1] The former Bull Moose
Progressive and onetime campaign manager for Alfred M.
Landon defended Benson and promised to write some commendatory editorials in support of the latter's policies.

The President acknowledged William Allen White's
letter and expressed his own appreciation for the favorable
sentiments made about Benson. "A magazine article by you
should be effective ammunition against some of his at-
tackers," wrote Ike. Thanking his fellow Kansan for his

entreaties to run for a second term, Eisenhower quipped, "My lapels are getting pretty worn--on both sides!"[2]

With the eyes of Congress focused on fall elections, the President's farm program was not so much bogged down as overloaded. Defying White House wishes, many GOP congressmen were eager to revive high price supports and favored incorporating these proposals into the Soil Bank bill so that farm income might be given a sudden boost. Republican leaders such as Senator William Knowland and Representative Charles Halleck simply could not control their congressional cohorts from padding the farm bill for their own political benefit. To save the situation, Senator George Aiken (R-Vt.), ranking GOP member of the Upper Chamber's Agriculture Committee, thought only a strong statement by the President would head off legislative disaster. Eisenhower responded by sending him a letter to be made public, saying: "I should be gravely concerned if the Soil Bank should be coupled with the restitution of production incentives certain to nullify the great benefits that the Bank can bring."[3]

Despite Aiken's last minute gambit, the measure finally passed by Congress and sent to the President was so repugnant that Eisenhower sarcastically called it a "private relief bill for politicians."[4] The Democrats, expertly led by Majority Leader Lyndon Johnson in the

Senate and Speaker Sam Rayburn in the House, were likewise in no mood to submit meekly to Eisenhower's austere demands. The President got his Soil Bank but only in a legislative package which surreptitiously returned price supports back to 90 per cent of parity. Almost en masse the Midwestern members of Congress had voted for the enactment of this farm bill.

Representing the sentiment of his farm bloc colleagues, Representative H. Carl Anderson (R-Minn.) urged the President to sign the measure. "You will note the solidarity of Republican Senators and Congressmen from the Midwest--our great farm belt--in favor of this bill," reasoned Anderson. "The fundamental issue on this question of price supports . . . is actually the price level of feed grains rather than the merits of flexibility in the price support program."[5]

In all other respects Representative Anderson was quite pro-administration in his voting record. He was adamant on this one question, however, and reminded the President: "You will recall that on July 28, 1953, I led a group of Midwest farm Congressmen into your office for a discussion with you on this vital issue [which included Clifford R. Hope (R-Kans.), August H. Andresen (R-Minn.), Charles B. Hoeven (R-Ia.), Ralph Harvey (R-Ind.), William S. Hill (R-Colo.), and Harold O. Lovre (R-S.D.)]. . . . I redicted then that if you followed the advice of Secretary

enson on this issue of price supports, the agricultural

idwest--so long the strong backbone and rallying point of

he Republican party--might well be lost to us in 1956."

alling it "the best possible compromise under the circum-

tances," Anderson pleaded, "In a democracy such as ours,

e must always compromise."[6]

    After listening to the counsel of Ezra Taft Benson,

ho steadfastly advised a veto, the President decided the

mnibus farm bill would undo all that had been accomplished

y the Agriculture Act of 1954. Eisenhower relayed his

ecision to Representative Anderson by writing: "After

tudying every detail of the bill over many long hours, and

earching my mind and my conscience, I felt that I had no

lternative but to veto it. In the short run it would have

urt more farmers than it would have helped. In the long

un it would have hurt all farmers."[7]

    Secretly many Democrats were delighted when the

esident vetoed the bill. By doing so they hoped he would

nerate an unpopular image of the Republican party in

ral areas. Whether or not Eisenhower considered the bill

political trap, he could only go so far on the road of

litical expediency and refused to go any further.

dressing himself especially to the farm population, he

id: "I know you are depending on me to tell you the

truth as I see it--and the truth is: I have no choice. I could not sign this bill into law because it was a bad bill. . . . It was a bad bill for the country. It was confusing in some respects, self-defeating, and so awkward and clumsy as to make its administration difficult and impractical."[8] He summarily asked the Congress to serve the interests of all Americans by passing a Soil Bank bill immediately--a measure without any debilitating provisions attached to undermine the long-range stability of agriculture.

Clifford Hope, now ranking Republican on the House Committee on Agriculture, was disappointed over what Eisenhower had done. He confided to Harry Riffel of Kansas, President of the Dickenson County Farm Bureau, "I have been in Washington for a long time but I have never seen any farm bill so grossly misrepresented as this one." This veto was "pretty discouraging," he admitted, particularly in view of the "almost unanimous support of the members of Congress from the Middle West."[9] To another constituent Hope acknowledged his disagreement with the President and pledged to reintroduce the "Domestic Parity Plan as a separate bill."[10]

In order to insure passage of some type of acceptable farm bill, Eisenhower did a little maneuvering of his own. The President let it be known that whereas he would not stand for an attempt to raise parity back to the

90 per cent figure, it did not necessarily have to be set at
75 per cent. He indicated his willingness to allow it to
remain at the 82.5 per cent figure as a compromise. Democratic leaders still wanted to sweeten up the package, but
they did not want to place themselves in the awkward position of having blocked all farm legislation for the session.
Ike commanded too much loyalty on Capitol Hill for any
likely success of overriding a veto, so on May 23 the Agriculture Act of 1956 was sent to the White House.

Although not entirely pleased with all aspects of
the new act, President Eisenhower did sign it into law. He
justified his actions on the basis that the provisions for
a Soil Bank outweighed all other undesirable additions. A
three-year authorization for a Soil Bank had been granted
with $750 million provided for the Acreage Reserve and $450
million appropriated for the Conservation Reserve.

Unwanted portions of the farm act included import
restrictions on long-staple cotton and authority for the
Commodity Credit Corporation to sell upland cotton in the
world market at prices lower than those at home. Acreage
allotments for rice and cotton were frozen for the crop
years of 1957 and 1958 at the 1956 level; transition of
corn, wheat, and peanuts to modern parity was frozen for
one year; price supports for feed grains were authorized;
and a two-price plan for rice could become operative at the

discretion of the Secretary of Agriculture.

Relative to surplus disposal the Department of Agriculture was authorized to both process food commodities, e.g. convert grain into flour, and to pay ocean freight on donations under Title II of PL 480. In addition the Secretary of Agriculture was directed to initiate studies pertaining to the desirability of a food stamp plan as well as the feasibility of establishing strategic stockpiles of food and fiber either at home or abroad.

The Rural Development Program once again received only token support from Congress. This was unfortunate, since it was a well-conceived policy that could have become a fundamental instrument for helping the very farmers most in need of substantial aid. Congress once again failed to see its enormous potentiality in solving the human dilemma of those farmers trying to eke out a meager existence on land that would not support them. Too many urban liberals thought it just another farm program, not realizing its long-range implications for their own communities. A viable Rural Development Program would have slowed the growth of countless urban ghettoes inhabited by former sharecroppers, cotton pickers, small farm operators and owners of marginal land.

Along with the USDA, the Budget Bureau and Council of Economic Advisors endorsed the new Soil Bank act. In so

doing, CEA chairman Arthur Burns was not particularly enthusiastic and indicated the Soil Bank would entail heavy
Treasury costs and enormous administrative tasks. Furthermore, he cautioned that any "expectations of achievement
should be moderate rather than large, and the possibility of
disappointing performance should be borne in mind."[11]

Both the Commerce and State Departments registered
their opposition to the new agricultural act. Sinclair
Weeks objected strenuously to those provisions calling for
dumping cotton abroad and putting import restrictions on
long-staple fiber. He also noted that the two-price system
for rice would discriminate against Cuba, a nation the U.S.
was then trying to keep out of the Communist orbit. In
their entirety, the sections dealing with trade, he concluded, "are in direct conflict with the foreign economic
policy of the United States, its commitments and obligations
under GATT and other international undertakings, and U.S.
efforts to free international trade of objectionable govern-
mental participation, regulation, and restrictions."[12]

State Department objections were presented by
Assistant Secretary Robert C. Hill, who likewise pointed
out that Cuban rice would suffer serious losses as a result of any U.S. market manipulation with a two-price plan.
Restrictions on long-staple cotton would, he forewarned,
have adverse effects on the economies of Egypt, Peru, and

Sudan. Implementing a full-scale policy of dumping, he admonished, could result in a disastrous downward spiral of world cotton prices. Without doubt, he opined, "The consequences of such a price decline could be extremely grave for the economic health and political unity of the free world."[1]

Noteworthy was the fact that a considerable number of Midwestern Republicans and Southern Democrats with rural constituencies were supporting a change in U.S. trade policy. Because American farmers were in economic difficulties, many representatives of agricultural interests were for both dumping surpluses overseas and protectionism at home for farm commodities. Contrary to the specific provisions of the General Agreement of Tariffs and Trade (an agreement frequently violated in spirit by many nations), the farm bloc moved ahead with its determination to alleviate the undue economic burden borne by U.S. farmers. In terms of agriculture, the price paid for certain Cold War policies seemed too high to bear. It would not be too long when even withdrawing the prohibitions against selling to Communist nations would be advocated by the farm bloc. They were thus partially instrumental in pushing the Eisenhower administration toward a rapprochement with the Communist bloc--a trend further implemented by the Nixon administration in the 1970's.

Harold D. Cooley (D-N.C.), chairman of the House
Agriculture Committee, did not miss the opportunity to get
in a few political shots by attaching a report to the Soil
Bank bill in which the Eisenhower administration was blamed
for creating a recession in the agricultural sector of the
economy. The President was furthermore criticized for his
veto of the first bill, which allegedly lost the farmers over
one billion dollars in income. Policies of Ezra Taft Benson
were faulted in elaborate fashion and blamed for causing
ruinous conditions for American agriculture. Written for
political effectiveness, the majority report stated: "While
this committee is presenting the soil bank in this legislation, it must be remembered that this program will pay farmers only about one-half of the gross income they would earn
if they cultivate the acres that are put into the soil bank;
and that every dollar invested in the soil bank program will
decrease the farmers' purchasing power by one dollar."[14]

After the President signed the Soil Bank Act into
law, he categorically denied the charges made by Democrats
by asserting: "The heart of the bill is the soil bank." It
would "check current additions" to our price-depressing,
market-destroying surplus stocks of farm products. Putting
forth the best construction he could, Ike concluded that the
Soil Bank was a concept "rich with promise" for "improving
our agricultural situation."[15]

After having finally gotten the Soil Bank passed, it
then had to be implemented before any economic advantage,
real or token, was to be gained. Secretary Benson therefor
proceeded to announce that farmers were eligible to sign up
for the Acreage Reserve through June and up to July 27.
Some one-half million farmers took advantage of the opportunity to deposit eleven million acres in the Soil Bank's
Acreage Reserve. Also about one and one-half million acres
were placed into the Conservation Reserve. Since the
planting season was over, most farmers would receive no
immediate financial benefit from the new farm program. Thi
was the price Eisenhower paid in political terms when he
vetoed the first farm bill.

A brief comparison of the agricultural planks of
the two parties revealed a marked difference in tone and
emphasis. The Democrats, being in a favorable position to
find fault, scored the Eisenhower administration for its
alleged defeatist attitude and refusal to take effective
action to assure the well-being of farm families. This the
Democrats could purport to do by deftly claiming: "We condemn its fear of abundance, its lack of initiative in
developing domestic markets, and its dismal failure to
obtain for the American farmer his traditional and deserved
share of the world market. Its extravagant expenditure of
money intended for agricultural benefit, without either

direction or results, is a national calamity."[16]

This type of criticism was totally unwarranted and unjustified. It was the Eisenhower administration which did initiate an aggressive trade policy and if it deserved criticism at all, this was certainly not the appropriate area for it. Decline in farm commodity sales overseas had in a very real sense taken place under the Truman administration--not Eisenhower's.

Both sides vied for maximum political advantage on the farm issue. After having been foiled in their attempt to gain legislative provisions for retention of 90 per cent price supports on most basic commodities, the Democrats audaciously labeled the Soil Bank as nothing but a GOP "vote-buying scheme." Hence they promised a return to high support levels and pledged with a flourish of electioneering cant to "enact a comprehensive farm program which, under intelligent and sympathetic Democratic administration will make the rural homes of America better and healthier places in which to live."[17]

The theme of the Republican farm plank, on the other hand, reflected Benson's fundamental thinking when it maintained: "Agriculture, our basic industry, must remain free and prosperous." Credit was duly taken for extending Social Security to cover farm workers; refunding gasoline tax amounting to $60 million; and making available $225 million in Soil Bank payments. It was proudly pointed out that the Eisenhower administration had disposed of $7 billion worth of price-depressing surplus farm products. As could be expected, Democrats were censured for their deliberate tactics of obstruction and delay in hamstringing passage of the Soil Bank.

By and large the remainder of the GOP platform dealing with agriculture sought to explain why quick solutions were impossible of attainment. Realistically it asserted there was no simple, easy resolution for complex farm problems. Likewise, the affirmation that Republicans did not envision making farmers dependent upon direct government payments for their incomes indicated movement away from federal management of every aspect of farming. Reiterating the benefits stemming from such a reform the Republican party committed itself: "To work toward full freedom instead of toward more regimentation, developing voluntary rather than oppressive farm programs; To encourage agricultural producers in their efforts to seek solutions to their own production and price problems; [and] To provide price supports as in the Agriculture Act of 1954 that protect farmers, rather than price their products out of the market."[19]

For use by campaigners, the Republican National Committee issued a "Farm Policy Summary" consisting primarily of public statements made by Secretary Benson. An attempt was made to defuse the farm issue by focusing on its complexity. Furthermore Benson's rhetoric was utilized to underscore positive aspects of the question while refuting the demagoguery connected with farm policy. "Agriculture is not for sale" or "Our agriculture is neither Republican nor Democrat--it is American," were slogans geared to counteract the purely partisan approach. Similarly assertions such as "Food is a good buy" were essentially correct or "It was under . . . price supports that our present farm problem developed" accurately stated the basic cause of the farm problem.[20]

When Secretary Benson took to the campaign trail himself, he for all intent and purposes intended to enlighten farmers. Instead of a host of promises couched in flowery rhetoric, Benson spoke plainly of past failures and present problems. In speaking to the National Federation of Republican Women in Chicago on September 7, 1956, Ezra Taft Benson labeled the Democrats' farm plank a "cynical, pessimistic document." He related how the Eisenhower administration had "been kept busy for $3\frac{1}{2}$ years putting out the fires, cleaning up the debris of unwise and unrealistic farm programs of the past, and attempting to rebuild our agricultural economy on a sound foundation--and all this in the face of continuing opposition." Setting forth what he believed to be the fundamental objective of the GOP, he attested: "Our approach is to help farm people help themselves."[21]

Continuing to accentuate the theme that agriculture needed reforming, Benson talked to a group commemorating the seventy-fifth anniversary of the Minneapolis Grain Exchange. Insisting that a "government warehouse is not a market," the Agriculture Secretary proclaimed, "The biggest threat we have today to our private marketing system is government itself." He made it abundantly clear he regarded stifling government controls a reactionary policy which caused rather than solved problems. Contemporary farmers needed freedom to react to the demands of real markets--not politically inspired promises of federal money. If the federal subsidization of farming continued, as seemingly advocated by the Democrats, he direly predicted that "freedom would be gone--farmers would be reduced to a government dole."[22]

The Agriculture Secretary was valiantly trying to explain the weaknesses of the price support system which had frozen production into uneconomic patterns by ignoring new consumer preferences and market demands. This had resulted in an accumulation of stored surpluses almost impossible for the Commodity Credit Corporation to sell simply because they were not in demand in the domestic or world market. Posturing himself as a rational reformer amid the passion of a presidential campaign was meritorious, but it could not compete with those who told farmers they had a right to federal subsidies. Benson's opponents created a false image of him as a callous businessman interested only in serving large landowners or big corporations. This strategy was very effective and Democrats got extraordinary political mileage from this technique. In the farm belt they campaigned against Benson instead of Eisenhower and it worked to their advantage.

Casting the Secretary of Agriculture as the foe of small farmers did him a great injustice. Deep in his heart he believed the family farm contributed much to the moral quality of American life. The economic riddle plaguing him was how to achieve prosperity for all farmers without causing undue hardship on small-scale units. His predicament was similar to that in the retail business where the trend for bigness caused the so-called "Mom and Dad" food stores to decline because of supermarkets. Increase in size and scale of operation was an inexorable economic necessity of the Industrial Revolution. It was ironic that while Democrats claimed the family farm declined drastically during Eisenhower's two terms due to his (and Benson's) disinterest, the following eight years (combining John F. Kennedy's and Lyndon B. Johnson's terms) the rate increased even further. Yet no one could accurately claim Secretary of Agriculture Orville Freeman was an enemy of the family farm.

Once when Treasury Secretary George Humphrey sent him a letter from R. E. Wood (Chairman-Finance Committee of Sears, Roebuck and Company) with a study entitled "Memorandum Prepared by T. V. Houser Analyzing the Current Farm Problem from Standpoint of National Policy," Benson rejected its main proposition "that there are probably even yet some millions too many farm workers."[23] The Agriculture Secretary, reflecting his own innate agrarianism, told Humphrey, who did have a big business viewpoint, that this view about family farms would rightfully be "opposed by the many people who believe that the small farm has social and other advantages which offset its economic disadvantages."[24] Humphrey, looking at small, inefficient farm units as poor business, disagreed. He continued to insist that any government policy encouraging continuation of little farms would be "not only bad politics but bad judgment."[25]

Returning from the annual conference of the American Farm Economic Association, Don Paarlberg reported to the Secretary of Agriculture (who sent Gabriel Hauge a synopsis of it) that opinion there was very favorable to the administration. Most agricultural economists, who understood the complexities involved, supported flexible price supports as the only realistic way to achieve balanced production. They did not attribute the current decline in farm income to Benson's programs but blamed it on the "unwise legislation

176

of the past" and to an "onrush of agricultural technology."[26] Unfortunately for Ezra Taft Benson such professional opinion could not compete with the oversimplified political rhetoric of his detractors.

Many issues were at stake in the 1956 presidential election. Not the least of these was the President's cooling down of the Cold War. That, plus Eisenhower's personal popularity with the American people, led to his second triumph over the Democratic challenger, Adlai E. Stevenson. Ike pulled 35,590,472 popular votes to his opponent's 26,022,752, and in the electoral college the tally was 457 to 74. The voting statistics were interesting in six farm states, however, because they showed a slight decline in Ike's rural strength from the previous presidential election. A comparison revealed the following slippage in plurality and percentage of popular vote:[27]

	1952	1956
Iowa	63.8% 357,393	59.1% 227,329
Kansas	68.8% 343,006	65.4% 270,561
Minnesota	55.3% 154,754	53.7% 101,777
Oklahoma	55.1% 88,188	54.6% 87,106
South Dakota	69.3% 113,431	58.4% 49,281

There was no doubt about Dwight D. Eisenhower's standing with the electorate. Although losing Missouri in 1956, a farm state he had won narrowly in 1952, the President displayed a magnetic appeal throughout the various sectors of the population. Even his pre-election heart attack did little to dampen voter enthusiasm about keeping him in the White House for another four years.

While speaking at the annual convention of the National Grange shortly after the election, Secretary Benson (now serving his second term in office) declared, "Needless to say, I am gratified with the November 6th decision of the American people--and especially with the verdict from the men and women on farms." All in all Benson was of the opinion that Republicans had held the rural sector quite well despite misleading electioneering by Democrats. He pronounced a failure the desperate effort "made by certain prophets of doom and gloom to whip up a farm revolt and spirit of farm depression."[28]

Benson sent presidential aide Wilton B. Persons a post-election copy of the Farm Journal with an analysis of the rural vote. According to this paper's assessment no real farm rebellion was in evidence, but only typical voter reaction to drought and low commodity prices. In other words some farmers did react to the immediate scene, no matter who was to blame, and this translated itself into an anti-Republican congressional vote. The Agriculture Secretary felt vindicated by the election results, so much so he penned an accompanying note to General Persons saying, "The headlines in agriculture are not all bad."[29]

The Democrats retained control of both houses with a modest increase of two seats in the House and one in the Senate. Speaker Sam Rayburn recognized Ike's political drawing power when he confided to Senator Kenneth D. McKellar (D-Tenn.), "the election proved one thing, and that is that the people like and want President Eisenhower, but they do not like or want the Republican party as demonstrated by their votes in electing a Democratic Senate and House."[30]

Following the renewal of his mandate, Eisenhower sent Benson a personal note of thanks for his vigorous campaign efforts. Knowing his Agriculture Secretary did not relish politics but nevertheless did his duty, the President wrote: "I shudder to think of those hundred-odd appearances in the farm area--though I suspect that they not only helped the campaign greatly but added to your information as to actual conditions there. I am sure you feel, as did I, a sense of reward in the verdict of the American people to retain the principles and policies of the administration for another four years."[31]

Chapter IX
The President's Political Loyalty

The GOP campaign slogan of 1956 was "Peace, Progress and Prosperity." Good times did generally prevail and Republican campaigners in the farm belt had relied heavily on the new farm act as an answer to the pocketbook issue. Whereas GOP congressmen representing Middle America were banking heavily on the Soil Bank to speedily put money into the hands of farmers, Ezra Taft Benson was more interested in getting more flexibility in the parity system. Only the latter (whatever value the land retirement program had) could, in his judgment, lay the foundations for long-time agricultural prosperity.

Much to Benson's dismay his future status depended almost entirely on results obtained from the Soil Bank. That is, the withdrawal of acreage from production would have to help in the adjustment of agriculture while at the same time contribute to farm income.

This approach had built-in pitfalls. First, without further reducing parity levels farmers would merely intensify efforts to increase productivity on less acreage. In other words land retirement per se did nothing to get at the fundamental reason for overproduction. Secondly, the Soil Bank was bound to be a costly venture with no assurance of success unless total production was reduced in line with market demands. To make the Soil Bank work at all meant committing the USDA to huge outlays of money. Benson needed $5 billion for fiscal 1958 just in order to implement the acreage and conservation reserve programs.

A 1957 survey entitled, "Facts About Price Supports," confirmed Benson's worst expectations. It predicted failure for the Soil Bank unless production was cut drastically. This, the report went on, could be accomplished only by a further lowering of parity. With certainty it was stated that "price supports at the levels specified by the old basic law continue to generate surpluses which must be disposed of at a heavy loss."[1]

A breakdown of disbursements for price supports in 1957 indicated that a lion's share of the $3.3 billion actually received for Soil Bank purposes went to only 1.3 million farmers. These large-scale farm recipients averaged $2,000 in parity payments while 2.7 million small operators received about $100 annually. Benson had always maintained that federal subsidies did not really help the small operator. Yet Congress stoutly resisted imposing a ceiling on the amount large farmers could receive. With such a disparity in distribution, it was also obvious that if a farmer owning only two or three hundred acres placed much of his acreage in the Soil Bank he would not benefit nearly as much as a big land owner. Any substantial loss of income by a tenant or small-scale farmer could not be supplemented sufficiently by Soil Bank subsidies to make land retirement a profitable venture. Even more disturbing evidence indicated that 80 per cent of the cost of price support and commodity stabilization programs revolved around only four basic crops; namely, wheat, cotton, corn, and dairy products. Of this amount 48 per cent was spent on the support of just two crops--cotton and wheat.[2] Farm bloc representatives of the regions associated with these two crops were the most vehement in opposing flexible price supports. Thus Benson was caught in a bind not of his own making.

In a cabinet meeting called on April 4, 1957 for the purpose of discussing current problems in agriculture, Benson reported that sign-ups for the acreage reserve were proceeding faster than had been anticipated. He then announced that despite the Soil Bank and vigorous surplus disposal activities (under the new provisions of PL 480), excess food and fiber in storage was still mounting at an unreasonable level.

The Agriculture Secretary suggested taking the initiative in contacting Senator Allen J. Ellender, Chairman of the Senate Agriculture Committee, to request corrections in existing legislation so that a reduction of price supports might proceed as first implemented in 1955. Benson repeated his belief that it was the partial return to high, rigid supports tacked on to the Soil Bank Act which accounted for increased surpluses. President Eisenhower indicated agreement with Benson and gave his approval for getting in touch with Senator Ellender.[3]

Hoping the Southern Senator would prove cooperative, the Agriculture Secretary had a letter drafted for presentation to Ellender. It informed the Louisiana Democrat about the dire need for continued reform. The crux of Secretary Benson's arguments was set forth as follows:

1. Controls are not effective in reducing overall agricultural production, despite the severe restrictions they impose on farmers' freedom to produce and market.

2. Agricultural products are likely to continue to be abundant. Under such conditions they cannot be successfully priced

as if they were scarce.

3. The present legal formulas governing
   acreage allotments and price supports
   are obsolete.[4]

In defending his basic assertions, Benson reasoned
that the "technical explosion" taking place on farms had
doubled the productive ability of each farm worker during
the past fifteen years. "This creates a new dimension in
farm policy," he contended, "and makes it virtually impossible to curtail agricultural output with the type of controls acceptable in our society." He agreed that farmers
should be protected from unexpected price variations, weak
bargaining power, and economic liabilities connected with
high productivity. Pleading for rational action Benson reminded the Senator that "it would be well to address ourselves to the inadequacies of the present law while the
soil bank and the disposal programs are available to facilitate the transition."[5]

Acreage allotments and marketing quotas had failed
in gaining their objectives, he insisted, because increased
yields per acre nullified all meaningful production controls. The use of hybrids, pesticides, herbicides, and
greater use of fertilizers constantly increased yields. To
get around this Benson suggested that at least acreage

allotments should be replaced with "quantity allotments."
This contemplated using allotments by units, i.e. bushels or
bales, rather than by designating some specified number of
acres. Beseeching the Senator to lay aside politics and
take statesmanship-like action, the Agriculture Secretary
claimed: "Of any proposed solutions, I ask these questions:
Will it work? Is it good for farmers? I have no doc-
trinaire solution for agricultural problems."[6]

In a series of public speeches the Agriculture Secretary reiterated over and over again the circumstances
forcing farmers to adjust to technological progress. To the
Economic Club in New York City, Benson noted that as farmers
had grown more efficient, fewer farm people were needed to
supply the nation's food and fiber. He labeled "reaction-
aries" those who feared the "fruits of advancing technology."[7] Included within this definition were rural
representatives who wanted to cling to a legislative
apparatus fashioned in another era. By definition he meant
use of strict production controls, high price supports,
government interference in preventing market oriented production, and federal obstruction in the role of decision
making relative to consumer demands.

Benson called for a reorientation of thinking and
basic legislative reforms in order to allow agriculture to
make needed adjustments. These included elimination of all

restraints on freedom of choice or free play of the market place in determining commodity prices. To his way of thinking farmers could not be shielded from reality. The means were at hand to temper dislocations but change could not be forestalled without incurring even more serious repercussions. His peroration posed the question: "Will historians write that abundance lost freedom, destroyed initiative or will they write that these free institutions were put to the test, that they survived the time of trial, somewhat modified no doubt, but intact and strengthened?"[8]

Benson never relented in his attempt to educate farmers as to why certain problems existed. Despite objections from those interested only in political reaction to his speeches, he embarked upon an endeavor to convince farmers that Congress was not dealing realistically with farm issues. In an address to a farmers' convention at the University of Tennessee, the Agriculture Secretary explained how technology affected their lives. He informed them that from 1935 to 1957 the farm population had declined 26 per cent and predicted this trend would continue unabated into the foreseeable future.

Speaking of the "human problem" this posed, he pointed to a way in which this dislocation could be cushioned. Five counties in the volunteer state had Rural Development projects in operation.[9] They were being run not by Washington but by local rural development committees composed of leaders from both farm and non-farm segments of the county's economic and social life. He inferred that the inaction of RDP by Congress contributed to human distress while rhetoric about the family farm solved nothing. Had Soil Bank funds been matched by a massive program to retrain and relocate farmers victimized by the technological revolution in agriculture, a positive step would have been taken at least to alleviate the plight of those unable to earn a living from the land.

Others in the Eisenhower administration working to resolve agricultural issues soon came to the similar conclusion that the Soil Bank by itself was not really capable of solving agriculture's main problem. In order to keep surpluses at bay Gwynn Garnett of the Foreign Agriculture Service recommended to Clarence Francis that Title I of PL 480 be extended through June 30, 1959, and that an additional $2 billion be sought from Congress to implement it. This would be necessary, Garnett reasoned, since neither the "acreage or reserve program" nor the flexible price support mechanism as modified by Congress were "expected to reduce accumulated surpluses fast enough to eliminate the need for disposals through foreign currency sales when programming of the present $1 billion authorization is completed this fiscal year."[10]

Former congressman Jack Z. Anderson, now on the White House legislative liaison staff, likewise perceived what Benson had been driving at all along. Considering the USDA budget was a whopping $5 billion for fiscal 1957, Anderson penned a lament to Sherman Adams. He personally disliked the idea of paying farmers for doing something they should do anyway. Particularly disturbing was data indicating the bulk of government largesse was going into the pockets of big producers of basic commodities. He opined, "I am afraid that the Soil Bank is going to cost much more than it will be worth." Although he knew Congress would not act, Anderson recommended that the Rural Development Program be "expanded and strengthened."[11]

After attending a cabinet meeting at which agriculture was discussed, Clarence Francis put some of his thoughts down on paper and sent them to the administration's trouble-shooter--Sherman Adams. He perceived clearly any solution of the farm problem meant coordinating overall policy. He noted that both reduction of price supports and taking acreage out of production via the Soil Bank were but means to force inefficient operators to quit farming. "But the government would be guilty of cruel and inhuman treatment if it suddenly forced out of farming a lot of people it originally encouraged to go into it," contended Francis. "Furthermore, a probable majority of these farmers have no place

to go."[12] He envisioned the Rural Development Program as a
means for readjustment or rehabilitation of farmers. Using
the analogy of how the Veteran's Administration retrained
soldiers [i.e. the G.I. Bill of Rights], Francis recommended
telling the uneconomical farmer in plain language: "For
the good of the country we are compelled to reduce price
supports on such and such a schedule; but since the government was at least partly responsible for your predicament
the government will help you get out of it; we will help
you relocate, to get started in some other business, to go
to school to acquire some other skills--or whatever--and
meanwhile we will put your acreage in conservation reserve."[13]

This approach, which would have materially enlarged
the Rural Development Program, seemed to Francis the only
socially sound and economically feasible way to proceed with
any chance of truly solving the farm predicament. But it
was not pushed because the RDP was still only in the pilot
stage due to lack of congressional funding.

The White House staff had succumbed to GOP congressional pressure for a farm act with political appeal and now
they were amazed at the ensuing cost. John H. Hamlin, a
White House staffer, notified Sherman Adams that as of March
18, 1957 the USDA was surpassing its budget because of huge
amounts involved in Soil Bank payments.[14] Again on April 23rd

he informed Ike's top lieutenant that USDA expenditures had exceeded budget limitations by $50 million.[15] In addition to this overspending the Commission on Increased Industrial Use of Agricultural Products had recommended the tripling of money to be allocated for utilization research. This would mean a monetary increase from $16 million to $48 million.[16] Once the federal treasury was made a political pawn the end for expenditures was nowhere in sight. Secretary Benson had predicted this turn of events but his recommendations were considered impolitic.

Ezra Taft Benson was firmly convinced the reasonable way to eliminate excess production was to discourage the planting of certain commodities by further reducing their price support level. Politics could in no way repeal the law of supply and demand. Using his administrative authority a national allotment of 55 million acres was announced for wheat. Even then it was four times the amount actually needed but represented the statutory minimum established by Congress. The new parity level was to be set at 75 per cent. This meant farmers were guaranteed only $1.78 per bushel when they had been getting $2.00. According to Benson's reasoning, however, this move would force farmers to make economically sound decisions regarding how much they would plant or whether they would even put the plow to some of their land. Without this step Commodity Credit Corporation storage bins would be the recipients of most of this wheat and there was already too much on hand.

No sooner had Benson disclosed the news about lowering price supports on wheat when he was subjected to a new wave of anguished outcries from members of Congress. Protesting this decision directly to the President, Representative George McGovern (D-S.D.) labeled this move an "irresponsible action on the part of Secretary Benson." It was tantamount to reducing income for South Dakotans by 25 per cent, he claimed, and this proved the Agriculture Secretary was "totally out of sympathy with the economically depressed conditions of farm families."[17] McGovern ended his politically inspired telegram with a demand that Benson be fired and replaced by a new appointee more acceptable to Democrats.

Undaunted by verbal brickbats emanating from South Dakota Benson journeyed to that state in the fall of 1957 to speak at the National Mechanical Corn Picking Contest. Dissident Democrats and National Farmer Union critics had organized a protest group to attend that meeting in order to embarrass the Secretary of Agriculture. Events were soon to get out of hand. While addressing a crowd at Sioux Falls, several irate farmers pelted the Agriculture Secretary with eggs. Although Senator Francis Case publicly decried the event, saying, "I always thought we Americans believed in the right of everyone to express his own opinions,"[18] the anti-administration press tended to transform the guilty culprits into local heroes.

Governor Joe Foss of South Dakota was mortified by the publicity given to such rude behavior. He wrote President Eisenhower: "I want to sincerely apologize for this shameful treatment of a member of your cabinet while he was a guest in this state." Significantly Governor Foss added this comment, referring to communications sent to him about the incident, "Quite a few of the letters expressed opposition to Secretary Benson's agricultural policies, but . . . most of our citizens have a great deal of admiration and respect for . . . [his] personal integrity and courage."[19]

In nearby Wisconsin another unexpected turn of events took place. Incumbent Senator Joseph McCarthy died suddenly on May 2, 1957. This opened the way for a special election to fill an unexpired term. William Proxmire, who was relatively obscure on the national scene, gained the primary nomination of the Democratic party and geared his entire campaign for election on an anti-Benson theme. He denounced Benson all up and down the nation's leading dairy state with exaggerated accounts of how the Eisenhower administration had crippled dairy farmers. Farmers with small herds were highly receptive to his political pitch.[20]

His opponent, who emerged from a fierce seven-man primary battle, was Governor Walter J. Kohler. Proxmire had previously lost the gubernatorial race to him and was not favored to win. But several factors worked in favor of Proxmire. He had the support of organized labor and, while getting support from key Democrats, he kept his distance from the party organization. This, in a Republican state, gave him the image of being an independent.[20] Anticipating a heavy Democratic turnout in Milwaukee County, the GOP candidate expected to win by taking northern and western counties. This seemed probable since in his 1956 try Proxmire had received only 30 per cent of the rural vote. But in 1957 he drew nearly 70 per cent of it. This huge plurality plus his expected showing in urban areas gave the Democrat a surprise victory in what had been up to then safe GOP territory.

After his surprise triumph in the August 27th special election, the new Senator-elect from the badger state audaciously telegrammed President Eisenhower: "Respectfully but with great urgency, I appeal to you to take immediate action to replace Ezra Taft Benson as Secretary of Agriculture."[21]

Flush with victory it was to be expected that Democrats would interpret their win in Wisconsin as a rural repudiation of the Eisenhower-Benson farm program.

Representative Henry S. Reuss (D-Wis.) also got in some political licks by wiring Eisenhower: "I join with Senator Proxmire in respectfully requesting that you replace Secretary of Agriculture Benson. Under his administration the family-sized farmer has been consistently discriminated against."[22]

Wisconsin Republicans were panic-stricken over the election. Fearing political erosion of his own base of power GOP Representative Melvin R. Laird, a member of the House Agriculture Committee, sent an urgent entreaty to the President which read: "I want you to know that as one of the members of Congress who has supported your agricultural program that I believe it is most important that a change be made in the office of Secretary of Agriculture before the next session of Congress. . . . [Benson] has become the issue, not the program which he stands for."[23] Laird, soon to be followed by other members of the farm bloc, wanted Benson to be the scapegoat. They hoped that his dismissal would defuse the situation for the benefit of them all.

Senator Karl Mundt, who had fought Benson's basic policy for years, poured out his woes once again to Sherman Adams. Mundt took advantage of this election loss to place all the blame on the Agriculture Secretary. As for the future, he informed Adams, "I am completely convinced that we cannot even come close to electing a Republican House of

Representatives or a Republican Senate in 1958 unless Secretary of Agriculture Benson is replaced by somebody who is personally acceptable to the farmers of this country."[24] Without the dismissal of Benson, Mundt predicted in his own inimical way, the GOP did not have a "Chinaman's chance of winning the farm vote."[25]

Like an avalanche the protestations continued to pour into the office of Sherman Adams. Also fearing political repercussions at home Representative A. L. Miller (R-Nebr.) pressed the now recurrent complaint that Benson "represents a symbol of lower prices." He too pushed the dump Benson movement. As for the mid-term elections coming up in 1958, the Nebraskan calculated that from six to eight Midwest congressional seats would be lost unless Benson was replaced immediately. If someone had to be the burnt offering, he wanted the Agriculture Secretary to be the victim. "There is rough weather ahead," cautioned Miller with the final suggestion that Adams "certainly ought to talk it over with the boss."[26]

Another sharp response to recent events came in from Minnesota congressman H. Carl Andersen. He argued, with a touch of verbal overkill, that the Republican defeat in Wisconsin was "virtually without precedent and should be taken as one more warning to us that our party is in serious difficulties in rural America." The irate Minnesotan also called for the immediate ouster of Ezra Taft Benson. In a tone of Machiavellian Realpolitik Andersen queried: "Why must the Midwest Republicans be sacrificed so needlessly when this tide could be so quickly reversed by such a change?"[27]

Meade Alcorn, who had taken over for Leonard Hall as GOP National Chairman, analyzed the Wisconsin vote and re-acted as a professional politician is prone to do. He considered it a protest vote that had to be mollified.[28] It was not in his realm to suggest remedies for the farm problem but he considered it necessary for someone other than Eisenhower to bear the blame. Alcorn subsequently met with the President and strongly urged him to supplant Benson with someone not connected with the administration. Ike, as he had done many times before, absolutely refused to abandon his Secretary of Agriculture. The President had compromised on his farm program to placate Midwest Republicans but he would not repudiate Benson just to pacify them. Ike was in basic agreement with his Agriculture Secretary and in no way intended to disown him.

Ezra Taft Benson came to his own defense by denying the final vote tally in Wisconsin reflected a rural rebellion against his farm policies. He contended that Governor Kohler's defeat could be attributed to a considerable number of other factors such as: the bitter residue of a seven-man

primary contest; a "stay at home" attitude on the part of
the McCarthy wing of the party; narrowing margins of victory
for Kohler in previous gubernatorial elections; and the
"lies that were told to Wisconsin farmers" by Proxmire and
other Democratic campaigners. He might have added another
Kohler (a relative of the Governor) was involved in a labor
dispute which antagonized organized labor. The true test,
Benson declared, "will come next year when . . . the Republican candidate chosen in convention will more adequately
reflect the political philosophy of the Wisconsin electorate."[29]

Going about his business, Ezra Taft Benson ignored
the furor raging about him and made plans for another one
of his trade promotion junkets. He considered this type of
work as more productive in solving farm problems. This
trip, starting October 22 and terminating on November 16,
1957, scheduled visits for the following cities of the
world: Honolulu, Tokyo, Hong Kong, Karachi (Pakistan),
Amman (Jordan), Tel Aviv (Israel), Athens, Rome, Madrid,
Lisbon, Paris, and London. Not only did the Agriculture
Secretary check on the progress of existing PL 480 programs
but he sought once more to open new commercial channels of
trade for American-produced farm commodities.[30] Rivaling
John Foster Dulles in the amount of traveling he would do,
Benson probed every avenue for new outlets. Certainly his

critics at home could not fault him for his efforts to expand overseas farm trade.

The inflammatory issue of whether Benson should or should not remain as Secretary of Agriculture was suddenly reopened when another special election took place early in 1958. Occasioned by the death of Representative August Andresen of Minnesota, who died on January 14, Republicans fought a fierce political battle to retain the seat. Finally, after an all-out campaign, a GOP state senator by the name of Albert Quie won a hard fought contest by a margin of 44,309 to 43,641 votes. Democrats had once again used an anti-Benson campaign strategy to try and win this rural Republican district.

Led by A. L. Miller of Nebraska and Walter H. Judd of Minnesota, a caucus of some thirty GOP farm-state representatives decided to take matters into their own hands. Collectively they privately asked Ezra Taft Benson to resign voluntarily for the sake of the party. Because they knew Ike's stand on this they refrained from going to the White House to demand Benson's immediate dismissal.[31]

Not one to stand idly by after being invited to step down, Benson issued a public statement in which he, while admitting concern for the political fortunes of elected officials, vowed he never had nor would he ever play politics with agriculture policy. His duty, he reaffirmed,

was to serve farmers and the nation to the best of his
ability. With absolutely no intention of resigning, the
Agriculture Secretary attested to his basic principles: "I
have responsibilities which I take seriously. As long as
God gives me the strength I shall continue to do all within
my power to help our farmers through this severe struggle
to a better and brighter future. . . . And for that reason
I shall continue to fight for what I feel to be right."[32]

During a leadership conference with congressional
spokesmen, Senator Everett Dirksen suggested that the President put an end to the continuing controversy by making a
strong statement at his next meeting with the press.
Willingly Ike accepted this advice and at his February 26
news conference utilized the opportunity to endorse in a
forceful way the actions of his Agriculture Secretary. He
praised Benson by saying, "I believe he is honest in his
great effort to find proper, reasonable, sensible programs
that can be recommended by the Congress." With a tone of
finality, the President made this pronouncement: "When we
find a man of this dedication, this kind of courage, this
kind of intellectual and personal honesty, we should say to
ourselves, 'We just don't believe that America has come to
the point where it wants to dispense with the advice of that
kind of a person.'"[33]

At the March 7th cabinet meeting, the President laid to rest any lingering doubts that may have existed. He reaffirmed in unequivocal terms his support for Benson and repeated his firm intention of keeping his loyal Agriculture Secretary in his administration.[34] Yet every time the Agriculture Secretary announced further cuts in price supports to get balanced production, he was subjected to another torrent of politically inspired criticism. A telegram from Senator Edward J. Thye (R-Minn.), for instance, attacked Benson for reducing dairy supports in March, 1957. The Senator, thinking only of next year's mid-term election, wanted price support money flowing into the Midwest even though excess milk flowed from dairy farms. Senator Thye even resented Benson's attempt to explain to Congress why high supports were shortsided in terms of alleviating depressed farm prices. Thye twisted these responses by charging, "Your unwarranted attacks upon congressional committees is not the type of constructive action which will assist in solving our economic problems."[35]

The Senator from Minnesota had also wired the President and informed him of his opinion relative to Ezra Taft Benson. Ike in turn scolded Thye: "Naturally I am not unaware of your strong feelings in this matter; yet it seems to me that upon reflection you will concede to Mr. Benson not merely the right but more importantly the obligation vigorously to set forth the programs and concepts which, in his best judgment, are essential to the well being of our farm people. It is my opinion that if he failed to do so, he would be derelict in his responsibility, and though so doing may understandingly create some difficulties, I hardly see how he could effectively carry out his responsibilities in any other manner."[36]

Despite the turmoil to which he was subjected Secretary Benson quietly and methodically worked on recommendations for legislative consideration. These were unveiled on January 16, 1958 when the President sent a series of proposals to Congress for its approval. They included nine broad requests:

1. The Conservation Reserve Program of the Soil Bank should be strengthened, and the Acreage Reserve Program terminated after the 1958 crop.

2. Authority to increase acreage allotments for cotton, wheat, rice, peanuts, and tobacco should be provided.

3. Acreage allotments for corn should be eliminated.

4. The escalator clauses in the basic law should be abolished.

5. The overall range within which price supports may be provided should be substantially widened.

6. Price supports for cotton should be based on the average quality of the crop.

7. The membership of the Commodity Credit Corporation Advisory Board should be enlarged and the Board's responsibilities increased.

8. The Agricultural Trade Development and Assistance Act should be extended.

9. Research efforts aimed at increasing industrial uses of farm products should be expanded.[37]

Additional suggestions by the President encompassed requests for continuation of the special milk programs; extension of the National Wool Act; broadening the source of funds for the Rural Electrification Administration; requiring state participation in drought programs; and restricting federal financing of cost-sharing conservation practices to those with long-range benefits. President Eisenhower also indicated that "increased emphasis" was planned for the Rural Development Program already in progress.[38]

The so-called Food and Fiber Bill submitted by the President signaled a movement away from land retirement and a return to flexibility. An end of the Acreage Reserve was being proposed because it was both expensive and ineffectual. To stop overproduction, Eisenhower wanted to step up the transition to lower price supports by terminating all delaying devices and widening the parity range to a spread of from 60 per cent to 90 per cent. Heretofore the lowest figure at which it could be set was 75 per cent. It was predictable that this would meet opposition in Congress. Farm bloc representatives of both parties believed themselves vulnerable in their home districts unless they supported high and rigid price supports.

It soon became clear that administration farm proposals faced tough sledding. Each member of Congress was thinking of his own survival and not about agriculture's overall welfare. Because it was an election year, GOP National Chairman Meade Alcorn felt compelled to make a series of suggestions to Ezra Taft Benson. His directive included precise instructions on how to gear USDA activities in order to achieve maximum political effectiveness. They read:

1. All speeches, releases, and literature
   from the Department of Agriculture should

adopt an affirmative approach . . . [and] stop "defending" our position.

2. A head-on attack on the National Farmers Union and its left-wing leadership would be timely.

3. A major farm conference should be held in the heart of the farm states to which the Secretary should invite the nation's farm leaders.

4. A series of small conferences should be held with Republican members of the Senate and House--and not confined to the leaders necessarily.

5. The Department of Agriculture should prepare and release at the earliest possible time a series of educational films designed to show the constructive steps the administration is taking to strengthen the economy.

6. The President should be requested to make a major farm policy speech.

7. The Secretary of Agriculture should consider inviting a top-level, highly confidential panel of public relations experts, skilled in the farm problem, to

meet with him at intervals of at least
once a month (and oftener, if possible)
to evaluate the manner in which the administration's story is getting through to
the voters.

8. If the Secretary does not now have a top
public relations man in his own Department, one should be obtained at the
earliest possible time.[39]

Benson resented the very idea of politicizing his
every word and deed but acceded to that portion of Alcorn's
recommendations which dealt with the National Farmers
Union. On April 14, Benson did send Sherman Adams an outline of a plan to counter this farm organization's publicity.
He contended the NFU, through its Grain Terminal Association, possessed a political war chest of $2.5 million.
Furthermore, asserted the Secretary of Agriculture, the NFU
deliberately propagated "misinformation and untruths"[40] via
radio and television broadcasts. To counter this line of
false propaganda, Benson suggested using film clips, radio
tapes, and distribution of a commercially prepared news-
letter. He also recommended making use of Republican Farm
Councils and field men of the Republican National Committee
to take the administration's message directly to farm groups.

The total cost of this modest public relations venture was but a mere $75,000.

The vote-hungry mood of Congress manifested itself when both houses voted to forestall any lowering of price supports by freezing parity levels. In the Senate eleven Republicans allied with thirty-nine Democrats to pass Senate Joint Resolution 162. The House concurred, but limited the freeze to only one year, when forty-four GOP members joined one hundred sixty-seven Democrats. Minority Leader Charles Halleck voted against the measure, but informed Eisenhower he would make no statement about Republican defections lest "it might make your situation more difficult in opposing the bill or vetoing it."[41]

In no frame of mind to placate either Congress or GOP members of the farm bloc, Benson took advantage of an invitation to speak to the Farm and Home Week forum at Ohio State University. He ripped into Congress for passing a "do-nothing bill . . . which would freeze supports and allotments in present uneconomic patterns." His verbal volleys took them to task for their attempt to hamper the transition to a more flexible system of price supports. Intimating strongly that Eisenhower would probably veto their resolution, Benson insisted "we must improve the farm program--not freeze it."[42]

Very shortly thereafter the President notified the Upper Chamber that he was returning Senate Joint Resolution 162 without his approval. In his veto message Eisenhower backed Benson by claiming, "with regard to government controls, what the farm economy needs is a thaw rather than a freeze."[43]

To get the administration's message over to the general farm population, Ike utilized the medium of television. In a national broadcast he defended his action by explaining: "If I had signed the freeze bill, it would have been a 180-degree turn--right back to the very problems from which our farm people are beginning to escape. Instead of doing that we should build on what we have done to meet the problems that remain."[44]

Although the Senate GOP Policy Committee had voted 17 to 14 to recommend presidential approval of SJ Res 162, Eisenhower's veto was nevertheless sustained. Democrats then proceeded to concoct an omnibus bill in the House which would have altogether sidetracked the administration's Food and Fiber Bill. This conglomerate proposed a two-price system for wheat; allowed dairy farmers to set their own quotas; and provided options for feed-grain farmers to choose either supports with production controls or unlimited output with no guaranteed price supports.

Secretary Benson, while speaking to a campaign rally in Baltimore, called this hastily contrived measure an "economic monstrosity and a political hodgepodge."[45] It met defeat in the House on June 26th by a vote of 214 to 171. Twenty-one Republicans voted for it (actually a roll call on H Res 609 calling for debate), signifying even at this time a substantial GOP bloc eager to go beyond the Eisenhower-Benson recommendations.

Democrats in Congress tried hard to capitalize on the lingering mood of insurgency still smoldering in the breasts of Midwest Republicans. Secretary Benson's tenacity, plus President Eisenhower's refusal to capitulate, forced GOP dissidents to work out a compromise acceptable to administration backers. Speaker Sam Rayburn, writing to his brother Dick (back in Texas), revealed Democratic strategy when he indicated "we will have time next year to pass a bill with reference to farm products when we will, in all probability, have more men in Congress who will agree with us."[46] In other words Democrats were willing to yield temporarily to Ike with the expectation of revising farm legislation after they had made hoped-for mid-term gains.

The Agriculture Act of 1958 again fell short of what Eisenhower desired but it was a measure the Chief Executive could live with. The minimum parity level was lowered from 75 per cent to 65 per cent; cotton and rice acreage allotments were frozen at 16,000,000 and 1,653,000 acres respectively; price supports for feed grains were made mandatory; and a referendum was provided for whereby farmers would determine for themselves whether production restrictions on corn would remain or be removed. Other legislative action included passage of a measure for more humane methods of slaughtering at packinghouses; extension of provisions dealing with wool; renewal of PL 480; and establishment of a two-year program for purchase of surplus dairy products by the armed forces.

In an address to the American Institute for Cooperation, given on August 25, Benson indicated that the farm bill just passed by Congress, while not in any way perfect, constituted a positive step toward gaining freedom for farmers. It at least continued the movement away from attempted control over farming by rigid government formula. Despite some limitations, he praised the new farm act because it was based on sound principles that led to expanded markets. Benson urged this major representative of cooperatives to enlarge its activities by stepping in to replace the role played by government in agriculture. Co-ops were both "free enterprise" and "democracy in action," contended Benson, and should "help farmers reap the benefits of advancing technology and expert management."[47]

The Secretary of Agriculture prodded co-ops to get
a quick start in the fast-growing movement toward vertical
integration. This technique involved close cooperation and
coordination between producers and processers. Whereas
individual farmers were securing contracts to raise specific
crops for processers, Benson suggested that individual co-
ops should initiate programs linking production, processing,
and marketing of commodities for its members. This type of
collective action furthered efficiency, hence increased
profits, while operating within the framework of economic
freedom. If cooperatives organized agriculture vertically,
that is linked the producer to his marketing agent, it
would make the price support-acreage allotment mechanism
unnecessary.

Since Benson's own background was so closely associated with cooperatives, his outlook always reflected a faith
in the ability of farmers to work together and manage their
own affairs. Co-ops gave farmers more profits by cutting
out middlemen. They could promote research and advertising.
Some marketing co-ops gained control over the amount,
quality, and retail price of their commodities. Others
provided professional and special services to members at
less cost than otherwise would be the case. In an era
where expertise and technological knowhow were so important,
co-ops provided a means for them to combine for their mutual

benefit. Benson continually urged farmers to organize in this manner in order to profit economically from such organization.

Among those few Democrats supporting Benson's reforms were two former Agriculture Secretaries. Senator Clinton P. Anderson (D-N.Mex.), of Truman's cabinet, and Henry A. Wallace, who served F.D.R., both believed some flexibility had to be reintroduced into the price support system. The elderly Wallace, architect of the original New Deal apparatus being reformed by Benson, addressed a Farm Institute in Iowa and claimed, "I am sure that eventually the ever-normal granary of 1938, abnormally as it has been distorted, can also be proved to be a blessing if properly handled."[48] To Wallace the storage device, i.e. Commodity Credit Corporation, was the equivalent of an ever-normal granary. He agreed that steps had to be taken to prevent excessive carry-overs but felt that some stored surpluses were genuine protection against famine or future shortages. The one-time New Dealer was of the opinion that a combination of the Soil Bank, cross-compliance enforcement, flexible price supports, and maintenance of a reasonable ever-normal granary constituted the best answer to agriculture's problems. Wallace praised Benson for his fine effort to expand markets abroad for he too had worked toward that end. F.D.R.'s Agriculture Secretary spoke kindly of his

successor and refused to engage in namecalling. When James
A. Farley urged him to criticize Benson's policies in a
partisan manner he refused to comply. As the elder states-
man among agricultural secretaries he knew Benson was doing
what needed to be done. Although not agreeing with every
action he admired Ike's Secretary for being both courageous
and conscientious.[49]

Having gained a modicum of victory from Congress,
Ezra Taft Benson hit the campaign trail in the fall of 1958
with optimistic expectations for a GOP triumph at the polls.
Speaking in Wisconsin, the Agriculture Secretary lavished
praise on the voting record of Republican Senator Alexander
Wiley but voiced disapproval of Senator William Proxmire.
The scheme to "socialize farming," as Benson labeled
Proxmire's impractical parity income deficiency payment
program, would require a "horde of bureaucrats" to enforce
it and would cost $18 billion to carry it out. Basically
what the Wisconsin Democrat proposed was a comprehensive
system involving high price supports, acreage controls, and
stringently enforced marketing quotas. This would have
meant total management of agriculture by the government.
Benson closed his canvass by stating his hope that the
people of the badger state would soon relegate William
Proxmire to the status of an "ex-Senator."[50]

Speaking to a large rural audience in Tekamah, Nebraska, the Secretary of Agriculture admitted forthrightly that farmers were not sharing fully in the national prosperity. He hastened to remind his listeners that fundamental causes were such factors as the cost-price squeeze, soft wage settlements for unionized labor, and increased productive capacity stemming from technological developments in all facets of farming. Commensurate with high productivity an updated parity was needed. Agriculture could prosper if it modernized and adjusted to the new economic milieu. "Today's farm worker provides food and fiber for himself and twenty-three other persons," explained Benson. "Never in history have so many depended on so few to feed and clothe us so well."[51]

Benson informed Nebraskans of recent developments originating from the USDA's utilization research program. Patience had begun to pay off in this area, he announced. New uses had been found for cornstarch; safflower was being recommended for commercial use; and witchweed (found in seventeen counties in North and South Carolina) had been kept from entering the Corn Belt. More news would be forthcoming he predicted as research activities took time before useable results were evident.

Moving on to Arizona, Benson spoke well of Senator Barry Goldwater. Giving the Arizonan a most enthusiastic endorsement, the Agriculture Secretary maintained all who believed in freedom and free enterprise would vote for Barry Goldwater. The Senator's election and those of like-minded congressmen, Benson vowed, would further the cause of "prudent government dedicated to fiscal integrity, a stabilized dollar, balanced budgets and a greater proportion of the tax revenue expended at the state and local level."[52] Denouncing Democrats Benson called for the election of responsible Republicans. To a cheering crowd of enthusiastic Arizonans he claimed, "This nation will soon decide whether it shall have a truly American or a left-wing dominated Congress for the next two critical years."[53]

Received with acclaim by an equally enthusiastic group of Young Republicans in Wyoming, Benson renewed his attack on Democrats. He lashed out at left-wing extremists whose social philosophy was even to the left of the New Deal-Fair Deal. Identifying certain labor leaders with that radical element, he bluntly queried, "Do we want Walter Reuther controlling and naming the next President?"[54]

Closing out his campaign tour on the West coast, the Agriculture Secretary addressed a gathering of farm and business leaders in Fresno, California. Benson declared the 1958 farm act was passed in spite of left-wing opposition. The assemblage was assured agricultural policy would continue to reflect a philosophy of faith in the ability of farm people to decide for themselves as opposed to a regimented plan of complete dependence on government. Only under socialism or communism, asserted Benson, is the government everything and the people nothing. He argued passionately: "The government cannot guarantee all farmers a fixed level of income any more than government can guarantee every businessman a profit or every worker a high annual wage--or every doctor so many patients, or every manufacturer so many customers."[55]

When the polls closed on election day the results indicated a major victory for the Democrats. Counted among Republican casualties was a considerable number of the farm bloc. GOP losses in the House totaled forty-seven (of which twenty-three were located in the Midwest). In the Senate the Republicans dropped thirteen states. Democrats scored heavily in all states and not just where farming was an important industry.

Rural discontent no doubt played a part in Democratic gains but there were other important factors also. A sluggish economy, Southern resentment over Eisenhower's use of federal troops at Little Rock, Arkansas (to foster integration of public schools), trouble over Quemoy and Matsu in the Formosa Straits, Soviet success in orbiting the first space satellite (Sputnik), and the resignation of Sherman Adams (the Bernard Goldfine incident)--all contributed to

the trouncing suffered by the GOP. Some states also had
right-to-work propositions on the ballot and this antagonized
organized labor.

The unadorned statistics certainly augured ill for
any hopes Benson might have harbored relative to pursuing a
policy of further ridding agriculture of federal controls
involving rigid price supports. Realistically, all he could
expect was more resistance--not increased receptivity--to
his agricultural policies.

Chapter X

Profile of Courage

Featured at a fund raising dinner in Newark, New
Jersey to help pay off election debts, Ezra Taft Benson admitted to fellow Republicans that "we were licked pretty
thoroughly from coast-to-coast." In a philosophical tone
he reminded them, "It takes adversity sometimes to bring
into focus the principles for which we stand."[1] Undaunted
by political defeat and intractable when it came to devi-
ating from his own set of principles, the Agriculture Secretary never entertained the idea of quitting under fire.
Nor did he even consider lowering his profile or softening
his advocacy of what to him was best for America.

This was very much in evidence when Benson spoke to
a group of students at Rutgers University. Countering the
liberal philosophy so current among young people he warned
that a "planned and subsidized economy . . . weakens initiative, destroys and discourages industry, destroys character,

217

and demoralizes the people."[2] Cognizant of the fact that college students oftimes regarded material security over true individual freedom, despite their protestations over restrictions on personal behavior, Benson rendered fatherly advice on the value of preserving genuine freedom for all. He loved to talk to America's youth and found it easy to speak to them. Young audiences may not have always agreed with him but they appreciated his honesty and sincerity.

Within the ranks of the GOP feeling toward Secretary Benson crystallized in an unexpected way. Many conservatives in all parts of the country began to look upon the Agriculture Secretary as their spokesman within the Republican party. Benson began to receive letters from the rank and file encouraging him to seek the presidential nomination so that he might be the party's standard-bearer in 1960.

To one such enthusiastic supporter, Benson confided that the "thought of running for elective office has never tempted me." He did acknowledge an abiding concern for the preservation of certain principles as guiding beacons for his party. One cardinal precept enunciated by him was that "No man can make full use of the God-given talents with which he is endowed unless he has freedom to make his own decisions--and learn from the consequences, good or ill." For that reason, Benson explained, he had never succumbed to the "mistaken idea that farmers were willing to exchange freedom of choice for security." Upholding fiscal responsibility and free enterprise as the cornerstones of a sound political philosophy, he let it be known his inclination was to reduce federal control over the affairs of individual citizens. He did not approve of the welfare-state philosophy and told his well-wisher: "History teaches us that freedom of initiative is stifled in such a climate, and we must continue to strive for local responsibility [which] is the sort of government envisioned by the framers if the Constitution is to survive."[3]

That portion of the press representative of the conservative viewpoint also began to build up Benson as one worthy of a future leadership role. His advocacy of more local democracy and less centralized government appealed also to the Jeffersonian tradition within the Democratic party. A Waco Times-Herald editorial took partisan issue with the Republican party but commended the Agriculture Secretary for remaining true to his principles. The Texas newspaper commented:

> For spreading that philosophy in the
> past Benson has been laughed at, scorned at,
> rejected by members of his own party,
> farmers have thrown eggs at him, he has been

declared a political liability and one
politician claims Benson is doing all this
because he wants to become President of the
United States.

Yet Benson continues in his own way to
attack those who believe the government
should continue to aid the farmer. If you
want to argue with Benson, you'd better have
your facts well in hand. He has his facts
that way, and unless you can quote him
facts, he can tear your arguments into rib-
bons.[4]

The pressing decision confronting Secretary Benson
with regard to the 86th Congress was simple enough--should
he try in 1959 to push for more changes in agriculture,
when the House and Senate were completely dominated by the
opposition party, or should he just sit out the rest of his
tenure and do nothing? It appeared as if the President
would react negatively to any request for positive action.
Prior to the election Eisenhower had advised members of the
cabinet that before preparing any measures for legislative
approval they should consider the following two questions:

1. Is the proposal essential at the present
   time, considering the certainty of a

large budget deficit and our firm policy
of strict economy in federal spending?

2. Can enactment of the proposal be reason-
    ably expected within the two year span
    of the 86th Congress?[5]

In all previous attempts by Ezra Taft Benson to prepare farm legislation these efforts prompted conflict within
the administration and provoked acrimonious attacks on him
from members of Congress. Besides, with the GOP weakened
by election losses, the prognosis for implementation of
further reforms seemed hopeless. Democrats were already
posturing themselves for the 1960 presidential election and
part of their strategy was to persist in making Benson a
whipping boy. Yet he felt duty bound to press for more
congressional authorization to free agriculture from remaining impairments.

Dwight D. Eisenhower yielded to Benson's plea and
on January 29, 1959 the President submitted a special
message on agriculture to Congress. Disregarding the obviously hostile political climate, it called for an end to
all delay and swift transition to modern parity. Ike's
recommendations included the proposition that either "prices
for those commodities subject to mandatory supports be related to a percentage of the average market price during the
immediate preceding years" or "the Secretary [of Agriculture]

should be given discretion to establish the level in accordance with the guidelines now fixed by law for all commodities except those for which supports presently are mandatory."[6] In each case it was obvious that price supports would be drastically reduced.

When Ezra Taft Benson appeared before the House Subcommittee on Agricultural Appropriations to defend these legislative proposals, he was given a cool reception. Ignoring repeated interruptions and impervious to partisan taunts, he launched into a detailed discourse on why the old price support-acreage control mechanism needed total overhauling. His appeal to reason amid such an atmosphere was as courageous as it was futile. With grudging admiration the legislators listened while the Secretary arrayed his facts in a tour de force of logic. The mélange of government restraints, he concluded, "has placed ineffective bureaucratic controls on farmers, destroyed markets, piled up surpluses, and imposed heavy burdens on taxpayers."[7]

Since limitations on acreage had proved ineffective in preventing surpluses, particularly with regard to the 1958 wheat crop, Benson asked for a tough double-barreled approach: "(1) Basing price supports on a percentage of average market prices of the immediately preceding years; (2) Eliminating all acreage allotments and marketing quotas for wheat as soon as price supports are adjusted to levels

that will move the crop into use in average years."[8] It
seemed clear to the Agriculture Secretary that further
changing the parity base and eliminating all acreage allotments would check overproduction and materially reduce
government expenditures.

What Benson desired was a termination of government's managerial role, with its corollary of unenforceable
controls, so that the perennial wheat problem could at long
last be solved. Technology had rendered the acreage allotment approach obsolete and he was asking legislators to
recognize this obvious fact.

Persuading the President to relax his prohibitive
injunction on proposals adding to the budget, Benson pushed
for a one-year renewal of the Soil Bank's Conservation Reserve. Some twenty-three million acres had already been
retired at a cost of $265 million (averaging $11.50 per
acre). Also requested was a one-year extension of PL 480
with a price tag of $1.5 billion. Such expenditures were
huge but a necessary part of extricating agriculture from
its inherited plight. It gave the lie to those of Benson's
critics who claimed his parsimony worked to the detriment of
farmers. When federal disbursements aided agriculture, he
supported such outlays of money. When they did not, he
energetically opposed them.

223

The Democratically controlled Congress disregarded his recommendations and went its merry way. The bill finally sent to the President's desk coupled a 25 per cent reduction in acreage allotments to a price support level set at 90 per cent of parity. Reform was ignored in favor of restoration of the old system. This was totally unacceptable to the Secretary of Agriculture and he strongly urged Eisenhower to veto it. On June 25, 1959, following Benson's advice, Ike released a veto message which read in part: "The bill disregards the facts of modern agriculture. The history of acreage control programs--particularly in the case of wheat--reveals that they do not control production. . . . The poorest acres would be retired from production and all the modern technology would be poured onto the remainder."[9]

On the same day the President also struck down S. 1901, a tobacco price support bill. He defended this veto action by claiming the measure took a "long step backwards by resurrecting 90 per cent of 'old parity' as one basis for determining the support level for tobacco" and that "the deterioration of our tobacco sales abroad can be directly attributed to the high level of price supports that are required by existing laws."[10] After rejecting the work of the Congress on bills pertaining to agriculture, Eisenhower requested reconsideration of his original proposals. Unable to override the presidential veto, Congress ignored White House suggestions and a stalemate on farm legislation ensued.

Another major donnybrook erupted when Congress sought, through passage of S. 144, to take certain powers from the Secretary of Agriculture related to loan approvals made by the Rural Electrification Administration. Keying in on Benson the Democrats portrayed the Secretary as an enemy of REA. The stratagem worked insofar as it added another stroke to the adverse image Democrats were painting of Benson, but it failed because of a presidential veto. After Eisenhower turned down the bill intended to weaken the Secretary of Agriculture's control over REA loans, Speaker Sam Rayburn used his tremendous influence in the House to obtain enough votes to override it (with six Republicans joining in). Even as a lame duck President, Ike had enough political clout to get his veto sustained in the Senate. Only six GOP Senators defected and enough Democrats came to his aid to foil this bid to deprive the Executive full control over the activities of the REA.

Midwest Republicans were running scared and their nerve was shaken. Ben Jensen, representing Southwest Iowa, got thirty-two House members to sign a petition reaffirming their support for this agency. Giving credence to the effectiveness of the Democratic tactics they disassociated themselves from Benson. Within the context of the public power versus private enterprise argument (and this involved the agency's increased interest in supplying telephone service for all rural Americans) these GOP farm bloc members gave the following reasons for giving the REA a free hand:

1. The value of this program is well understood by everyone.
2. Adequate funds, irrespective of what
   might appear in the budget, will be
   readily granted by the present Congress.
3. The program is progressing along desirable lines under the present administration.[11]

The REA fracas was but one incident of many where an anti-Benson coalition exploited any incident presented to them for political capital. Benson baiting continued whenever any opportunity presented itself. Democrats had a field day for example when Comptroller General Joseph Campbell sent his report on the Agricultural Marketing Service to the Congress. This audit found evidence of certain technical violations in the administration of AMS's Food Distribution Division. In two counties in Alabama investigations discovered the following unsatisfactory conditions:

1. Storage areas not clean.
2. Presence of insects and weevils in commodities and rodents in storage areas.
3. Cheese not stored under refrigeration.
4. Inventories in excess of needs.
5. Applications and certificates of eligibility incomplete or not properly prepared.[12]

Here was an instance where Secretary Benson received the brunt of criticism for the inadequacies of a Southern state under the control of a Democratic administration. In Alabama the Department of Education took charge of the school lunch program while the Department of Pensions and Security handled distribution of federal surplus food. Not noted for its leadership in welfare projects, the personnel and facilities were considerably below national standards. Corrections could be forced only by threat of withdrawing government support. Such drastic action would certainly have precipitated retaliation in Congress, since many Southerners occupied positions of power on the various agricultural committees. Consequently the USDA was really powerless to prod states south of the Mason-Dixon Line to reform local administrative practices.

Just prior to Thanksgiving in 1959 the Food and Drug Administration (part of the Department of Health, Education, and Welfare) alertly seized a large lot of contaminated cranberries. It had been discovered that an herbicide named aminotriazole caused thyroid cancer in tests on animals. Residues of this weed killer were found in canned cranberries. To prevent consumption of this potentially dangerous food, some cans were recalled from food stores. Once news about this affair was released the public at large refused to purchase any cranberries. Secretary Benson was criticized by cranberry producers and political head-hunters alike for an administrative decision beyond his control. In an era when the concern for ill effects of food additives was not widespread, this incident was elevated into a source of embarrassment instead of a scientific search for safe food.

Ezra Taft Benson placed great reliance on research. His endeavors were directed into channeling a proportionate amount of effort into ways and means of finding new uses for food and fiber. The USDA's traditional concern was for techniques to increase production. Thus departmental scientists continued to develop chemicals and methods for increasing productivity. Little interest or concern was given to the toxic effects these substances were contributing to the pollution of the rivers and streams, thus contaminating fish and wildlife.[13] At a time when ecology was not yet a popular subject, the established scientists in the Department of Agriculture defended the use of pesticides and weed-control sprays as both safe and necessary for farm use. Indeed many were, but the wider use of them by the general public for home use made precautionary investigations necessary. If USDA scientists had information regarding the overall harmful effects of such chemicals, it was not made available to Benson. He sincerely believed that with proper safeguards there was no danger involved from residues that remained in the water or soil.[14] We know now that many scientists underestimated the threat indiscriminate use of these substances posed to the total environment.

Two other reports submitted to Congress by the Comptroller General caused the Secretary some momentary anguish. The first, filed on March 23, found fault with the Foreign Agricultural Service. This USDA agency supervised the operations involved in carrying out Title I of PL 480, which dealt with sales or disposition of surpluses for foreign currency. Indicating the existence of administrative laxity in carrying out its tasks, the FAS was criticized primarily for not keeping adequate records. To correct this defect it was suggested that in the future all "factors considered as the base for determining the estimated commodities and quantities available for sale for foreign currency should be adequately documented and recorded."[15] Another hortatory admonition asked that FAS personnel draw on foreign currency deposits instead of dollars to cover travel expenses while performing overseas duties.

The second report of the Comptroller General, sent to Congress on December 31, took the USDA's Commodity Stabilization Service to task for the way in which this agency executed provisions of the Soil Bank Act. Instances of questionable managerial procedures were cited as follows: significant errors in computations noted throughout North Dakota; incomplete information for seventy-three land retirement contracts in Vernon County, Missouri; and land leased from the states of Colorado, New Mexico, and Texas was accepted for placement in the Conservation Reserve. Noted also were violations of the congressional stipulation that annual rental payments should in no case exceed 20 per cent of the total value of the land being retired from production. "We do not believe that this limitation was effectively carried out," stated the report. In the Comptroller's judgment many of the administrative weaknesses disclosed "could have been detected and corrected had an adequate program of review and supervision been in effect."[16] With all of the political controversy over farm policy and the enormous task of administering the many agricultural acts, no one in the USDA was particularly happy about these additional criticisms.

Laws passed by Congress were complex and oftimes confusing. Many agencies were often involved in carrying out provisions of any single act. Knowing his department was huge and cumbersome, Benson had not only tried to reorganize it but had counseled USDA employees to perform in a conscientious manner. Some had resented his advice at the time; now the Secretary had to accept responsibility for both judgmental errors and procedural mistakes. Benson denied that there had been deliberate misinterpretation or malfeasance in the land retirement program. He claimed USDA rules were well within the spirit of the law and "that everything . . . done is consistent with the Soil Bank Act."[17]

Certain interpretations had to be made in the handling of such an enormous job. But in addition to the routine administrative foul-ups that occur in any bureaucracy, local politics again entered the scene. This often placed USDA officials on the horns of a dilemma. Farmers protested to their congressmen when strict interpretation prevented them from receiving income from land they wanted to include in the Conservation Reserve. Members of Congress in turn pressured the USDA to treat their constituents generously when it came to accepting acreage for placement in the Soil Bank. The combination of these factors sometimes resulted in acceptance of land for retirement which might have been excluded with the application of narrow and rigid interpretive practices.

The difficulties experienced by Benson in keeping track of the many endeavors of his huge department added to his burdens but did not sidetrack his own efforts to enlarge overseas markets for U.S. agricultural commodities. In 1959 the Secretary made two more trade trips to Europe, the first from June 25 to July 6 and the second extending from September 23 to October 9. The initial leg of his journey on the continent covered four cities in Switzerland (Lausanne, Bern, Basel, and Zurich); three cities in Germany (Cologne, Bonn, and Frankfurt); and two cities in Denmark (Copenhagen and Aalborg). During the fall junket he visited Yugoslavia, Germany, Poland, Finland, Norway, and the Soviet Union. The fourfold purpose of his travels abroad was to check personally on the operations of PL 480 programs; to investigate the possibilities of increasing American exports; to meet with government officials in order to remove trade barriers; and finally to make observations on the status of agriculture in the countries visited.

Benson's brief stay in the Soviet Union made a deep impression upon him. With his wife and two daughters accompanying him, the Agriculture Secretary had a firsthand opportunity to observe collective farms. He came away

more convinced than ever, as his report stated, of the
"superiority of our agricultural system of privately owned
family-sized farms, the profit system, freedom for the
farmer to decide what to grow and market, and competitive
markets." The Secretary got the distinct impression the
Soviet Union had openly challenged the United States to
peaceful competition in agricultural production and trade.
He thought the Eisenhower-Krushchev meetings had been fruit-
ful in cooling the Cold War and that cultural contacts between the two nations were worthwhile. While admitting the
Soviets might liberalize their views to some degree because
of relaxed tensions, Benson nonetheless held to his conviction that "the basic Communist ideology and strategic
objectives of world domination for Communism remained the
same."[18]

The most intense emotional experience without doubt
came when he was invited to occupy the pulpit of the Central
Baptist Church in Moscow. At a worship service at which
Russian Christians were in attendance, Benson gave a vivid
testimony of his personal religious faith. He told the
congregation that: "This life is only a part of eternity.
We are eternal beings. . . . We will live again after we
leave this life. Christ broke the bonds of death and was
resurrected. We will all be resurrected." As he departed
from their midst the congregation sang "God Be With You Til

We Meet Again." It was truly a heartwarming and soul-satisfying event for Benson. "We shall never forget this victory of the spirit over tyranny, oppression, and ignorance," he recalled upon returning home. "We can never forget the ultimate deliverance of the Russian people."[19]

Shortly after his latest trip abroad the Secretary of Agriculture began to suffer from acute intestinal pains. At first he attributed his illness to overwork. Long hours at his office, much traveling, and the partisan controversy that constantly surrounded him were tension-producing factors that could have easily eroded away his ability to work under immense pressure. When he became too sick to carry on, he entered Walter Reed Hospital for a physical examination. Doctors immediately diagnosed his infirmity as an inflamed gall bladder. A cholecystectomy was performed successfully on December 4th. Because he was in such good physical condition, his recovery was quick and without complications. Tarrying only ten days after his operation, the Agriculture Secretary returned to his job intent as ever on fighting for his farm policy objectives. By now he had come to regard his position as the "hot spot."[20]

With a Democratic Congress holding the reins chances for more reform legislation dwindled. Another obstacle was the attitude of the President. Eisenhower seemed intent upon drastically reducing expenditures during his final years in the White House. He told his cabinet, on November 22, 1959, future "watchwords should be frugality, economy, [and] efficiency." In what amounted to a directive he stressed: "I have only fourteen months left to serve in this office. I want to send up a tough, balanced budget. If the budget I send up should be unbalanced, or substantially raised, I would be defeated. I don't want to be defeated. I haven't often been defeated."[21]

Within this retrenchment frame of mind, it became increasingly difficult for White House aides to interest the President in propositions to enlarge existing programs. Don Paarlberg, having replaced Gabriel Hauge as Ike's Special Assistant for Economic Affairs (the latter had accepted a position with the Manufacturers Trust Company of New York City), wanted to have the Rural Development Program enlarged. He felt the RDP deserved more publicity and further funding.[22] But to have talked seriously about expansion would have meant increased expenditures. Even if Congress would have been interested, which was doubtful, the President refused at this time to consider further development of any program involving large financial outlays.

Having intimate knowledge of the attempts under PL 480 to get rid of surpluses, Paarlberg felt this too should be given more attention. It could be done without spending more money but merely by focusing the spotlight on

projects then in existence. Paarlberg's public relations
suggestion was good politics and it met with Ike's approval.
Not only was it a good move for a pre-presidential election
year, but it prevented the Democrats from claiming credit
for something already started by the Eisenhower administration. Senator Hubert Humphrey (D-Minn.) had submitted a
report to the Senate Agriculture and Forestry Committee entitled "Food and Fiber as a Force for Freedom."[23] Now he
was pressing for renewal of PL 480 on a three-year basis
with more emphasis upon its foreign aid aspects. When the
President established his own Food for Peace Program, with
Don Paarlberg named as coordinator, it took the play away
from the Democrats.

As one very interested in helping the GOP establish
a good political posture for 1960, Vice-President Richard
Nixon gave Paarlberg considerable support in selling the
President on the idea of a Food for Peace Program. With the
know-how of one experienced in politics Nixon told the
cabinet: "A farmer who knows that his wheat is going
abroad, to meet human need, as a part of the foreign policy
of the United States, is likely to be happier than a farmer
who is told that his wheat is simply creating a storage prob
lem for the United States government."[24]

Ezra Taft Benson accepted the foreign aid program o
the predication that it was a humanitarian gesture. He had

once supervised an overseas program for his church after World War II and knew its value to the citizens of underdeveloped nations. He supported the reemphasis given to the Food for Peace Program by justifying it on the basis "We are making our God-given bounty available to the less fortunate --not in the spirit of a wasteful give-away but rather in the spirit of genuine helpfulness."[25]

In keeping with the President's determination to hold the line on spending, his agricultural message to Congress, sent to Capitol Hill on February 9, 1960, was both modest and moderate in tone. The Food for Peace, utilization research, and the Rural Development Program were given brief mention but no substantial sums were requested to expand them. Eisenhower did ask for an enlargement of the Conservation Reserve to 60 million acres with provisions for making government payments in kind (i.e. in produce) if farmers desired it. Once again, at the insistence of Benson, Ike called for legislation to correct the overproduction of wheat. Inviting compromise, the President concluded his message on agriculture by stating: "If the Congress wishes to propose a plan as an alternative to the course here recommended, so long as that plan is constructive, as I have indicated herein, I will approve it."[26]

Appearing before the House Committee on Agriculture on February 18, Secretary Benson elaborated on the reform proposals which had been submitted by the President. He indicated the Conservation Reserve should be renewed for three years with authorization for federal payments to farmers in surplus corn, wheat, or other feed grains when desirable. Reiterating desires made known many times before, Benson asked that Congress enact legislation immediately to eliminate acreage allotments for wheat while at the same time lowering the price support payment to 75 per cent of parity. The formula to be used for the computation of parity was to be based upon the price-cost ratio of the past three years. Secretary Benson wanted these needed reforms to be encompassed in a three-year program for maximum effectiveness and he also asked that parity for tobacco be formulated on the basis of contemporary figures.

In his testimony Benson sought certain corrective amendments to PL 480. He wanted authorization to allow underdeveloped countries to stockpile food under Title I and sought permission to use surplus commodities as payments for wages in foreign aid projects. Other petitions included renewal of the Sugar Act and legislation preventing the REA from paying interest in excess of those amounts paid by the U.S. Treasury Department on long-term obligations.[27]

On his own Benson tried to spur grass roots support for these proposals. Speaking to a Farmer-Businessman Dinner at Yankton, South Dakota, the Agriculture Secretary tried to convince that state's wheat growers of the soundness of his position. He argued, "It doesn't make sense to me that this traditional wheat area should be deprived of productive and economic wealth by unsound farm programs that lose markets and depress prices through imbalance of natural production here in this country."[28] Admitting that he differed on farm policy with Senator Karl Mundt, Benson continued to press his own case for reduced price supports. He maintained farmers not only benefitted from Eisenhower's farm policy but also by the President's efforts to control inflation. The Agriculture Secretary contended that the cost of living had risen 133 per cent during the years from 1939 to 1952, but went up only 4 per cent since 1952.

Benson acknowledged to this assemblage that his worst misfortune was that of "being misrepresented" by political foes. Trying to dismiss the myth that he was not sympathetic to their cause, the Secretary insisted that his main objective was to secure a lasting prosperity for them and all of the rural sector. Political opponents had done much to malign him, he claimed. "They have distorted my actions--sought to create a false image of the Secretary of Agriculture [and] . . . have tried to force me out of office. . . ."[29] Although Benson had personally reconciled himself to the unfair abuse aimed his way, he still resented the harm it did to effective action. By setting up a straw

239

man, Benson's critics flailed away at this fictitious image with dogged determination. But in so doing they detracted from his ability to promulgate lasting and telling reforms. In that respect farmers were the real losers.

Secretary Benson was the constant victim of bad press. Liberal commentators and columnists within the public media found it easier to attack him than to criticize Eisenhower. In this sense, Ike was wise in keeping Benson in the cabinet. It kept much vitriol from reaching the White House.

Once when the well-known Edward R. Murrow asked the Secretary and his family to appear on the widely-watched television show "Person-to-Person," Benson regarded it as an honor. It gave the Bensons an opportunity to testify to their faith, which they did by demonstrating a family devotion in the home. Four months later, however, the Agriculture Secretary was dismayed at another Murrow-produced TV program called "See It Now." In a documentary-like show titled "Crisis of Abundance," the Eisenhower-Benson farm policy was (as they say in the trade) given a hatchet-job. Benson objected strenuously to a contorted sequence which portrayed one Iowa farm being auctioned off, seemingly representing a bankruptcy when in actuality it was just an ordinary sale. So twisted and distorted was the program in the Secretary's opinion, he asked for and received equal time from the Columbia Broadcasting System to correct erroneous impressions.[30]

Secretary Benson received two jarring setbacks in 1960. First, after the death of Senator William Langer (R-N.D.) on November 8, 1959 a special election was held the following June. Quentin N. Burdick, a one-term Democratic congressman, defeated former GOP Governor John E. Davis in a closely contested election. The significant aspect of the campaign was the Democrat's slogan: "Beat Benson With Burdick."[31] This Republican defeat once more stirred talk of getting rid of Ezra Taft Benson lest the party ruin its chances in the fall presidential election. The verbal venom flowed freely from the corridors of Congress.

Always eager to discomfort the Secretary of Agriculture, Democrats initiated a probe into the workings of the Commodity Credit Corporation. The CCC had been involved in scandals during the Truman administration and seemed a likely place for political ammunition. After an investigation a subcommittee of the Senate Agriculture and Forestry Committee found some evidence of mismanagement and conflict of interest. CCC costs for its transactions ran close to a billion dollars a year and was a vast operation. With that kind of money being spent it was inevitable that some waste would occur. In fact Benson had repeatedly warned Congress of the losses involved due to spoilage and loss of quality

241

in stored products. Congress charged the CCC with paying excessively high amounts for storage, especially when contracts were let to privately owned warehouses. Such facilities were at a premium during periods of bumper harvests. Without delay Benson announced revisions in the Uniform Grain Storage Agreement to effect a 19 per cent reduction in rent payments to warehousemen.[32] Needless to say the Agriculture Secretary did not appreciate this type of faultfinding since if he had had his own way the large volume of commodities handled by the CCC would be unnecessary.

Congress again ignored Benson's express wish to pursue reforms when it came to agricultural legislation in 1960. When President Eisenhower sent proposals for such action, it refused to expand the Soil Bank's Conservation Reserve and balked at lowering price supports on wheat. Instead two laws were passed and sent to the President. The first was a tobacco support bill which froze supports at the 1959 level with provisions for raising it thereafter according to the increase in the cost of living. A second measure raised price supports on dairy products from 77 per cent to 80 per cent. To Benson these bills reversed what he had been trying to achieve during his whole tenure of office One might have expected Ike to veto them, but to the surpris of many he did not. Many pressures were brought to bear on

Eisenhower. Vice-President Richard Nixon for one advised

him to sign them as did Senator Thruston B. Morton (R-Ky.),

who was then serving as Chairman of the Republican National

Committee.

It became increasingly clear to Benson that Richard

M. Nixon, the obvious leader in the Republican race for the

presidential nomination, was trying to placate all factions

of his party. In the mind of the Agriculture Secretary

steadfast adherence to principle and not political expediency

was the key issue. As for Nixon the dilemma was quite dif-

ferent. He did not want to defend Benson, as did Eisenhower,

but rather saw a chance of avoiding this alternative.

While agreeing in essence with Benson's policy he was willing

to temper parity with politics. For this reason the Vice-

President began to exert more influence on agricultural

affairs so that he could start his campaign in the farm belt

with no political encumbrances.

Chapter XI

Richard Nixon and the 1960 Election

Once he became aware of the likelihood that his
Vice-President would be the GOP candidate for the presidency
in 1960, Dwight D. Eisenhower proffered some advice to his
would-be successor. In a memorandum dated January 13, the
President counseled Richard Nixon in many areas including
suggestions on how to conduct his presidential campaign.
On the topic of agriculture he wrote: "The man who stands
highest, so far as knowledge of this subject and integrity
of purpose are concerned, is of course, Secretary Benson.
Many Republicans think that any public appearance by him
would be a detriment in the Middle West. Nevertheless it
is possible that he could be used efficiently in the
metropolitan areas because his viewpoint is that of the nation and not of the local voters."[1]

Mentioned also by Ike as potential speakers in farm
areas were: Allan B. Kline, President of the AFBF; William

I. Myers, Chairman of the NAAC; Representative Leslie Arends of Illinois, House Whip; and Representative Charles B. Hoeven of Iowa. The President included his brother Milton in the list with the comment "if he can be induced to participate in the political campaign." These men by and large were in perfect agreement with Benson's outlook on agricultural policy. Nevertheless the fact that Ike forewarned Nixon about the attitude of Midwest Republicans impressed the Vice-President. Consequently he redoubled his efforts to prepare a political scenario geared to soften this issue.

Secretary Benson was not oblivious to the maneuvers of the Vice-President and it worried him. Was Nixon going to jettison his policy? Evidence mounted when already in 1959, as the Agriculture Secretary saw it, Nixon influenced the President to moderate his final farm message to Congress. After the first cabinet meeting in March, at which time differences on agricultural policy were again aired, Benson wrote in his diary: "I wish I had more confidence in the Vice-President's ability to provide wise leadership for the nation."[2]

When ex-Governor Victor E. Anderson of Nebraska approached Benson about the advisability of retiring just before the 1960 elections, the Agriculture Secretary sensed that he had been sent by Nixon. Moreover after Benson sent some materials to White House aide Don Paarlberg, who was helping prepare a Republican farm plank, they were rejected in a rather abrasive manner. Paarlberg sent them back with the comment, "I would suggest an entirely different pitch, positive, not negative; opportunity-oriented, not problem-prone." On one page of the proposed Benson draft Paarlberg had the notation: "I count eighteen places in the manuscript in which the Congress and political activity generally are ridiculed. One doesn't catch flies with vinegar."[3] His negative reaction to Benson's contributions closed with an injunction the Agriculture Secretary read over carefully the contents of the so-called Percy Report.

Charles H. Percy, the young executive who headed Bell and Howell Company, was chosen Chairman of the Republican National Platform Committee. Prior to this assignment Percy, who represented the liberal wing of the party, had helped formulate a detailed statement on agricultural policy. The Percy Report did seek to place the blame on Democrats by charging: "The Republican administration has acted vigorously to cope with the consequences of this self-defeating program and to modernize it. But these efforts have been defeated by the persistent refusal of the Congress, controlled by the opposition . . . , to face up to the problems posed by the onrush of farm technology."[4] But it was also more studded with compromising rhetoric and vague phrases

capable of being interpreted in various ways. It was a
document attuned to the exigencies of politics.

Richard Nixon, as Chairman of the Cabinet Committee
on Price Stability for Economic Growth, again crossed swords
with the Secretary of Agriculture over another issue. Other
members in addition to Secretary Benson included: Robert
B. Anderson, Secretary of the Treasury; James P. Mitchell,
Secretary of Labor; Frederick H. Mueller, Secretary of Commerce; Raymond J. Saulnier, Chairman-Council of Economic Advisors; Arthur E. Summerfield, Postmaster-General; and W.
Allen Wallis, Special Assistant to the President (Executive
Vice-Chairman). Counseled by Arthur Burns, former Chairman
of the CEA, Nixon sought to persuade this group to urge both
a tax cut and a relaxation on government spending. There
were signs, so Burns indicated to the Vice-President, that
unless these steps were taken the country would slide into
a recession just about the time the presidential election
would be in progress.[5] This, of course, would be disastrous
to Nixon.

It was Benson's conviction that neither cutting taxes
nor increasing federal expenditures were wise at the moment.
This was also in line with President Eisenhower's thinking.
In Benson's judgment the real enemies of the farmer were
still inflation and an unbalanced budget. The committee's
final report praised this aspect of the Eisenhower

247

administration claiming it had blunted the inflationary thrust. Furthermore it affirmed: "Economic progress requires that we also promote competition, reduce wasteful subsidies, eliminate rigidity and immobility in our economic system, stimulate research and innovation, encourage saving and investment, and pursue similar positive programs for the cultivation of economic growth." To prevent any future rise in the cost of living, the Committee on Price Stability for Economic Growth recommended only a continuation of "persistent efforts to enforce competition in all markets, to control unwarranted upward cost pressures, and to root out many government induced impediments to economic change and efficiency. . . ."[6]

Upon reading this report Don Paarlberg sent the following evaluation of it to Philip E. Areeda (an assistant to Special Counsel David W. Kendall): "This draft was discussed by Nixon and the Committee with the President this morning and is soon to be released. It breaks no real new ground but emphasized matters already a part of the President's program. Your reactions if you wish."[7]

Areeda's assessment of the document was contained in the unenthusiastic response: "Not bad as a release--though it does make abundantly clear that the Committee is doing nothing of significance. That, I suspect, will be the main reaction to the release."[8] Government and politics seemingly are interrelated and policy making is never completely divorced from this context; yet in this instance the line was held.

No small part of the predicament faced by Richard M. Nixon was the stand-pat attitude of Eisenhower during his final months as President. The blow-up of the Paris summit conference and the ominous signs of a slow-down in the economy placed the Vice-President in the painful position of having to defend past actions rather than to be able to propose new and positive policies. Philip Areeda's prediction that Nixon's economic report would be panned came true. The Democratic nominee for the presidency, Senator John F. Kennedy, ridiculed it with telling effect in one of his 1960 campaign speeches. Amid a recession he made political hay by saying:

> Finally, last year, the Republicans decided to do something bold. They appointed a committee to study the problem. They called it the Cabinet Committee on Price Stability for Economic Growth and for chairman they picked the Vice-President of the United States.
>
> The New York Times called this Mr. Nixon's "first formal executive role" . . .

The Committee met--and talked--and studied
--and, as a result, they acted. They
didn't bring prices down. They didn't
send our growth rate up. But they did
file a report.

The Wall Street Journal said it was
fine except it had no recommendations on
what it was appointed to do. Today, as
the 1960 campaign goes on, we hear a lot
about experience--but somehow the Committee is never mentioned.[9]

With considerable dexterity Richard Nixon tried to
put together a farm plank that would for all intent and purposes bypass Ezra Taft Benson without repudiating his farm
policy. Ironically, whereas Nixon was trying vainly to
disassociate himself from Benson as a political liability,
his own stand on agriculture was not unlike that of Ike's
Agriculture Secretary. His later administration proved the
merits of the Benson policies by bringing them to a successful culmination. The midterm losses of 1958 had persuaded
the Vice-President to reduce Benson's profile by restricting
his role in any future campaign. Commenting on that election where many Midwestern Republicans had gone down to defeat, Nixon told the party faithful: "Take the farm issue,

for example. What we have proposed and what we have done has been right for the farmer and the nation. The farmer has never had it so good. But, some way, somehow, our Democratic friends have done such a good job on Ezra Benson that they have the farmers thinking he and the Republican party are against them. We took the worst shellacking in the farm states."[10]

The word "new" in politics is a catchy slogan inferring bold and fresh ideas. As such the "New Frontier" was but one more catch phrase even as were the New Deal and Fair Deal. Nixon eschewed coining a political shibboleth but he did latch onto the word "new." In his election-year book, The Challenge We Face, the Vice-President gave as one of his five points for assuring a prosperous America, "We must develop a new [italics added] program for agriculture rather than adopting the unworkable political approach of freezing America's farmer in an obsolete, rigid system which can only lead to a dreary cycle of surpluses, controls, and depressed farm income."[11] In so doing Nixon attempted to put an up-to-date face on his farm policy while removing Benson as a symbol of controversy in order to placate critics.

The GOP farm plank as finally hammered out contained Benson's policies and Nixon's rhetoric. The Republican party formally committed itself "to develop new [again the

magic word] programs to improve and stabilize farm family
income." Promises were made to intensify Food for Peace
activity, strengthen surplus disposal programs, and
reorganize the marketing operations of the Commodity Credit
Corporation. With the accent on words implying future
action, the platform continued with the following pledges:

A crash research program to develop industrial and other uses of farm products. Use
of price supports at levels best fitted to
specific commodities, in order to widen
markets, ease production controls, and help
achieve increased farm family income.

Acceleration of production adjustments, including a large-scale land conservation
reserve. Continued progress in the wise use
and conservation of water and soil resources.
Use of marketing agreements and orders . . .
to assist in the orderly marketing of
crops.

Stepped-up research to reduce production
costs and to cut distribution costs.
Strengthening of . . . educational programs.
Improvements of credit facilities.
Encouragement of farmer owned and operated

cooperatives including rural electric and
telephone facilities.

Expansion of the Rural Development Program.[12]

Convening in the Los Angeles Sports Arena the Democratic Convention met amid an aura of optimism. The youth
and glamour of their presidential candidate generated an
atmosphere of effervescence throughout the convention hall.
With little debate delegates approved a lengthy platform
containing an agricultural plank aimed at winning the farm
vote. It was a tour de force in semantics. Deftly written
it castigated the GOP while assuming a stance as sole
champions of the rural population. "The right [their magic
word] of every farmer to raise and sell his products at a
return which will give him and his family a decent living,"
was presented as the basic position of the Democratic party.
By defining the economic need of the farmer as a "right,"
it dispelled any notion that rural people had their hands
out for government subsidies or that Democrats intended to
buy their allegiance.

Rhetoric exceeded reality when the plank charged,
"We will no longer view food stockpiles with alarm but will
use them as powerful instruments for peace and plenty."
Additional promises were made such as: increasing domestic
consumption, improving school lunch and milk programs,

maintaining food reserves for national defense, expanding research for new industrial uses for agricultural commodities, greater use of American food abroad, and expansion of foreign trade. There was really not much more the Democrats could do in these areas not already done but nevertheless past efforts were labeled "unimaginative, outmoded Republican policies."[13]

A cleverly worded attack upon Ezra Taft Benson was contained in the plank's phraseology when it asserted: "All these goals demand the leadership of a Secretary of Agriculture who is conversant with the technological and economic aspects of farm problems, and who is sympathetic with the objectives of effective farm legislation not only for farmers but for the best interests of the nation as a whole." What were the goals toward which new and progressive legislation should be directed? Democrats committed themselves to enactment of a program which would "include production and marketing quotas measured in terms of barrels, bushels, and bales, loans on basic commodities at not less than 90 per cent of parity, production payments, commodity purchases, and marketing orders and agreements." In calling for a revival of the old system of high, rigid price supports the farm plank claimed: "We are convinced that a successful combination of these approaches will cost considerably less than present Republican programs which

254

have failed."[14]

When Democratic delegates cheered wildly at the acceptance speech of their youthful-looking presidential nominee, few realized how much at odds he had been with their farm plank. While representing the state of Massachusetts, Senator John F. Kennedy had registered twenty-seven key votes in favor of Benson's farm program. In 1956, for example, when the Democrats with rural constituencies were trying to attach a high price support amendment to the Soil Bank Bill, J.F.K. rose on the Senate floor to state: "I am opposed at this time to any farm program calling for high price supports fixed at 90 per cent of parity until such time as the flexible support program and the new soil bank program have had a sufficient opportunity to prove themselves. To those of my colleagues who call upon me to support the 90-per cent program, despite its shortcomings, as a means of stabilizing farm income during the current farm recession, I can only point to the decline in farm prices and income which has taken place during the operation of that 90-per cent program."[15]

Making a one hundred eighty degree reversal, J.F.K. now canvassed throughout farm territory on an anti-Benson motif. Electioneering in Carbondale, Illinois, Kennedy made this campaign statement: "Mr. Benson is an honest man, but he has not been a successful Secretary of Agriculture. I

could not disagree more with the agricultural policy pursued
by this administration, which has got for its basis, a
steady drop of support prices as a method of eliminating
overproduction. Mr. Nixon proposed his plan a week ago and
he put in the same basic feature, which is that the support
price shall be tied to the average of the market place. If
it goes down, so does the support price." Taking his stand
on rigid price supports coupled with strict production controls, the Democrat candidate unabashedly announced: "My
own judgment is for our agricultural program that we should
tie support price to parity price. Then the support price
is fixed. But along with that we should have effective controls on production."[16]

    All throughout the farm belt John F. Kennedy did his
best to link Ezra Taft Benson with Richard M. Nixon. At a
farm conference in Des Moines, Iowa, J.F.K. pointed out:
"Here in the Middle West, Mr. Nixon hardly speaks to Mr.
Benson. He disowns the man he once called 'the best Secre-
tary of Agriculture we ever had.' But in Portland, Maine a
week ago, he talked along different lines. The reason Mr.
Benson has not been successful, he said, is because the
Democratic Congress has never given his program a chance."
Then riveting the audience's attention on Ike's Secretary of
Agriculture, Kennedy evoked applause with a punch line laden
with ridicule: "Congress did give Mr. Benson's program a

chance--but Mr. Benson's program never gave the farmer a chance."[17]

The quandary facing Richard Nixon was that of a political tightrope walker. He wanted to maintain a proper distance from Benson but still not disown him. In his memoir-like book, Six Crises, Nixon outlined in explicit terms the crux of his dilemma: "The Democrats for eight years had done a vicious hatchet-job on Ezra Taft Benson. They had created the impression, not only among Democratic farmers but among Republicans as well, that Benson had no sympathy for the farmers and their problems and that his attitude was simply that the farmer should 'grin and bear it.' The Republican farm bloc leaders respected him as a man of high principle. Scarcely a one of them had any alternative to offer. But almost to a man they told me-- 'The farmer has not been getting his fair share of America's increasing prosperity. He is hurting.' He will not vote for a presidential candidate who says, in effect, 'we are doing all we can and things will work out in time.'"[18]

Biting the bullet as the saying goes, Nixon approached Eisenhower on the advisability of sending Secretary Benson on several overseas trade missions during the course of the campaign. Perhaps remembering his own Kasson pledge gambit of 1952, the President agreed to do this as long as neither Benson nor his farm policy were openly renounced by the Nixon-Lodge team. To this arrangement the Vice-President readily gave his assent.

Commencing on July 30, Ezra Taft Benson was out of the country for eighteen days while he toured France, Belgium, West Germany, Egypt, Jordan, Israel, and the Netherlands. Upon returning, he was eager to get into the campaign. The Agriculture Secretary felt sure he could contribute much to elect a Republican to the presidency.

Speaking at the Chesterfield County Fair Grounds in Virginia, Benson pointed out the incredible reversal of position displayed by John F. Kennedy. Labeling the Democratic nominee a captive of the Farmers Union, he told the crowd before him, "Senator Kennedy made a complete flip-flop in his farm voting record." Secretary Benson called for the election of the GOP team because "the stability, dependability, and capability of the Nixon-Lodge ticket is the nation's best hope." He reaffirmed his own personal endorsement of the Republican party's presidential nominee by predicting Richard Nixon would be a "great and beloved President."[19]

This was a generous gesture on Benson's part because at the GOP National Convention in Chicago he had been approached by Governor Nelson Rockefeller of New York as a potential vice-presidential running mate as a part of his nomination efforts. Even though Nixon had appointed Fred

Seaton his agricultural advisor--not Benson or someone associated with him--the Agriculture Secretary very much wanted to play a major role in the campaign. This was not to be the case.

Just when Benson thought he would hit the electioneering trail in earnest, Secretary of State Christian A. Herter asked the Secretary of Agriculture to embark on a special trade mission to Latin America. Aware now that he was being sidelined, Benson then devoted himself to official duties. Before his departure to South America (to include stops in Argentina, Brazil, Uruguay, Chile, and Peru), Benson proffered this final advice to the Vice-President:

> I feel the time has come for you to hit hard and be tough but be sure you are right. You need to keep emphasizing the basic differences between your philosophy and your opponent's and by letting the American people know there is a real choice. You need to keep pointing out the Democratic record when Truman was President and our record since. . . .[20]

While not being present physically during the greater part of the fall campaign, Ezra Taft Benson's presence was manifest in other ways. He had prepared his own

personal statement for distribution to the delegates of the
GOP National Convention and it was still being circulated.
With the title, "Where We Stand," Benson warned fellow
Republicans, "Never must this choice nation be permitted
to fall prey to a government by decree to create and dispense health, wealth, and happiness to a subservient
people."[21]

In a more detailed book-length work, published under
the title Freedom to Farm, Benson elaborated in detail on
all facets of his political philosophy. "My concern is two-
fold," he wrote concerning farm policy, "that efforts to aid
farmers contribute to making their future brighter, not
serve to compound their problems; and that agriculture be
unhampered in its continuing technological advancement."
He circumscribed the difficulties by asserting, "The nub
of our present problem is unrealistic support prices and
futile attempts to control production." Indicating the
failure of the old parity formula based on the 1910-1914
period, Benson advised movement toward market-oriented farm
prices. He contended that the "efficient commercial farmer
can more nearly get income parity if he is allowed to
operate in a relatively free market."

What was to happen to the small-scale farmer? His
answer was the frank assessment that: "It doesn't matter
whether we give that man 100 or 200 per cent of parity

through the price support program, his income problem will
not be solved. His problem is one of volume, not price.
He does not have an economic farm unit. He is not able to
grow the volume of crops to benefit substantially by price
supports. What he needs is an opportunity for full employment. Undersized, undercapitalized, and underequipped farms
cannot furnish such employment, nor can those who operate
them possibly earn an adequate income without part-time work
in other occupations."[22]

Reactions to Freedom to Farm ranged from lavish
praise to total condemnation. Herschel D. Newsom, Master of
the National Grange, was typical of many farm leaders who
formed the old Agrarian Establishment. He could not adjust
to new ideas. Newsom wrote to the Agriculture Secretary and
told him: "I have always valued your friendship, and I
always will. I have always felt that fundamentally we have
many purposes in common. On the other hand, I concede that
there must be a deeper seated difference of philosophy between me and some of my good, personal friends than I have
ever thoroughly understood."[23] In his mind the family farm
was associated with the retention of price supports and
federal subsidies.

Press coverage included both kudos and adverse
criticism. A book review in the Newark Leader compared
Benson favorably with Herbert Hoover in his desire to stand

on principle, rather than to play politics with agriculture.[24] "There are few grays in Benson's spectrum," declared the Washington Post, "and that is why he has had such difficulties with Congress."[25] The Des Moines Register noted, "Benson believes so strongly that price supports and government production controls are morally wrong that he sometimes closes his eyes to facts which do not fit his beliefs."[26] Similarly the Minneapolis Tribune commented, "Once his mind is made up that a course of action is right, he is a hard man to dissuade."[27]

In the Nebraska Farmer a caustic critic wrote, "But if Ezra Benson believes the majority of farmers want the government to abandon agriculture, he's sure been talking to different farmers than we have."[28] Dr. Willard W. Cochrane of the Department of Agricultural Economics at the University of Minnesota, and one of John F. Kennedy's principal farm advisors, summed up Benson's book for the Saturday Review by curtly stating, "In short, a return to the good old days around Preston, Idaho [the Agriculture Secretary's home town] would resolve the farm problem."[29]

Equally biting was the observation of the Reading Guide (published by the University of Virginia Law School) that a "certain querulousness of tone, together with an impatient sense of mission, creeps into the discourse." It was also noted that farmers in the period from 1920 to 1932 possessed a total freedom to farm, "but by 1935 they were buried in worse surpluses than is the case today."[30]   In Illinois the Springfield State Journal announced with an overtone of approval: "The most controversial member of President Eisenhower's cabinet . . . [is] slated for retirement by the next President."[31]

Applauding Eisenhower's Secretary of Agriculture, who along with Postmaster General Arthur E. Summerfield were the only two original cabinet appointees to last eight years, the editor of the Weekly Star Farmer wrote: "It was this kind of dedication that Benson, an elder in the Mormon Church, took with him into government service and only by realizing this can it be understood how stubbornly he has stood by convictions he thinks are right, though politically unpopular."[32]   The Wall Street Journal considered the book well "timed to set the record straight."[33]   Giving it an excellent review, the Richmond Times-Dispatch queried, "Will the Republicans heed the advice of the man who has steadfastly fought for a return to sanity in agriculture?"[34]   In the far West the Arizona Republic hailed Benson as the "voice of sanity" while denigrating the Democratic farm plank as "the ultimate in bribery and vote-buying."[35]   Nicholas King, writing in the New York Herald Tribune, claimed: "Mr. Benson has the great advantage not always shared by high government officials, of knowing exactly what he is talking about."[36]

After reading a copy of Freedom to Farm, Assistant
Secretary Earl Butz endorsed it wholeheartedly. But concerning the election, he was worried. He wrote: "It would
appear that if the Democrats are successful that the eight
years of effort to get some order out of the farm program
goes down the drain. I wish I better understood what Vice-
President Nixon has in mind but this I don't know and I have
been unable to determine whose advice he is actually taking
in preparing the program."[37]

Long-time friend William I. Myers congratulated
Benson by telling him, "I might quibble with you a little
about some of your interpretations of minor events but I
think it is an excellent book and deserves wide public recognition." Added as a postscript, Myers made the comment:
"I hope and believe Nixon's farm program will be in general
agreement with yours. He has some excellent advisors, one
of whom assures me that his farm speech will be satisfactory. I surely hope so for the Democratic program is ter-
rible."[38]

Farm journals throughout the countryside were also
speculating as to the nature of Nixon's agricultural policy.
Jay Richter, in an article entitled "The Next President and
Southern Agriculture," written for the Progressive Farmer
just before the election, made a prediction that a future

GOP program would reflect the views of Nixon's advisors.
Both of the Vice-President's farm advisors, Fred A. Seaton
and Henry L. Allgren (Director of Extension-University of
Wisconsin), he claimed, supported "indemnity payments" for
taking land out of production and wanted "to bring supply
and demand into such relationship that farmers will no
longer find it profitable to produce for government." It
was highlighted as significant that the Vice-President "has
broken with Benson and is said to feel that surpluses must
be brought under control quickly, even at considerable
cost."[39]

The Wallaces Farmer, blanketing the Midwest, perceived accurately that Nixon's strategy in the farm belt was
to "disassociate himself with Benson's supposed unpopularity
without really straying far from Benson-type farm programs."[40]
Agreeing with its Iowa counterpart, the Prairie Farmer of
Illinois asserted: "Vice-President Richard M. Nixon promises
an expanded soil bank to fit production to consumption.
He would also use other voluntary supply-management devices
to increase consumption." Noted too was the fact that
Nixon's proposed farm program resembled closely Secretary
Benson's concept of "adjustment through low-price dis-
couragement."[41]

In reality Richard Nixon intended to depart very
little from Benson's basic policies of flexible price

supports with land retirement and market expansion as corollaries. But he sought to couch his words in a milder, less concrete tone. Likewise having once been in Congress he planned to work more closely with congressional leaders. The Vice-President (resembling Eisenhower) was willing to temporize and to implement plans more slowly as political events dictated, yet in the main he believed a fundamental adjustment was necessary to keep surpluses within reasonable limits. When Nixon was elected to the presidency in 1968 he ultimately attained many of the goals for which Benson worked so hard and so patiently.

Because newsmen noticed Ezra Taft Benson's conscpicuous absence from a large part of the campaign, Chicago <u>Daily News</u> reporter William McGaffin brought up the question at the President's August 10th press conference. McGaffin asked Eisenhower point blank, "Do you regret having kept Ezra Taft Benson on as Secretary of Agriculture in view of the unresolved farm problem that is giving Mr. Nixon such a hard time in his campaign?"[42]

Ike responded quickly: "Ezra Benson has, to my mind, been very honest and forthright and courageous in trying to get enacted into legislation plans and programs that I think are correct. And, therefore, for me to regret that he has been working would be almost a betrayal of my own views in this matter. I think we must find ways to give greater freedom to the farmer and make his whole business more responsive to market, rather than just to political considerations."[43] As it turned out even President Eisenhower did not play a large role in the election campaign. To some extent, the Vice-President no doubt wanted to carry the major responsibilities of the campaign to establish party leadership on his own.

Many factors determined the outcome of the 1960 presidential election and the farm issue could at best only be considered of secondary importance. Yet because John F. Kennedy eked out such a narrow victory with a plurality of only 118,550, more votes from any source would have materially aided Nixon. J.F.K. won such states as Illinois, Michigan, Minnesota, and Missouri, where large rural populations existed, by the slimmest of margins. On a percentage basis he drew 50 per cent in Illinois, 50.9 per cent in Michigan, 50.6 per cent in Minnesota, and 50.3 per cent in Missouri. It must be said, however, that J.F.K. drew most heavily in urban and not rural areas.

Richard Nixon was the first to admit that it was not the so-called farm revolt that defeated him. The ill-fated television debates, Kennedy's mod style, the issue of religion which seemed to work in Kennedy's favor, and international affairs, plus indeterminable elements, all played their role. The people of America had spoken through the

ballot, but as is the case in a democracy it was somewhat
difficult to ascertain just what type of mandate was presented to the victor.

After the President-elect named the former Governor
of Minnesota, Orville L. Freeman, to be next Secretary of
Agriculture, Ezra Taft Benson knew for sure that some of his
policies were going to be altered. Freeman had been known
to favor high price supports coupled with production controls. Benson wrote a gloomy letter to William I. Myers,
in which he confided, "I must admit to some concern that the
prospect ahead for agriculture is not as bright at the
moment as I would like to have it."[44]

In his formal letter of resignation, dated January
3, 1961, Benson told Eisenhower, "It has been a great honor
and high privilege to serve our farm people. . . . I am
deeply grateful for your support and humbly proud of my
association with you personally." To the Chief Executive
who had remained so loyal to him in times of adversity, he
wrote, "your place among the great and beloved Presidents
of this choice land and among the truly noble of our age is
secure." After cataloging what he considered to be his
major achievements during the past eight years, Benson concluded with the proud assertion: "We have halted and reversed the trend towards a regimented agriculture. We have
introduced the principle of flexibility . . . and restored

to our people some of their lost freedom to plant, to market, to compete, and to make their own decisions."[45]

Replying to Benson, Dwight D. Eisenhower wrote, "As Secretary of Agriculture for the past eight years, you have been of immeasurable aid to me and in accepting your resignation, effective January 20, 1961, I wish to thank you for the many contributions you have made to the nation, and especially to its rural population." He praised his departing Agriculture Secretary for the many "vital programs" implemented from 1953 to 1960. Ike closed with the cordial commendation: "Although agriculture still faces many problems, through your determined and dedicated work, and the efforts of your fine staff, the way has been pointed toward solution of our problems."[46]

Ezra Taft Benson dutifully gave a farewell message to fellow Mormons in Washington, D.C. With deep affection, he told his co-religionists attending a Stake Conference: "And so my brethren and sisters I go back to my duties in the Twelve . . . and I've been grateful beyond my power of expression for the support I've had in my own home during very crucial and difficult times from my wife and my children, and especially from my oldest son Reed who has been my counselor and advisor and helper through thick and thin." Recounting his many trials and tribulations, Benson told them:

269

It was a difficult thing to try and
reverse a trend of many years, moving in
[the] direction of more and more centrali-
zation of authority in the federal government [and] more and more control of price
fixing in the field of agriculture.

Feeling he had worked conscientiously to do what he
deemed best for the welfare of all farmers, Ezra Taft Benson
vowed, "If I had it to do over again, I would follow very
much the same course."[47]

Conclusion

After the arduous eight years of public service, the preparations for returning to Salt Lake City brought great happiness to Ezra Taft Benson. He longed to get away from politics and return to the Mountain America of his Mormon-pioneer heritage. Seeing once again the magnificent Temple in the center of Utah's capitol city quickened his spirit. This six-spired edifice rested on the floor of a beautiful valley and was so monumental in size it seemed to rival the majestic mountains which ringed the area. Atop the Temple stood a statue of the heavenly messenger Moroni with trumpet upraised as if to signal a mighty welcome for all the faith-ful who had been away. Silhouetted against the blue sky the towering Temple indeed symbolized the grandeur of men's faith in things spiritual. Benson and his family were home again and they had no plans ever to leave it again.

Addressing the April conference of his church, Benson confessed openly: "I am so happy . . . to be with

271

you today back here in the bosom of the Church." Reminiscing aloud he spoke with assurance in declaring, "I have had a conviction, through all this period, my brethren and sisters, that I was where the Lord wanted me to be." He admitted there had been criticism, but his reaction was simple and straightforward: "I have been convinced I was doing the thing that seemed to me, at least, to be right. . . . I have no bitterness today. . . . I have prayed--we have prayed as a family--that we could avoid any spirit of hatred or bitterness." The former Secretary paid public tribute to Dwight D. Eisenhower by saying, "I am grateful for the support I have had from the Chief Executive during these eight years, for his loyalty, for his deep spirituality, for his determination to do that which he believed to be right, and to approve my doing so as well."[1]

Ezra Taft Benson served faithfully on the Eisenhower team (a term Ike preferred) and in turn his chief stood by him. Although different in temperament and ability they complemented one another.

Dwight D. Eisenhower possessed the native instinct for adapting to the exigencies of politics. Training as Supreme Allied Commander and heading NATO gave him valuable experience in the art of negotiation and compromise. His inclination was to be slow and cautious rather than impetuous and reckless. While in retirement he reflected upon his two terms and admitted that many people "thought I was moving too slowly about matters close to their hearts." He explained the reason for his circumspect behavior as follows: "Behind every human action the truth may also lie behind some other action or arrangement, far off in time or place. Unless circumstances and responsibility demanded an instant judgment, I learned to reserve mine until the last proper moment."[2]

While serving as Chief Executive, Eisenhower held to a definite set of principles. He did, however, allow himself sufficient latitude when applying them in order to remain flexible. In what Ike termed "modern Republicanism" he defined his modus operandi in the following manner: "While our principles have remained unchanged for a hundred years, the problems to which these principles must be applied have changed radically and rapidly."[3] While subscribing to the need always "to encourage the full and free energies of labor and industry" among the people, Eisenhower acknowledged also that "where the job before us, or any part of it, is one that only the federal government can do effectively, this government must and will act promptly."[4]

To his Secretary of State, John Foster Dulles, Ike once wrote: "The time has come for clear-cut, determined action in setting this nation on a moderate but definite course--avoiding the extremes of both Right and Left, but always steadily pushing ahead the broad Center--where there is room for all men of good will."[5] In foreign policy as well as domestic this was Eisenhower's method of operation. He was truly an "artist in iron"[6] moving the nation slowly and surely through a period of postwar adjustment. What he started in international affairs, namely defusing the Cold War, was consummated during the administration of Richard M. Nixon. His domestic programs laid the groundwork for a durable prosperity which has continued, with minor variations, long past his lifetime. He was a good politician and a great leader of men.

Ezra Taft Benson was given a post which was demanding and impossible of fulfilling without incurring the wrath of certain special interests. Ike's instincts for judging character were excellent. He wanted someone tough and tenacious, and a person who would be selfless in serving the best needs of agriculture. Thus he chose Benson. Being a man with a fortress-like faith and possessing superb expertise in his field, Benson broke through the inertia of established tradition and entrenched attitudes to show the way toward agricultural reform. His very habits of not compromising and never giving up made him valuable in the political arena where selling out is too often elevated into a fine art.

Following the dictates of his conscience, no matter what the obstacles, made Benson a tower of strength. When Ike asked for an opinion he knew his Secretary of Agriculture would tell him the unvarnished truth. Working for long-range goals was not enjoyable because immediate praise or commendation for success were usually absent. Being the recipient of political assaults brings joy to no one but Benson took comfort in the knowledge that in the end he would be vindicated. What he strove so valiantly to achieve was accomplished in large measure by his successors in the Nixon administration.

Democracy remains essentially a decision-making process. It was never a political system with absolute means or immutable ends. Via popular sovereighty mandates are bestowed upon leaders by an electorate and through rather imperfect means the government responds to the will of the people. Elected officials, and their appointees, cannot either be culpable cowards who bend with every capricious wind of public opinion nor can they be entirely aloof from the expressed wants of the populace.

A fine line exists, and no one can pinpoint it with exactitude, between reacting to the legitimate needs of constituents and merely serving as their senseless errand boy. Statecraft therefore becomes a difficult art. It means guiding purely selfish wishes of voters into acceptable channels through intelligent and imaginative leadership in order to serve the general welfare. Both Ezra Taft Benson and Dwight D. Eisenhower worked for the good of the entire nation as they envisioned it. Each "did his thing" (as the contemporary saying goes) but in a different manner. The former bore the brunt of the burden for wielding the cutting edge of reform while the latter won popular plaudits for carrying the soothing balm of compromise to ease the shock emanating from change. Together they served the people admirably by enhancing the national interest. Their service is now a part of our recorded past and testifies to the merit of their lasting accomplishments. The Eisenhower-Benson farm policy gave a significant thrust to reform and American agriculture has indeed benefitted from it. Ezra Taft Benson, along with Henry A. Wallace, are the two pivotal men who changed the direction of agriculture at key junctures in American history. Both should rank in the "great" category and both should be remembered for a long time to come. Thus the annals of history may reward Eisenhower's Secretary of Agriculture far more than his contemporaries. This would be a fitting tribute to Ezra Taft Benson, the man who put the people's welfare above party politics.

FOOTNOTES

Introduction

[1]Report of Isaac Newton, January 1, 1863, as quoted
in Ross B. Talbot and Don F. Hadwiger, The Policy Process
in American Agriculture (San Francisco, 1968), 227.

[2]Ezra Taft Benson, The Red Carpet (Derby, Conn.,
1963), 171. Noteworthy was the motto in President Eisenhower's
office. It contained a quotation from Abraham Lincoln,
"Gentle in manner, strong in deed."

Chapter I

[1]See the Papers of Charles Murphy for the farm
speeches of President Truman in 1948, Harry S. Truman
Library (Independence, Missouri).

[2]Senator Carlson wrote Milton Eisenhower on July 16,
1952: "I am firmly convinced that Dewey lost the last election because the farmers in a small group of states out in
this part of the country lost confidence in his position on
price supports." Papers of Frank Carlson (Kansas Historical
Society, Topeka). In a radio broadcast Representative Hope
likewise insisted: "Four years ago, President Truman surprised most people and won the election by carrying Iowa,
Illinois, Ohio, and Wisconsin. . . . Farmers' votes can very
well be decisive in states like Oklahoma, Tennessee,
Missouri, and Kentucky, and even in Texas, Florida, and
Virginia." Statement by Clifford R. Hope, September 9,
1952, Papers of Clifford R. Hope (Kansas State Historical
Society, Topeka).

[3]See "House GOP Agricultural Leaders Propose Strong
'52 Farm Plank," Papers of Clifford R. Hope and "Senate

Minority Memo: Will the Democrats Fool the Farmer Again?"
Papers of Robert A. Taft (Library of Congress, Washington,
D.C.).

[4]The problem confronting Clifford Hope was that
whereas his own position on farm policy was clear, he did
not really know where Ike stood. Hope wrote in "A Farm
Program for '52--And the Future," prepared for the June,
1952 issue of Country Gentleman, that: "More than twenty
years of experience with various programs . . . demonstrates
that a system of price supports for basic storable commodities, geared to the principle of parity prices and operated
through commodity loans, is the most feasible method. The
present price-support system, inaugurated in 1938 and re-
vised from time to time, has been well tested." Yet Hope
had to admit to James C. Farmer of the Grange Mutual Insurance Company, in a letter dated March 1, 1952, that although
"General Eisenhower has outlined his basic views on govern-
mental matters on many occasions, . . . I am unable to find
that he has ever had the occasion or opportunity to express
himself on specific agricultural questions." While Hope was
preparing campaign materials for Ike, he presumed the GOP
candidate was in basic agreement with him on farm policy.
This was not actually true and only after the election would
Hope discover his early and sustained support for Eisenhower

carried with it no promises for continuing high price supports as a major aspect of future farm programs. See Clifford R. Hope to Henry Cabot Lodge, Jr., February 28, 1952; Dwight D. Eisenhower to Clifford R. Hope, March 8, 1952; and "Farm Background of Dwight D. Eisenhower by Clifford R. Hope for Eisenhower Headquarters--April 2, 1952," Papers of Clifford R. Hope.

[5]Text of Address at Kasson, Minnesota, OF 106 Agriculture-Farming, Dwight D. Eisenhower Library (Abilene, Kansas).

[6]Text of Address at Memphis, Tennessee, OF 106 Agriculture-Farming, Eisenhower Library. Representative Hope pressed for a deeper commitment on the part of Eisenhower when he advised Senator Carlson: "I think the tobacco law ought to be mentioned. . . . Senator Cooper of Kentucky introduced an amendment providing that the support price on tobacco, if marketing quotas were in effect, should be 90 per cent of parity. . . . It would undoubtedly be helpful . . . if General Eisenhower could endorse the provision." Clifford R. Hope to Frank Carlson, September 8, 1952, Papers of Frank Carlson.

[7]"1952 Republican Platform," in Kirk H. Porter and Donald Bruce Johnson, compilers, National Party Platforms

1840-1960 (Urbana, 1961), 501.

[8]"1952 Democratic Platform," Porter and Johnson, compilers, National Party Platforms 1840-1960, 479.

[9]Herbert J. Muller, Adlai Stevenson: A Study in Values (New York, Evanston, and London, 1967), 99-100. Democrats had traditionally supported high price supports although not necessarily the 90 per cent of parity figure. From 1933, when the original Triple-A Act was passed, the Democratic party did stand committed to the concept of assuring farmers an income commensurate with that of other sectors of the economy. The GOP, notwithstanding conversion of some Midwestern Republicans to the principle of high price supports, generally stood for more flexibility and lesser federal involvement in agricultural affairs. The controversy over rigid, high supports versus low, flexible ones constituted a larger issue--namely, whether the government should or should not guarantee a minimum income to any one economic group. Thus the farm problem (of overproduction) was complicated by the bigger question of how far government should go to subsidize a particular element of the population. For a summation of agricultural policy during the 1920's and 1930's see the authors' Henry A. Wallace of Iowa: The Agrarian Years, 1910-1940 (Ames, 1968);

for the late 1940's and early 1950's see Allen J. Matusow, Farm Policies and Politics in the Truman Years (Cambridge, Mass., 1967); and for a succinct but comprehensive coverage of earlier years see Gladys Baker, et al., Century of Service: The First 100 Years of the Department of Agriculture (Washington, D.C., 1963).

[10]Text of Address at Kasson, Minnesota, OF 106 Agriculture-Farming, Eisenhower Library.

Chapter II

[1]Senator Taft wanted assurance that the budget
would be cut; there would be no repeal of the Taft-Hartley
Act; that neither Paul Hoffman nor Thomas E. Dewey would be
appointed Secretary of State; equal representation for his
side in the cabinet; and "no commitment to anything like the
Brannan Plan or even a flat 90 per cent guarantee. We
should stand by our conservative farmer friends in the Farm
Bureau and Grange." Robert A. Taft to Everett M. Dirksen,
August 6, 1952, Papers of Robert A. Taft (Library of Congress, Washington, D.C.). Senator Carlson felt one of his
great accomplishments "was to work out the Taft-Eisenhower
meeting, which was held yesterday and I think [it was] most
satisfactory. I know from visiting with Bob Taft that he
feels well pleased over the outcome and certainly General
Eisenhower [felt] the same." Frank Carlson to Merle J.
Trees, September 13, 1952, Papers of Frank Carlson.

[2]Eisenhower's brother suggested the following men
for consultation on agricultural policy: William I. Myers,
Allan Kline, Herschel Newsom, John Davis, Chester Davis,
Alfred P. Stedman, Edward O'Neal, James McConnell, Francis

Wilcox, and Clinton Reynolds. This group was more inclined
to pick Ezra Taft Benson than a representative of those
backing retention of high price supports. Milton Eisenhower
to Frank Carlson, August 1, 1952, Papers of Frank Carlson.

[3]Milton Eisenhower to authors, September 23, 1969.

[4]Senator Taft supported Frank Carlson but worked
actively against the naming of Clifford Hope as Agriculture
Secretary. When Ezra Taft Benson was named to the post,
Taft wrote his friend Louis J. Taber: "It is a good thing
that we have a sound man like Benson as Secretary of Agriculture. I hope he can lead the extreme farmers into a
more reasonable attitude than some of their representatives
are adopting at the present time. Price supports are all
right, but if carried too far they amount to a complete
government controlled economy." Robert A. Taft to Louis J.
Taber, February 12, 1953. See also Taft to George D. Aiken,
August 13, 1952, Papers of Robert A. Taft. Senator Milton
Young (R-N.D.), soon to become an outspoken critic of Ezra
Taft Benson, wrote the President-elect: "In my opinion,
Congressman Clifford Hope of Kansas is probably the most
qualified man that could be selected for this important
position. Senator Carlson also would be an able Secretary
although not as experienced in this field as Congressman

Hope." Had Young reversed his recommendations, his Senate colleague would have had a better chance for selection. Carlson would certainly have been a clever compromise choice as events were soon to prove. Milton R. Young to Dwight D. Eisenhower, November 11, 1952, Copy in Papers of Frank Carlson.

[5]Some insiders felt Milton Eisenhower's counsel was the deciding factor in Ike's final decision to appoint Ezra Taft Benson to his cabinet as Secretary of Agriculture. Milton certainly could have vetoed any individual, but whether he had the influence to promote a candidate is debatable. Gabriel Hauge to authors, September 19, 1969 and Interview with Sherman Adams, August 13, 1969.

[6]Ezra Taft Benson, Cross Fire: The Eight Years With Eisenhower (Garden City, 1962), 11. See also Dwight D. Eisenhower, The White House Years: Mandate for Change, 1953-56 (Garden City, 1963), 90.

[7]Ibid.

[8]Ibid.

[9]Ibid., 12.

[10]Quoted by Ezra Taft Benson, "The L.D.S. Church and Politics," Address to Brigham Young University Student Body, December 1, 1952, Papers of Ezra Taft Benson (Archives of The Church of Jesus Christ of Latter-day Saints, Salt Lake City). Hereinafter cited as ETB-LDS.

Chapter III

[1]Ezra Taft Benson, "The Beef Cattle Situation in the Northern Range Area in its Relation to the Iowa Feeder," Unpublished Master's Thesis, Iowa State College, 1927, p. 103.

[2]Joseph Fielding Smith, Essentials in Church History (Salt Lake City, 1950), 702.

[3]Ezra Taft Benson, "The Least Among You," Address at the 114th Semi-Annual General Conference, Salt Lake City, October 1, 1943, ETB-LDS.

[4]Doctrine and Covenants, 36: 12. See also letter from Brigham Young to Charles C. Rich, August 2, 1847 for its reference to Ezra Taft Benson, Copy in Bureau of Information and Museum (Salt Lake City, Utah).

[5]Quoted in Harold H. Martin, "Elder Benson's Going to Catch It," The Saturday Evening Post, Vol. 225 (March 28, 1953), 110. See also Ezra Taft Benson, "The L.D.S. Church and Politics," Address to Brigham Young University Student Body, December 1, 1952, ETB-LDS.

[6]Address of Harold B. Lee at Washington Stake Conference, March 1, 1953, ETB-LDS.

[7]Address to Student Body of Brigham Young University, Provo, Utah, December 1, 1952, ETB-LDS.

[8]Other prominent Mormons achieving national office prior and after Ezra Taft Benson included not only Reed Smoot but James H. Moyle as Assistant Secretary of the Treasury under President Wilson; William Spry was Commissioner of Public Lands under both Harding and Coolidge; J. Reuben Clark, Jr. served as Undersecretary of State in the Hoover administration; Marriner Eccles in the Roosevelt administration; Stewart Udall as Secretary of the Interior in the Kennedy administration; David Kennedy--Treasury Secretary and George Romney, Secretary of Housing and Urban Development in the Nixon administration.

[9]It should be explained that another major Mormon group calling itself the Reorganized Church of Jesus Christ of the Latter Day Saints has its headquarters in Independence, Missouri. They followed the leadership of Joseph Smith's son rather than Brigham Young. Hyrum Smith's sons went with the Salt Lake migration. Hyrum was the older brother of Joseph and he too was killed by the mob who stormed the Carthage jail and murdered the Prophet Joseph.

[10]Address and Dedicatory Prayer given by Ezra Taft Benson at the Dedication of the Daughters of Utah Pioneers Building, Salt Lake City, July 23, 1950, ETB-LDS.

[11]Ezra Taft Benson, "Principles of Cooperation," Address at the 116th Semi-Annual General Conference, Salt Lake City, October 7, 1945, ETB-LDS.

[12]Ezra Taft Benson, "Raising Our Sights," Address to Dairyman's League, Syracuse, New York, October 12, 1950, ETB-LDS.

[13]Ezra Taft Benson, "Cooperative Goals," Address to the American Institute of Cooperation, Madison, Wisconsin, August 22, 1949, ETB-LDS.

[14]Ezra Taft Benson, "The Challenge for Cooperatives Today," Address to the American Institute of Cooperation, Logan, Utah, August 26, 1950, ETB-LDS.

Chapter IV

[1]Reconstructed extemporaneous prayer given at the cabinet meeting of January 12, 1953 in New York City, ETB-LDS.

[2]For further information on Eisenhower's religious views see Merlin Gustafson, "The Religious Role of the President," Midwest Journal of Political Science, XIV (November, 1970), 708-722.

[3]Quotation in Miscellaneous File, ETB-LDS.

[4]Quotation in Miscellaneous File, ETB-LDS.

[5]Quotation in Miscellaneous File, ETB-LDS.

[6]Senator Young and Secretary Benson quoted in "Behind the Committee Doors: The Senate Questions Ike's Cabinet," The New Republic, Vol. 128 (February 2, 1953), 1-2. See Ezra Taft Benson, Cross Fire, 36-39. Clifford Hope, then Chairman of the House Committee on Agriculture, spoke well of Benson and tried to act as peacemaker. He said of the new appointee: "[Benson] is an able man and

unusually well qualified for the difficult and important position to which he has been appointed." On another occasion Hope maintained "it is a reassuring thing to have in the President's cabinet a man who possesses the moral and spiritual qualities of Ezra T. Benson." Address to PMA Committees, Wichita, Kansas, January 28, 1953 and Address to Texas and Southwest Cattle Raisers Association, Houston, Texas, March 17, 1953, Papers of Clifford R. Hope.

[7] Ibid.

[8] Ibid.

[9] Ibid.

[10] Ibid.

[11] Ibid.

[12] Ibid.

[13] Ibid.

[14] Memorandum No. 1320, January 21, 1953, ETB-LDS.

[15] General Statement on Agricultural Policy, February 5, 1953, Papers of Ezra Taft Benson (Dwight D. Eisenhower Library). Hereinafter cited as ETB-DDE.

[16] Ibid.

[17] Address before the Annual Meeting of the Central
Livestock Association, St. Paul, Minnesota, February 11,
1953, ETB-LDS.

[18] Quoted in Time, LXI (February 23, 1953), 25.

[19] Letter from Senator Frank Carlson dated February
16, 1953, in Papers of Sherman Adams (Dartmouth College).
Fellow Kansan Clifford Hope also thought the St. Paul speech
an enormous blunder. He confided to a friend: "The trouble
is it is going to take so much more now to win back the
confidence of the farmer than it would have taken to establish that confidence in the first place." Clifford Hope to
Wilbur N. Renk, July 3, 1953, Papers of Clifford R. Hope.

[20] Quoted in Ezra Taft Benson, Cross Fire, 70.

[21] Memorandum from Bryce N. Harlow to General Wilton
B. Persons with enclosure (Senator Mundt's letter being returned), March 26, 1953, Adams Papers.

[22] Memorandum for the Record, March 28, 1953, Adams
Papers.

[23]"Procedure Used in Selecting State PMA Committee Members," n.d., OF 1-M, Eisenhower Library.

[24]Sherman Adams, First-Hand Report: The Story of the Eisenhower Administration (New York, 1961), 82.

[25]Telegram, Frank L. Chelf to Ezra Taft Benson, October 22, 1953, Copy in Adams Papers.

[26]Telegram, Frank L. Chelf to Dwight D. Eisenhower, October 22, 1953, Adams Papers.

[27]Interview with Sherman Adams, August 13, 1969; Frank L. Chelf to Sherman Adams, October 22, 1953, Adams Papers.

[28]Sherman Adams to Frank L. Chelf, October 27, 1953, Adams Papers. Secretary Benson also got involved in a protracted dispute over drought aid to farmers in the state of Missouri. See correspondence of Senator Stuart Symington, Speaker Lester A. Vonderschmidt, and Governor Phil M. Donnelly in Papers of Phil M. Donnelly (Western Historical Manuscript Collection, University of Missouri-Columbia).

[29]Handwritten memorandum dated May 15, 1953, Adams Papers.

[30] Sherman Adams, First-Hand Report, 205.

[31] Dwight D. Eisenhower, The White House Years, Mandate for Change 1953-1956 (New York, 1963), 354.

[32] Address by Ezra Taft Benson to 123rd Annual Conference, Salt Lake City, April 4, 1953, ETB-LDS.

[33] Ibid.

[34] Oral History Interview of Don Paarlberg (1969), Eisenhower Library.

[35] Serving as Secretary of Agriculture from 1969 to 1971 Clifford M. Hardin pressed for flexible price supports and expansion of agricultural trade. But as reflected by the Agriculture Act of 1970 large amounts of federal subsidy payments were made to farmers. He concluded programs under his direction were similar in some ways and different in others from those advocated by Ezra Taft Benson in the 1950's. Clifford M. Hardin to authors, October 4, 1972.

[36] A transition in agricultural policy paralleled the shift in top echelon USDA personnel. Some New Deal oriented employees regarded it as an undesirable change from the "Iowa State" to the "Purdue" school of thought. Iowa State

University had produced many agricultural economists, including Henry A. Wallace, who favored considerable government intervention on behalf of farmers, while graduates of
Purdue University tended to favor free market operations.
If Richard S. Kirkendall, in his Social Scientists and Farm
Politics in the Age of Roosevelt (Columbia, 1966), is
correct in asserting that agricultural economists who served
in the Department of Agriculture during the New Deal
innovated planning, government management, and brought the
social service (welfare) state to farmers, then the Benson-
Butz school constitutes a reform of the reformers. Using
the Kuhnian paradigm, as outlined in Thomas S. Kuhn, The
Structure of Scientific Revolution (Chicago, 1970), the New
Deal acreage restriction-production control mechanism represented the conventional wisdom or accepted model. A new
paradigm, the open production-free market outlook, began to
compete for acceptance when the old New Deal approach no
longer provided acceptable solutions to farm problems of another era. Agricultural historians also find it difficult
to adjust their outlook. They have "hang-ups" relative to
accepting historical evidence countering older beliefs or
longstanding political faiths. Dwight D. Eisenhower and
Ezra Taft Benson are on the "enemies list" of certain
liberal intellectuals and pro-Democratic academicians because the former dared to defeat Adlai E. Stevenson and the

latter dared to reform a corrupted and unworkable system of farm programs.

[37]Ezra Taft Benson to Dwight D. Eisenhower, August 28, 1953, OF 1-Agricultural Department, Eisenhower Library.

[38]Interview with M. L. Wilson, July 17, 1966.

[39]Statement of Ezra Taft Benson before Senate Committee on Government Operations, May 19, 1953, ETB-LDS. See Journal of Farm Economics, XXXVI (February, 1954), for comments of former USDA personnel on Benson's reorganization plans. Charles Brannan, Truman's second Secretary of Agriculture, had sought to reorganize the USDA according to some of the recommendations of the Hoover Commission. He had requested a new Assistant Secretary and an Administrative Assistant Secretary in order to provide for "general integrating . . . at the Secretarial level of (1) Our conservation and production adjustment activities . . . ; (2) Research . . . ; (3) Credit . . . ; (4) Marketing and regulatory activities; and (5) Staff services." Statement by Secretary of Agriculture Charles F. Brannan before the House Committee on Agriculture, March 20, 1952, Papers of Clifford R. Hope.

[40]Memorandum to All Department Employees with Attachments Relative to Reorganization and Policy Statements, October 13, 1953, OF 1, Eisenhower Library.

[41]Bernard M. Shanley to Sherman Adams, April 6, 1953, OF 1-J-2 (1953-55), Eisenhower Library.

[42]Bernard M. Shanley to Milton Eisenhower, May 11, 1953, OF 1-J-2 (1953-55), Eisenhower Library.

[43]Lee Metcalf to Dwight D. Eisenhower, October 27, 1953, Adams Papers.

[44]Homer H. Greunther to General Wilton B. Persons, March 25, 1953, OF 1-J-3, Eisenhower Library.

[45]Address by Ezra Taft Benson before the National Ranch Congress of the Denver Chamber of Commerce, Denver, Colorado, April 7, 1953, ETB-LDS.

[46]T. H. Graves to Ezra Taft Benson, April 16, 1953, Office of the Secretary of Agriculture Correspondence-1953, RG 16, National Archives (Washington, D.C.).

[47]Mrs. Clive Chamberlin to Dwight D. Eisenhower,
May 20, 1954, Copy in Office of the Secretary of Agriculture
Correspondence-1954, RG 16, National Archives.

[48]William I. Myers to Ezra Taft Benson, January 9,
1953, National Agricultural Advisory Commission-1953, RG 16,
National Archives.

[49]Memorandum, Ezra Taft Benson to Don Paarlberg,
July 23, 1953, Office of the Secretary of Agriculture
Correspondence-1953, RG 16, National Archives.

Chapter V

[1]Ezra Taft Benson to George A. Aiken and Clifford
Hope, July 31, 1953, Office of the Secretary of Agriculture
Correspondence-1953, RG 16, National Archives. Later in
the fall Clifford Hope announced his own "plans for a 2,000
mile tour of Western agricultural areas, as part of a na-
tionwide study to determine what long-range agricultural
policy farmers want." Press Release, October 21, 1953,
Papers of Clifford R. Hope.

[2]Senator George A. Aiken to authors, September 27,
1969.

[3]Fred Seaton to Dwight D. Eisenhower, June 9, 1953,
OF 1, Agriculture Department-1953, Eisenhower Library.

[4]Dwight D. Eisenhower to Senator Arthur V. Watkins,
November 9, 1953, OF 1, Agriculture Department-1953,
Eisenhower Library.

[5]Clifford R. Hope to George E. Sokolsky, November
6, 1953, Papers of Clifford R. Hope. His letter asserted:

"I have not opposed Secretary Benson; I am not opposing him now; and I challenge anyone to cite a single critical word that I have spoken of Secretary Benson since he took office."

[6]Gabriel Hauge to Clifford R. Hope, November 23, 1953, Papers of Clifford R. Hope.

[7]Press Release of Address by Senator Wallace F. Bennett to the Salt Lake City Rotary Club, October 27, 1953, Copy in Papers of Clifford R. Hope.

[8]Clifford R. Hope to Gabriel Hauge, November 27, 1953, Papers of Clifford R. Hope.

[9]Clifford R. Hope to Wallace F. Bennett, November 27, 1953, Papers of Clifford R. Hope.

[10]Wallace F. Bennett to Clifford R. Hope, January 5, 1954, Papers of Clifford R. Hope.

[11]Clifford R. Hope to Wallace F. Bennett, January 8, 1954, Papers of Clifford R. Hope.

[12]National Agricultural Advisory Commission, December, 1953, RG 16, National Archives.

[13]True D. Morse to Ezra Taft Benson, July 8, 1954, NAAC-1954, RG 16, National Archives.

[14]D. W. Brooks to True D. Morse, July 12, 1954, NAAC-1954, RG 16, National Archives.

[15]D. W. Brooks to Don Paarlberg, February 5, 1954, NAAC-1954, RG 16, National Archives.

[16]G. W. Wood to True D. Morse, September 20, 1954, NAAC-1954, RG 16, National Archives.

[17]William I. Myers to Dwight D. Eisenhower, December 15, 1953, NAAC-1953, RG 16, National Archives.

[18]Ezra Taft Benson, "Working Together," Address to American Institute of Cooperation, Columbia, Missouri, August 12, 1953, ETB-LDS.

[19]Ibid.

[20]Joseph M. Dodge to Dwight D. Eisenhower, August 3, 1953, OF 1, Agriculture Department-1953, Eisenhower Library. Treasury Secretary George H. Humphrey had advised the Budget Director: "No authority should be given for the adoption of any policy that costs any money except only in

cases of extreme emergency until we first have a complete statement of proposed expenditures for the entire fiscal year of 1954." George M. Humphrey to Joseph M. Dodge, n.d. [circa February, 1953], Papers of George M. Humphrey (The Western Reserve Historical Society, Cleveland, Ohio).

[21]Ezra Taft Benson to Dwight D. Eisenhower, June 26, 1953, OF 1, Agriculture Department-1953, Eisenhower Library.

[22]Ezra Taft Benson to Dwight D. Eisenhower, December 7, 1953, OF 1, Agriculture Department-1953, Eisenhower Library.

[23]"The White House, Emergency Drought Facts," n.d.; Statement of Secretary Ezra Taft Benson after conference with the President, October 7, 1953; "Summary, Conference on Emergency Hay Needs and Requirements in Drought-Stricken States, Hotel Meuhlbach, Kansas City, Missouri, October 13, 1953"; "Drought History," November 7, 1953. All in General Drought Correspondence and Data, Bryce Harlow File-Eisenhower Library.

[24]August H. Andresen to Dwight D. Eisenhower, February 27, 1954, Clarence Francis File-Eisenhower Library.

[25] Joseph M. Dodge to Sherman Adams and Bernard M. Shanley, March 1, 1954, Adams Papers.

[26] Sherman Adams to Ezra Taft Benson, March 3, 1954, Adams Papers.

[27] Message of the President to Congress, January 11, 1954, Copy of text in Adams Papers.

[28] Ibid.

[29] Ezra Taft Benson, "A Sound Farm Program," Address to National Council of Farmer Cooperatives, Chicago, Illinois, January 12, 1954, ETB-LDS.

[30] Ezra Taft Benson, "A Better Program--Farmers Deserve It," Address to National Farmers Union, Denver, Colorado, March 17, 1954, ETB-LDS.

[31] Ezra Taft Benson, "America Must Be Strong," Address to Farm and Home Week Conference, Ithaca, New York, March 24, 1954, ETB-LDS. For a detailed account of the basic farm program enacted during the New Deal period--see the authors' Henry A. Wallace of Iowa: The Agrarian Years, 1910-1940 (Ames, 1968)--particularly Chapters 11 and 15.

[32] Ezra Taft Benson, "A Brighter Day for Dairying," Cache Valley Breeding Association, Logan, Utah, April 3, 1954, ETB-LDS.

[33] Ezra Taft Benson, "Research Results in Progress," Address at 25th Anniversary Celebrating the Founding of the Frozen Food Industry, Washington, D.C., April 13, 1954, ETB-LDS.

[34] Statement of Secretary of Agriculture before House Committee on Agriculture, March 10, 1954, Papers of Ezra Taft Benson-Eisenhower Library. Hereinafter cited as ETB-Eisenhower Library.

[35] Statement by Secretary of Agriculture before Senate Committee on Agriculture and Forestry, January 18, 1954, ETB-Eisenhower Library.

[36] Statement by Secretary of Agriculture before Senate Committee on Agriculture and Forestry, April 21, 1954, ETB-Eisenhower Library.

[37] Ibid.

[38]Richard Haney, "JFK's Catholic Vote in the 1960 Wisconsin Presidential Primary," Paper delivered at the Wisconsin Association of Teachers of College History, Wisconsin State University, Stevens Point, Wisconsin, October 10, 1970. Professor Haney illustrated how Senator Hubert Humphrey sought to prove Kennedy's pro-Benson stance to Wisconsin farmers by revealing JFK's voting record on farm proposals. On twenty-seven specific occasions Kennedy had supported Benson's position while Humphrey had opposed them each time.

[39]Minutes of Cabinet Meeting, June 6, 1954, Adams Papers.

[40]Address by the President at the Opening Session of a meeting of the District Chairmen of the National Citizens for Eisenhower Congressional Committee, Washington, D.C., June 10, 1954, Adams Papers.

[41]Herschel D. Newsom to Karl D. Butler, February 23, 1954, Adams Papers. Butler, a member of the National Agricultural Advisory Commission, sent Newsom's letter to Adams for his information.

[42]"The Administration's Farm Program," Script for Richard M. Nixon, Vice-President of the United States, and Ezra Taft Benson, Secretary of Agriculture, over the American Broadcasting Company, June 28, 1954, ETB-Eisenhower Library.

[43]Ibid.

[44]Charles A. Halleck to authors, October 28, 1969.

[45]Statement by the President, Denver, Colorado (Lowry Air Base), August 28, 1954, Adams Papers.

[46]Report to Accompany H.R. 9680, Submitted by Mr. Hope, from the Committee on Agriculture, Report No. 1927, 83rd Congr., 2d Sess., June 26, 1954, Bills File-Eisenhower Library. In a telecast to his Kansas constituents Hope openly differed with Benson by declaring: "Let me say in the beginning that as between 90 per cent and flexible price supports, I favor 90 per cent, and have so voted on every occasion. . . . I believe there is a better program for wheat than either 90 per cent or flexible supports. I refer to the certificate form of a two-price system. Under this plan farmers receive full parity for the sale of all wheat consumed domestically. . . . The remainder would bring the

world price." Television broadcast over KTVH, October 26, 1954, Papers of Clifford R. Hope.

[47]Ezra Taft Benson, "New Tasks and New Tools," Address at Oregon State Fair, Salem, Oregon, September 10, 1954, ETB-LDS.

[48]Ezra Taft Benson, "Government and Prices," Address to Association of Commissioners, Secretaries, and Directors of Agriculture, Brainerd, Minnesota, September 13, 1954, ETB-LDS.

[49]K. B. Cornell to Ezra Taft Benson, October 25, 1954, Office of the Secretary of Agriculture Correspondence-1954, RG 16, National Archives.

[50]A. M. Mathieu to True D. Morse, September 15, 1954, Office of the Secretary of Agriculture Correspondence-1954, RG 16, National Archives.

[51]Ezra Taft Benson to J. Marion Harman, Sr., July 9, 1954, Office of the Secretary of Agriculture Correspondence-1954, RG 16, National Archives.

[52] Senator Everett M. Dirksen to Ross Rizley, September 21, 1954, Correspondence 1954, Commodities: Acreage Allotments--Marketing Quotas, RG 16, National Archives.

[53] Ross Rizley to Lyndon B. Johnson, August 16, 1954, Correspondence 1954, Commodities: Acreage Allotments-Marketing Quotas, RG 16, National Archives.

[54] Senator Arthur V. Watkins to Ezra Taft Benson, September 1, 1954 and Clyde A. Wheeler, Jr. (for Ross Rizley) to Arthur V. Watkins, September 28, 1954, Correspondence 1954, Commodities: Acreage Allotments-Marketing Quotas, RG 16, National Archives. Senator Clinton P. Anderson (D-N.M.), a former Secretary of Agriculture and a supporter of administration policy regarding lower price supports, fared better than his colleagues. He was informed that New Mexico farmers would be permitted to divert idle acres into bean production. Ross Rizley to Clinton P. Anderson, August 13, 1954, Correspondence 154, Commodities: Acreage Allotments-Marketing Quotas, RG 16, National Archives.

[55] Carl T. Curtis to Ezra Taft Benson, September 25, 1954, Correspondence 1954, Commodities: Acreage Allotments-Marketing Quotas, RG 16, National Archives.

[56]Ezra Taft Benson to Carl T. Curtis, October 12,
1954, Correspondence 1954, Commodities: Acreage Allotments-
Marketing Quotas, RG 16, National Archives.

[57]Carlos Campbell to Ezra Taft Benson, October 18,
1954, Correspondence 1954, Commodities: Acreage Allotments-
Marketing Quotas, RG 16, National Archives.

[58]George Goddard to Ezra Taft Benson, October 13,
1954, Correspondence 1954, Commodities: Acreage Allotments-
Marketing Quotas, RG 16, National Archives.

[59]USDA News Release, December 13, 1954, RG 16,
National Archives. The original announcement was issued
on September 15, 1954.

[60]Memorandum to Agency Heads and Employees of the
Department of Agriculture, December 23, 1954, RG 16,
National Archives.

Chapter VI

[1]Agricultural Trade Development and Assistance Act
of 1954, 83rd Congress, 2nd Session, January 6, 1954, Bills
File (Agriculture), Eisenhower Library. Senator Paul H.
Douglas (D-Ill.) led an attempt to broaden the domestic
distribution of surpluses. In a speech at Harvard, Illinois on June 5, 1954 he explained: "I proposed to use
$3 billion of surpluses to add to the diets of the unem-
ployed, disabled vets, those on relief, [and] old age
pensioners. . . ." Box 23, Papers of Paul H. Douglas
(Chicago Historical Society).

[2]Memorandum to the Cabinet from Maxwell M. Rabb,
December 15, 1954, Clarence Francis File, Eisenhower
Library.

[3]Notes on Oral Report of Trip to Caribbean by Secretary of Agriculture, February 19 to March 8, 1955, ETB-
LDS.

[4]Benson sought to keep Dulles informed on matters
of agricultural policy. See the Benson-Dulles correspondence

310

in the Papers of John Foster Dulles (Princeton University
Library, Princeton, New Jersey). For more insight into
Dulles's thinking on international trade see also the oral
history memoirs of: Milton Eisenhower, Samuel C. Waugh,
Harold E. Stassen, and Clarence B. Randall. All are in the
Dulles Oral History Collection (Princeton University
Library). William Appleman Williams and followers of his
Open Door interpretation accuse America of following a
policy of "free trade imperialism." In The Roots of Modern
American Empire (New York, 1969), pp. xvi-xvii, he sees the
agrarian expansionism (Frontier thesis) as leading to
industrial expansionism (Open Door thesis) resulting from
a market-oriented capitalist economy. In The Tragedy of
American Diplomacy (New York, 1962), p. 206, he accuses
the United States of employing "its new and awesome power
in keeping with the traditional Open Door Policy which
crystallized the cold war." On p. 275 he specifically
indicts Secretary Dulles for formulating the "definitive
statement" of this alleged imperialism. Although America
had lost many markets, while opening ours to foreign nations,
as a corollary to its leadership of the free world, Williams
ignores or impugns the enormous post-war assistance rendered
by the United States. He also was unaware that Dulles
opposed Benson's efforts to recapture lost markets--hence

in this sense was, economically speaking, an anti-imperial-
ist.

[5]Ezra Taft Benson, "Let Us Go Forward in Friendship," Address to Canadian Federation of Agriculture,
Regina, Canada, June 14, 1955, ETB-LDS.

[6]Ezra Taft Benson, "Good Neighbors Can Build a Great
Future," Address to Alberta Canadian Clubs, Calgary, Canada,
June 15, 1955, ETB-LDS.

[7]Ezra Taft Benson, "The Eyes, Ears, and Voice of
Agriculture Abroad," Address to Agricultural Attachés,
Paris, France, September 7, 1955, ETB-LDS.

[8]Ezra Taft Benson, "Agriculture in a Changing
World," Address to International Federation of Agricultural
Producers, Rome, Italy, September 9, 1955, ETB-LDS.

[9]"The Problem of Agricultural Surpluses," n.d.,
ICASD Materials, James M. Lambie, Jr. File, Eisenhower
Library.

[10]"Possible Alternatives," n.d., ICASD-1955, Lambie
File-Eisenhower Library.

[11]Ernest T. Baughman to Gwynn Garnett, August 12, 1955 with enclosures: "Study on Foreign Disposal of Domestic Agriculture Surpluses"; Ernest T. Baughman to Clarence Francis, September 2, 1955, both in Francis File-Eisenhower Library.

[12]*Ibid.*

[13]Earl L. Butz to Gwynn Garnett, n.d., "Subject: Baughman Report," and Earl L. Butz to James Lambie, March 1, 1956, both in Francis File-Eisenhower Library.

[14]Ralph W. E. Reid to Clarence Francis, March 13, 1956, Francis File-Eisenhower Library.

[15]Clarence Francis to Joseph M. Dodge, March 27, 1956, Francis File-Eisenhower Library.

[16]When Clifford Hope received a copy of the Baughman Report it contained the following disclaimer: "The study is a staff document, not one representing the position of the Interagency Committee on Agricultural Surplus Disposal. Its conclusions correspond to the views of the Chairman of ICASD. It has not been approved by any agency and its conclusions and analysis do not necessarily reflect the views of the administration." Earl L. Butz

to Clifford R. Hope, May 25, 1956, Papers of Clifford R. Hope.

[17]Minutes of Cabinet Meetings, August 5 and December 7, 1955, Adams Papers.

[18]Gwynn Garnett to Clarence Francis, September 21, 1956, Francis File-Eisenhower Library.

[19]Ambassador of New Zealand to Secretary of State, May 11, 1954, Agriculture Surplus Disposal Program Correspondence-1954, Eisenhower Library.

[20]Ambassador of New Zealand to Secretary of State, September 8, 1954, Agriculture Surplus Disposal Program Correspondence-1954, Eisenhower Library.

[21]Walter H. Judd to authors, April 13, 1970.

[22]Walter H. Judd to Ezra Taft Benson, October 20, 1954, Agriculture Surplus Disposal Correspondence-1954, Eisenhower Library.

[23]Walter H. Judd to authors, April 13, 1970. In a letter to the authors, dated September 24, 1969, Arthur E. Burns (Chairman of the Council of Economic Advisors during

part of the Eisenhower administration) conceded candidly, "All things considered it is likely that the surplus disposal program produced some results that an avowed dumping program would have produced."

[24]Memorandum, Clarence Randall to members of the Council of Foreign Economic Policy, November 11, 1956, Francis File-Eisenhower Library.

[25]"Reappraisal of PL 480," Council on Foreign Economic Policy Paper, November 9, 1956, Francis File-Eisenhower Library.

[26]John H. Davis to Clarence Francis, July 2, 1954, with enclosure: "Report of Agricultural Trade Missions to the Secretary of Agriculture on Foreign Trade of the United States in Agricultural Products," June, 1954, Francis File-Eisenhower Library.

[27]Memorandum, Maxwell Rabb to the Cabinet, February 16, 1955 with enclosure: "Supplementary Report on Surplus Commodity Distribution to Needy Families," Francis File-Eisenhower Library. It is interesting to note that the Nixon administration was confronted with many of the same problems of the Eisenhower administration--only in the area of industrial trade policy rather than agricultural.

[28]Ibid. Senator Paul H. Douglas (D-Ill.) had also
proposed legislation in which agricultural surpluses would
be used to: "Supplement and increase the diet of the needy
in this country such as those on relief, the unemployed,
aged pensioners, disabled veterans, children in orphanages,
sick people in hospitals, [and] old people in nursing
homes." Press Release, April 14, 1954, Box 23, Douglas
Papers.

[29]Interim Report to the Congress from the Commission
on Increased Industrial Use of Agricultural Products, April
19, 1957, Pursuant to Pl 540, 84th Congress, OF 106-N,
Eisenhower Library.

[30]Ibid.

[31]"Plan for the Use of an Additional $50 Million
for Utilization and New Crops Research in the First Year's
Implementation of the Program Proposed by the President's
Commission," June 6, 1957, Agriculture Surplus Disposal-
1957, Lambie File-Eisenhower Library.

[32]Ibid.

[33]Clarence Francis to Gabriel Hauge, July 9, 1957,
Francis File-Eisenhower Library.

[34]John Hamlin to Sherman Adams, April 12, 1957 with enclosure: "Elements of Production Research," OF 110-N, Eisenhower Library.

Chapter VII

[1] Statement by Secretary of Agriculture before the Senate Committee on Agriculture and Forestry, January 19, 1955, Francis File-Eisenhower Library.

[2] Joseph R. McCarthy to Dwight D. Eisenhower, August 24, 1955, Adams Papers. See also Washington *Star*, August 28, 1955.

[3] Maxwell M. Rabb to Cabinet, October 5, 1955 with enclosure: "Current Appraisal of the Farm Situation," Francis File-Eisenhower Library.

[4] Minutes of Cabinet Meeting, December 9, 1955, Adams Papers.

[5] Memorandum for the Secretary of Agriculture from the President, October 23, 1955, Adams Papers.

[6] Minutes of Cabinet Meeting, December 9, 1955, Adams Papers.

[7]Testimony of Melvin P. Gehlbach to House Agriculture Committee's Public Hearings, Bloomington, Illinois, October 17, 1953, Serial R, Part 8 (Washington, D.C.: Government Printing Office, 1955). Plans similar to the final Soil Bank program were arrived at independently by others. Senator Edward J. Thye (R-Minn.) pushed such a proposal as did Professor Harold C. Case of the University of Illinois Department of Agriculture. See Ezra Taft Benson to Harold C. Case, January 24, 1956 acknowledging receipt of "A Proposed Price Support Program Based on Soil Conservation and Production Control," in Papers of Harold C. Case (University of Illinois-Urbana).

[8]"Plans for Implementing the Soil Bank (Tentative)," 1956, Bryce N. Harlow File-Eisenhower Library.

[9]"Benson Announces New Farm Program Highlights," USDA Press Release, December 13, 1955, Harlow File-Eisenhower Library.

[10]James A. McConnell to W. E. Hamilton, November 2, 1955, Office of the Secretary of Agriculture, Correspondence-1955, RG 16, National Archives.

[11]W. E. Hamilton to James A. McConnell, November 28, 1955, Office of the Secretary of Agriculture, Correspondence-1955, RG 16, National Archives.

[12]Statement of the American Farm Bureau Federation Before the House Committee on Agriculture Regarding H.R. 12, A Bill Concerning Price Supports for Basic Commodities, by Charles B. Shuman, President, February 23, 1955, Correspondence-1955, Commodities: Price Supports--Commodity Loans, RG 16, National Archives. In a letter to the authors, dated August 18, 1971, Charles B. Shuman reflected: "I am also under the impression that Secretary Benson modified his recommendation on farm policy changes to conform with the wishes of the President and his advisors. They were politically oriented and realistically recognized the difficulty of making any constructive changes when the majority in Congress was opposed to the Administration. The result of this dilemma was that the Eisenhower-Benson years could be described as making very little progress towards what I think was the Secretary's goal of gradually phasing out government controls and price fixing in agriculture."

[13]"An Appraisal of the Political Situation That Faces Agriculture by Area and by Commodity," n.d., Harlow

Files-Eisenhower Library.

[14]Karl E. Mundt to Ezra Taft Benson, December 14, 1955, Copy in Adams Papers.

[15]Karl E. Mundt to Sherman Adams, December 14, 1955, Adams Papers.

[16]News Release from the Office of Senator Karl E. Mundt, December 14, 1955, Adams Papers.

[17]"A Weekly Report from Karl Mundt, Senator from South Dakota," January 18, 1956, Vol. 18, Howard Pyle Files-Eisenhower Library. Clifford Hope had also given advice to Benson, but he received only the qualified comment: "I was very pleased to know that the observations and suggestions made in your letter are being pretty well embodied in the recommendations made to the leaders yesterday, particularly in reference to the Soil Bank. It is of the utmost importance that we work closely together during this coming year. The administration needs your effective leadership in promoting the program which the President will recommend in his Special Message to Congress in January." Ezra Taft Benson to Clifford R. Hope, December 13, 1955, Papers of Clifford R. Hope.

[18]Karl E. Mundt to Sherman Adams, January 14, 1956, Adams Papers.

[19]Special Message to Congress, January 9, 1956, Copy in Adams Papers.

[20]Ibid.

[21]Ibid.

[22]Ibid.

[23]Ibid.

[24]Address by Ezra Taft Benson to the National Cattlemen's Association, New Orleans, January 10, 1956, ETB-LDS.

[25]Address by Ezra Taft Benson to the National Council of Farmer Cooperatives, Los Angeles, January 16, 1956, ETB-LDS. Treasury Secretary Humphrey had argued strongly against the plan to refund gasoline taxes to farmers. He protested to Benson: "We have opposed all excise tax reductions this year, and all other proposals for changes in the tax law which would involve revenue losses. I do not see how we could make an exception of the gasoline tax and endorse exemptions of gasoline consumed off the highways."

Papers of George M. Humphrey.

[26]Ezra Taft Benson to Dwight D. Eisenhower, April 26, 1955 with enclosure: "Development of Agriculture's Human Resources," OF 99-G-3, Eisenhower Library.

[27]Rural Development Program News, August, 1955, National Agricultural Library (Beltsville, Maryland). Three Democrats in the Senate, Paul H. Douglas (Ill.), Matthew M. Neely (W.Va.), and John F. Kennedy (Mass.) co-sponsored an Area Development Bill (S. 2663) which, if passed, would have: (1) Provided assistance to communities, industries, enterprises, and individuals in areas needing redevelopment; (2) created an Area Redevelopment Administration with administrator; (3) established local committees; and (4) made available loans, grants, technical assistance, retraining, and vocational education. Digest of Douglas-Neely-Kennedy Bill, Box 26, Douglas Papers.

[28]"Progress in the Rural Development Program, First Annual Report of the Secretary of Agriculture, September, 1956," National Agricultural Library.

[29]"Supplement to the Fifth Annual Report of the Secretary of Agriculture on the Rural Development Program, September, 1960," National Agricultural Library. See

also <u>Rural Development Program News</u>, November, 1960.

[30]Oren Lee Staley to authors, January 12, 1966 with enclosure: "National Farmers Organization, Its Origin, Aims, and Objectives."

[31]Earl L. Butz to Ezra Taft Benson, October 18, 1955, Pyle File-Eisenhower Library.

[32]"Preliminary Opinion of New Republican Farm Program by Farm Leaders and Editors," conducted by Research Department, Leo Burnett Company, Inc., January 16, 1956, Pyle File-Eisenhower Library.

[33]<u>Ibid</u>.

[34]<u>Ibid</u>.

[35]<u>Ibid</u>.

[36]Gabriel Hauge to Wilton B. Persons, August 25, 1955, OF 106, Agriculture-Farming, Eisenhower Library.

[37]"Memorandum of Reactions to Address by Under Secretary of Agriculture True D. Morse Before Trask Bridge Picnic, Pecatonica, Illinois, August 24, 1955, OF 106, Agriculture-Farming, Eisenhower Library.

[38]Ibid.

[39]Ibid.

[40]Val J. Washington to Gabriel Hauge, November 17, 1955, OF 106, Agriculture-Farming, Eisenhower Library.

[41]Howard Doggett to Gabriel Hauge, November 9, 1955 and Gabriel Hauge to Val J. Washington, November 14, 1955, OF 106, Agriculture-Farming, Eisenhower Library.

[42]USDA News Release, October 27, 1955, OF 106, Agriculture-Farming, Eisenhower Library. See also New York Times, October 27, 1955.

[43]Val J. Washington to Gabriel Hauge, December 6, 1955, OF 106, Agriculture-Farming, Eisenhower Library.

[44]Val J. Washington to Sherman Adams, January 20, 1956, OF 106, Agriculture-Farming, Eisenhower Library.

[45]Ezra Taft Benson to Gabriel Hauge, May 11, 1955, OF 106, Agriculture-Farming, Eisenhower Library.

[46]Gabriel Hauge to Andrew J. Goodpaster, June 3, 1955, OF 106, Agriculture-Farming, Eisenhower Library.

[47]Gabriel Hauge to Sherman Adams, May 16, 1955, OF 106, Agriculture-Farming, Eisenhower Library.

[48]Gabriel Hauge to True D. Morse, December 16, 1955 with enclosure of Governor Dan Thornton's communication, OF 106, Agriculture-Farming, Eisenhower Library.

[49]Interview with Sherman Adams, August 13, 1969.

[50]Statement by the Secretary of Agriculture Ezra Taft Benson Submitted to the House Committee on Agriculture, March 27, 1956, OF 106, Agriculture-Farming, Eisenhower Library.

[51]Ibid.

Chapter VIII

[1] William Allen White to Dwight D. Eisenhower, January 28, 1956, OF 106, Agriculture-Farming, Eisenhower Library.

[2] Dwight D. Eisenhower to William Allen White, February 2, 1956, OF 106, Agriculture-Farming, Eisenhower Library.

[3] Adams, First-Hand Report, 215.

[4] Eisenhower, The White House Years, I, 633.

[5] H. Carl Anderson to Dwight D. Eisenhower, April 12, 1956, OF 106-F, Eisenhower Library.

[6] Ibid.

[7] Dwight D. Eisenhower to H. Carl Anderson, April 15, 1956, OF 106-F, Eisenhower Library.

[8] Eisenhower, The White House Years, 664.

[9]Clifford R. Hope to Harry Riffel, April 20, 1956,
Papers of Clifford R. Hope.

[10]Clifford R. Hope to John N. Luft, April 28, 1956,
Papers of Clifford R. Hope. Congressman Hope made this
overt break with the Eisenhower administration because he
had already decided not to run for reelection.

[11]Arthur Burns to Roger W. Jones, May 28, 1956,
Bills File-Eisenhower Library.

[12]Sinclair Weeks to Director of the Budget, May 25,
1956, Bills File-Eisenhower Library.

[13]Robert C. Hill to Director of the Budget, May 25,
1956, Bills File-Eisenhower Library.

[14]A Report, No. 2077 (1956) 1956 Farm Bill, to
Accompany H.R. 10875, Submitted by Mr. Cooley, 84th Congress,
House of Representatives, Bills File-Eisenhower Library.

[15]Statement by the President, May 29, 1956, Francis
File-Eisenhower Library.

[16]"Democratic Platform 1956," in Kirk H. Porter and
Donald Bruce Johnson, National Party Platforms 1840-1960
(Urbana, 1961), 532-534.

[17]Ibid.

[18]"Republican Platform 1956," in Porter and Johnson, National Party Platforms, 550-552.

[19]Ibid.

[20]"Farm Policy Summary, and Indexed Summary of Statements by Ezra Taft Benson," Republican National Committee, 1956, ETB-LDS.

[21]Address by Ezra Taft Benson to National Federation of Republican Women, 9th Biennial Convention, Chicago, September 7, 1956, ETB-LDS.

[22]Address by Ezra Taft Benson to the Minneapolis Grain Exchange (75th Anniversary Dinner), Minneapolis, September 12, 1956, ETB-LDS.

[23]George M. Humphrey to Ezra Taft Benson, September 27, 1954; R. E. Wood to George M. Humphrey, September 17, 1954, Papers of George M. Humphrey.

[24]Ezra Taft Benson to George M. Humphrey, October 21, 1954, Papers of George M. Humphrey.

[25]George M. Humphrey to Ezra Taft Benson, October 25, 1954, Papers of George M. Humphrey.

[26]Ezra Taft Benson to Gabriel Hauge, September 4, 1956, OF 106, Agriculture-Farming, Eisenhower Library.

[27]Cited from Congress and the Nation, 1945-1964 (Washington, D.C., 1965), 64-65.

[28]Address by Ezra Taft Benson at the 90th Annual Convention of the National Grange, Rochester, New York, November 14, 1956, ETB-LDS.

[29]Ezra Taft Benson to Wilton B. Persons, December 3, 1956, OF 2, Eisenhower Library.

[30]Sam Rayburn to Kenneth D. McKellar, November 12, 1956, Papers of Sam Rayburn (Sam Rayburn Library, Bonham, Texas).

[31]Dwight D. Eisenhower to Ezra Taft Benson, November 12, 1956, OF 2, Eisenhower Library.

Chapter IX

[1]"Facts About Price Supports," December 10, 1957,
OF 1, Eisenhower Library.

[2]Ibid. Secretary Benson tried to save some money
by freezing the number of personnel in the USDA. This
gesture, however, saved very little when compared to departmental expenditures. Ezra Taft Benson to Heads of
Department Agencies, "Reduction of Expenditures," April 22,
1957, OF 2, Eisenhower Library.

[3]Minutes of the Cabinet Meeting, April 12, 1957,
Adams Papers.

[4]Ezra Taft Benson to Allen J. Ellender, May 2,
1957, with enclosure: "Need for Reappraisal of Farm Price
Support and Production Control Programs," Gerald Morgan
Files, Eisenhower Library.

[5]Ibid.

[6]Ibid.

[7]Address by Ezra Taft Benson to Economic Club, New York City, April 29, 1957, ETB-LDS.

[8]Ibid.

[9]Address by Ezra Taft Benson to Tennessee Farmers' Convention, University of Tennessee, Knoxville, June 19, 1957, ETB-LDS.

[10]Gwynn Garnett to Clarence Francis, n.d. [1957], Francis File-Eisenhower Library.

[11]Jack Z. Anderson to Sherman Adams, August 12, 1957, Jack Z. Anderson File-Eisenhower Library. The following chart compares agricultural expenditures of the Truman and Eisenhower administrations. Taken from Luther Tweeten, Foundations of Farm Policy (Lincoln, 1970), 317:

Year	Income Stabilization	Total Budget
	(Billions of Dollars)	
1948	.1	.6
1949	.3	2.5
1950	.5	2.8
1951	.5	.7
1952	.3	1.1
1953	.3	2.9
1954	.8	2.6
1955	3.1	4.7
1956	3.2	4.9
1957	2.5	4.2
1958	2.1	3.9
1959	4.7	6.2
1960	2.9	4.3

[12]Clarence Francis to Sherman Adams, November 22, 1957, Francis File-Eisenhower Library.

[13]Ibid.

[14]John H. Hamlin to Sherman Adams, March 18, 1957, OF 110-N, Eisenhower Library.

[15]John H. Hamlin to Sherman Adams, April 23, 1957, OF 110-N, Eisenhower Library.

[16]Ibid.

[17]Telegram, George McGovern to Dwight D. Eisenhower, April 20, 1957, Adams Papers.

[18]Quoted in Aberdeen American-News, October 22, 1957.

[19]Joe Foss to Dwight D. Eisenhower, October 22, 1957, OF 2, Eisenhower Library. In an era when disrupting a speaker was considered improper conduct, the unruly protesters were fined fifty dollars each and given suspended sentences of thirty days.

[20]William Proxmire to authors, September 22, 1969 and Martin Nolan, "Report from Washington," The Atlantic, Vol. 226 (December, 1970), 6-20.

[21]Telegram, William Proxmire to Dwight D. Eisenhower, September 12, 1957, Adams Papers.

[22]Henry S. Reuss to Dwight D. Eisenhower, September 12, 1957, Adams Papers.

[23]Melvin R. Laird to Dwight D. Eisenhower, October 22, 1957, Adams Papers.

[24]Karl E. Mundt to Sherman Adams, October 23, 1957, Adams Papers.

[25]*Ibid.*

[26]A. L. Miller to Sherman Adams, October 26, 1957, Adams Papers.

[27]H. Carl Anderson to Sherman Adams, August 28, 1957, Adams Papers.

[28]Memorandum "Wisconsin Farm Vote," William B. Prendergast to Meade Alcorn, September 23, 1957, Adams Papers and Meade Alcorn to authors, October 30, 1969.

[29]Ezra Taft Benson to Sherman Adams, October 17, 1957, Adams Papers.

[30]"Report on Secretary of Agriculture's Round the World Trip," 1957, ETB-LDS.

[31]Quoted in Benson, Cross Fire, 388-389.

[32]Statement to the Press by Ezra Taft Benson, February 21, 1958, OF 2, Eisenhower Library.

[33]The President's News Conference of February 26, 1958, Public Papers of the Presidents of the United States Dwight D. Eisenhower 1958, 187. Hereinafter cited as Eisenhower Public Papers. For other instances of where Senator Everett Dirksen defended Eisenhower appointees see Neil McNeil, Dirksen: Portrait of a Public Man (New York and Cleveland, 1970), 157.

[34]Minutes of the Cabinet Meeting, March 7, 1958, Adams Papers.

[35]Edward J. Thye to Ezra Taft Benson, March 8, 1958, OF 1, Eisenhower Library.

[36]Dwight D. Eisenhower to Edward J. Thye, March 13, 1958, OF 1, Eisenhower Library.

[37]"Special Message to the Congress on Agriculture," January 16, 1958, Eisenhower Public Papers 1958, 100-107.

[38]Ibid.

[39]Memorandum, "Improving Republican Strength in the Farm Areas," Meade Alcorn to Ezra Taft Benson and Sherman Adams, March 27, 1958, Adams Papers.

[40]Ezra Taft Benson to Sherman Adams, April 14, 1958, Adams Papers.

[41]Charles Halleck to Dwight D. Eisenhower, March 21, 1958, OF 106, Eisenhower Library.

[42]Address by Ezra Taft Benson at Farm and Home Week, Ohio State University, Columbus, March 25, 1958, ETB-LDS.

[43]President Eisenhower's Veto Message to the Senate, March 31, 1958, Adams Papers.

[44]Text of the Remarks of the President on the Veto of SJ Resolution 162, as Recorded for Radio and Television, March 31, 1958, Adams Papers.

[45]Speech by Ezra Taft Benson at Campaign Dinner, Maryland Republicans, Baltimore, June 17, 1958, ETB-LDS.

[46]Sam Rayburn to Dick Rayburn, August 9, 1958, Sam Rayburn Library (Bonham, Texas).

[47]Address by Ezra Taft Benson at Annual Meeting of American Institute for Cooperation, Pennsylvania State University, August 25, 1958, ETB-LDS.

[48]Henry A. Wallace, "Freedom and Prosperity for All," Address to Farm Institute, February 1, 1958, Des Moines, Iowa, Papers of Henry A. Wallace (University of Iowa, Iowa City). Wallace once wrote James A. Farley that a Democratic farmer informed him "that neither he nor his neighbors have any use for Benson. This is unfortunate and I told him that for the sake of the farmers and the nation we should pray for Benson's success. For Benson's sake I am sorry that he should have created this impression because I think that the flexible price idea so far as corn is concerned is probably sound." Henry A. Wallace to James A. Farley, January 29, 1954, Wallace Papers. For Wallace's later activities in the field of agriculture, see the authors' Prophet in Politics: Henry A. Wallace and the War Years, 1940-1965 (Ames, 1970)--particularly Chapter 15.

[49]Ibid.

[50]Address by Ezra Taft Benson at Wisconsin Fund Raising Dinner, Janesville, Wisconsin, September 17, 1958, ETB-LDS.

[51]Address by Ezra Taft Benson at Nebraska Corn Picking Contest, Tekamah, Nebraska, October 9, 1958, ETB-LDS.

[52]Address by Ezra Taft Benson at Public Meeting, Safford, Arizona, October 18, 1958, ETB-LDS.

[53]Ibid.

[54]Address by Ezra Taft Benson to Young Republicans of Washakie County, Worland, Wyoming, October 27, 1958, ETB-LDS.

[55]Address by Ezra Taft Benson to combined meeting of California Farm Bureau, Agriculture Council of California, and Chamber of Commerce, Fresno, California, October 31, 1958, ETB-LDS.

Chapter X

[1]Address by Ezra Taft Benson at Jersey Republican
State Committee Fund Raising Dinner, Newark, New Jersey,
February 25, 1959, ETB-LDS.

[2]Address by Ezra Taft Benson at the National Conference of Tau Kappa Alpha, Rutgers University, New Bruns-
wick, New Jersey, March 24, 1959, ETB-LDS.

[3]Draft of letter from Ezra Taft Benson to Otis T.
Lippincott, September 18, 1959, Correspondence of the
Secretary of Agriculture, RG 16, National Archives.

[4]Waco (Texas) Times-Herald, April 8, 1959.

[5]Memorandum, Dwight D. Eisenhower to Members of the
Cabinet, September 6, 1958, OF 1, Eisenhower Library.

[6]Special Message to the Congress on Agriculture,
January 29, 1959, Eisenhower Public Papers 1959, 149-150.

[7]Statement by Secretary of Agriculture before the
House Subcommittee on Agriculture Appropriations, May 7,

1959, OF 1, Eisenhower Library.

[8]Ibid.

[9]Veto of Bill Relating to the Wheat Program, June 25, 1959, Eisenhower Public Papers, 1959, 477.

[10]Veto of Tobacco Price Support Bill, June 25, 1959, Eisenhower Public Papers, 1959, 478.

[11]Ben Jensen to Joseph W. Martin, Jr. with enclosure, January 7, 1958, OF 1-Q, Eisenhower Library. The Iowan's dislike of Benson intensified after the fall elections when he lost seven out of fourteen counties to eke out a narrow 2,200-vote victory.

[12]Report to the Congress of the United States, Audit of Direct Distribution Program, Agricultural Marketing Service, USDA, Fiscal Year 1957, Ralph Campbell (Comptroller General) to Sam Rayburn (Speaker of the House of Representatives), September 30, 1958, 1-Q, Eisenhower Library.

[13]Rachel Carson, Silent Spring (Greenwich, Conn., 1968), 150, 201.

[14]Statement by Secretary of Agriculture on Cabinet Paper, January 22, 1960, ETB-LDS.

[15]Report to the Congress of the United States, Audit of Foreign Agricultural Service, Joseph Campbell (Comptroller General) to Sam Rayburn (Speaker of the House of Representatives), March 23, 1959, OF 1-Q, Eisenhower Library.

[16]Report to the Congress of the United States, Review of the 1959 Conservation Reserve Program, Commodity Stabilization Service, USDA, Joseph Campbell (Comptroller General) to Sam Rayburn (Speaker of the House of Representatives), December 31, 1959, OF 1-Q, Eisenhower Library.

[17]Secretary Ezra Taft Benson Comments on Soil Bank Report by General Accounting Office, January 7, 1960, ETB-LDS.

[18]Notes on Trip to Europe, June 25-July 6, 1959 and "General Comments, Observations, and Conclusions on Trip to Europe, September 23-October 9, 1959," ETB-LDS.

[19]Ibid. See also letter from Ezra Taft Benson to (Mrs.) Myrtle Olsen, October 28, 1959, Correspondence of the Secretary of Agriculture, RG 16, National Archives. In this letter Secretary Benson relates more on his personal feelings relative to the contact made with Russian Christians.

[20]True D. Morse to William I. Myers, December 4, 1959, Correspondence of the Secretary of Agriculture, RG 16, National Archives.

[21]Don Paarlberg to General Persons, November 28, 1959, with attachment: "Concentration and paraphrasing of the President's comments in Cabinet meeting on the general subject of the 1961 budget and related matters (November 22, 1959)," Paarlberg File-Eisenhower Library.

[22]Don Paarlberg to Wayne B. Warrington, October 14, 1958, OF 106-F, Eisenhower Library.

[23]Peter A. Toma, The Politics of Food for Peace, Executive-Legislative Interaction (Tucson, 1967), 42 ff.

[24]Comments by Cabinet Members on Food for Peace Program, July 1, 1960, Paarlberg File-Eisenhower Library.

[25]Cabinet Presentation on Food for Peace Program, July 1, 1960, Paarlberg File-Eisenhower Library.

[26]Special Message to the Congress on Agriculture, February 9, 1960, Eisenhower Public Papers 1960-61, 162-165.

[27]Statement by Secretary of Agriculture Ezra Taft Benson before the House Committee on Agriculture, February

18, 1960, Paarlberg File-Eisenhower Library.

[28]Address by Ezra Taft Benson at Farmer-Businessman Dinner, Chamber of Commerce, Yankton, South Dakota, March 1, 1960, ETB-LDS.

[29]Ibid.

[30]Alexander Kendrick, Prime Time, The Life of Edward R. Murrow (New York, 1970), 432-433. See also "Agriculture: See It Now," Time, LXVII (February 6, 1956), 18.

[31]Quentin N. Burdick to authors, November 16, 1970.

[32]Statement by Secretary Benson on Grain Storage, January 16, 1960, ETB-LDS.

Chapter XI

[1]Memorandum, Dwight D. Eisenhower to Richard M.
Nixon, January 13, 1960, as quoted in Dwight D. Eisenhower,
The White House Years Waging Peace: 1956-1961 (Garden City,
1965), 591.

[2]Benson, Cross Fire, 511-512.

[3]Don Paarlberg to Ezra Taft Benson, May 20, 1960,
Paarlberg File-Eisenhower Library.

[4]Charles H. Percy, "Decisions for a Better America,"
1960, Paarlberg File-Eisenhower Library.

[5]Herbert Stein, The Fiscal Revolution in America
(Chicago and London, 1969), 366-367.

[6]"Prospects for Price Stability," April 2, 1960,
Second Interim Report of the Cabinet Committee on Price
Stability for Economic Growth, Paarlberg File-Eisenhower
Library.

[7]Don Paarlberg to Philip E. Areeda, n.d., Paarlberg File-Eisenhower Library.

[8]Philip E. Areeda to Don Paarlberg, n.d., Paarlberg File-Eisenhower Library. See Arthur M. Schlesinger, Jr., A Thousand Days (Greenwich, Conn., 1965), 65-78.

[9]Campaign Speech by John F. Kennedy at Euclid Beach Park, Cleveland, Ohio, September 25, 1960, Final Report of the Committee on Commerce United States Senate Prepared by its Subcommittee on Communications, The Speeches, Remarks, Press Conferences, and Statements of Senator John F. Kennedy, August 1 Through November 7, 1960, p. 1053.

[10]Quoted in Earl Mazo, Richard Nixon: A Political and Personal Portrait (New York, 1959), 202.

[11]Richard M. Nixon, The Challenge We Face (New York, Toronto, and London, 1960), 152.

[12]"Republican Platform 1960," Porter and Johnson, National Party Platforms, 611.

[13]"Democratic Platform 1960," Porter and Johnson, National Party Platforms, 585-586.

[14]Ibid.

[15]Senate Speech, March 5, 1956, in John Fitzgerald Kennedy, A Compilation of Statements and Speeches Made During His Service in the United States Senate and House of Representatives (Washington, D.C., 1964), p. 384.

[16]Campaign Speech by Senator John F. Kennedy at Southern Illinois University, Carbondale, Illinois, October 3, 1960, in The Speeches, Remarks, Press Conferences, and Statements of Senator John F. Kennedy, August 1 Through November 7, 1960, p. 466.

[17]Campaign Speech by Senator John F. Kennedy given at Midwest Farm Conference, Des Moines, Iowa, August 21, 1960, Box 21, Papers of John F. Kennedy (John F. Kennedy Library, Waltham, Massachusetts).

[18]Richard M. Nixon, Six Crises (New York, 1962), Cardinal Edition, 359.

[19]Campaign Speech by Ezra Taft Benson, Chesterfield County Fair Grounds, Chesterfield, Virginia, September 5, 1960, ETB-LDS.

[20]Ezra Taft Benson to Richard M. Nixon, October 19, 1960, as quoted in Benson, Cross Fire, 544-545.

[21]Ezra Taft Benson, "Where We Stand," A Report by the Secretary of Agriculture to the American People, July 19, 1960, ETB-LDS.

[22]Ezra Taft Benson, Freedom to Farm (Garden City, 1960), 16, 23, 198-200, et passim.

[23]Herschel D. Newsom to Ezra Taft Benson, July 14, 1960, ETB-LDS.

[24]Newark Leader, July 17, 1960.

[25]Washington Post, July 17, 1960.

[26]Des Moines Register, n.d., Clipping File, ETB-LDS.

[27]Minneapolis Tribune, n.d., Clipping File, ETB-LDS.

[28]Nebraska Farmer, July 16, 1960.

[29]Saturday Review, July 25, 1960, Clipping File, ETB-LDS.

[30]Reading Guide, November, 1960, Clipping File, ETB-LDS.

[31]Springfield State Journal, February 24, 1960.

[32]Weekly Star Journal, n.d., Clipping File, ETB-LDS.

[33]Wall Street Journal, July 10, 1960.

[34]Richmond Times-Dispatch, n.d., Clipping File,
ETB-LDS.

[35](Phoenix) Arizona Republic, July 23, 1960.

[36]New York Herald Tribune, July 17, 1960.

[37]Earl Butz to Ezra Taft Benson, n.d. [1960],
ETB-LDS.

[38]William I. Myers to Ezra Taft Benson, August 27,
1960, National Agriculture Advisory Commission-1960, RG 16,
National Archives.

[39]Jay Richter, "The Next President and Southern
Agriculture," Progressive Farmer, Vol. 75 (October, 1960),
25.

[40]Wallaces Farmer, Vol. 85 (October 15, 1960), 6.

[41]Prairie Farmer, Vol. 132 (November 5, 1960), 49.

[42]The President's News Conference of August 10, 1960, _Eisenhower Public Papers 1960-61_, 621.

[43]_Ibid._

[44]Ezra Taft Benson to William I. Myers, December 21, 1960, National Agriculture Advisory Commission-1960, RG 16, National Archives.

[45]Ezra Taft Benson to Dwight D. Eisenhower, January 3, 1961, ETB-LDS.

[46]Dwight D. Eisenhower to Ezra Taft Benson, January 4, 1961, ETB-LDS.

[47]Address by Ezra Taft Benson at Closing General Session, 82nd Quarterly Conference, Washington Stake, December 4, 1960, ETB-LDS.

Conclusion

[1] Ezra Taft Benson, "A World Message," Address at April Conference of The Church of Jesus Christ of Latter-day Saints, April, 1961, ETB-LDS.

[2] As quoted by Richard Rhodes, "Ike: An Artist In Iron," Harper's, Vol. 241 (July, 1970), 77.

[3] "Modern Republicanism," Address by Dwight D. Eisenhower to the Republican National Conference, June 7, 1957, Eisenhower Public Papers 1957, 449.

[4] Campaign Speech by Dwight D. Eisenhower at Lexington, Kentucky, October 1, 1956, in Vital Speeches, XXIII (October 15, 1956), 2.

[5] Dwight D. Eisenhower to John Foster Dulles, December 30, 1953, Papers of John Foster Dulles.

[6] Rhodes, "Ike: An Artist In Iron," 76.

SELECT BIBLIOGRAPHY

<u>MANUSCRIPTS</u>

Anderson College (Anderson, Indiana): Papers of Charles E.
    Wilson

Archives of The Church of Jesus Christ of Latter-day Saints
    (Salt Lake City, Utah): Papers of Ezra Taft Benson

Chicago Historical Society Library: Papers of Paul H.
    Douglas

Dartmouth College (Hanover, New Hampshire): Papers of
    Sherman Adams

Dwight D. Eisenhower Library (Abilene, Kansas):

    Papers of Dwight D. Eisenhower

    Papers of Ezra Taft Benson

    Staff Files: Jack Z. Anderson; Clarence Francis;
        Homer Gruenther; Bryce N. Harlow; Meyer
        Kestnbaum; James M. Lambie, Jr.; Gerald
        Morgan; E. Frederic Morrow; Don Paarlberg;
        and Howard Pyle

    Oral History Project: Ezra Taft Benson; James M.
        Lambie, Jr.; True D. Morse; and Don
        Paarlberg

Harry S. Truman Library (Independence, Missouri):   Papers
of Charles Murphy

John F. Kennedy Library (National Archives and Federal
Records Center-Waltham, Massachusetts):
Papers of John F. Kennedy (Campaign of 1960)
Oral History Project (Interviews with John A. Baker,
Howard Bertsch, and Willard W. Cochrane)
Staff Files

Iowa State History Collection (Iowa State University-Ames,
Iowa): Ezra Taft Benson Collection

Kansas State Historical Society (Topeka, Kansas):
Papers of Frank Carlson
Papers of Clifford R. Hope

Library of Congress (Washington, D.C.):
Papers of Robert A. Taft

Minnesota State Historical Society (St. Paul, Minnesota):
Papers of Hubert H. Humphrey

National Archives (Washington, D.C.):
Correspondence of the Secretary of Agriculture
Files of Commodity Stabilization Service
Files of National Agriculture Advisory Commission

National Agricultural Library (Beltsville, Maryland):
Files of Rural Development Programs News
Reports of the Secretary on the Rural Development
Program

Princeton University (Princeton, New Jersey):

Papers of John Foster Dulles

The Dulles Oral History Collection: George D.
Aiken; Everett M. Dirksen; Andrew J.
Goodpaster; Charles A. Halleck; Milton
Eisenhower; Herbert C. Hoover, Jr.; George
M. Humphrey; Clarence B. Randall; Harold E.
Stassen, and Samuel C. Waugh

Stonehill College (North Easton, Massachusetts):

Papers of Joseph W. Martin, Jr.

The Sam Rayburn Library (Bonham, Texas):

Papers of Sam Rayburn

University of Missouri--Western History Collection (Columbia, Missouri):

Papers of Phil M. Donnelly

University of Illinois (Urbana):

Farm Foundation Archives

Papers of Harold C. Case

Papers of Garret L. Jordon

Papers of David E. Lindstrom

Papers of Charles B. Shuman

Tape Recorded Lecture by Charles B. Shuman, "Secretaries of Agriculture As I Have Known Them,"
April 26, 1973

University of Illinois (contd.)

Tape Recorded Interview with Charles B. Shuman,
March 1, 1974

University of Iowa (Iowa City, Iowa):

Papers of Henry A. Wallace

Wisconsin State Historical Society (Madison, Wisconsin):

Papers of Clark R. Mollenhoff

Papers of Morris Ryskind

Western Reserve Historical Society (Cleveland, Ohio):

Papers of George M. Humphrey

INTERVIEWS

Personal interview with Sherman Adams, August 13, 1969
(Lincoln, New Hampshire)

Personal interview with M. L. Wilson, July 17, 1966 (Washington, D.C.).

CORRESPONDENCE WITH AUTHORS

George D. Aiken, Meade Alcorn, Clinton P. Anderson, Leslie
C. Arends, Ezra Taft Benson, Charles E. Brannan, Herbert
Brownell, Robert Buck, Quentin N. Burdick, Arthur E. Burns,
Harold D. Cooley, Carl T. Curtis, Thomas E. Dewey, James O.
Eastland, Allen J. Ellender, Milton S. Eisenhower, A. B.
Evans, Paul Findley, Marion B. Folsom, Orville L. Freeman,
Thomas S. Gates, Charles A. Halleck, Clifford M. Hardin,
Ralph Harvey, Gabriel Hauge, Ben Hibbs, Oveta Culp Hobby,

Spessard L. Holland, O. B. Jesness, Walter H. Judd, Alfred
M. Landon, Arthur Larson, George McGovern, Flint McRoberts,
Albert K. Mitchell, Clark R. Mollenhoff, True D. Morse,
Hyde H. Murray, William I. Myers, Don Paarlberg, James G.
Patton, W. R. Poage, William Proxmire, Howard Pyle, Maxwell
R. Rabb, Charles B. Shuman, Wilmer Smith, Oren Lee Staley,
Robert Taft, Jr., Jamie L. Whitten, John J. Williams, and
Milton R. Young.

PUBLIC PAPERS AND COLLECTED WORKS

Public Papers of the Presidents of the United States Dwight
     D. Eisenhower Containing the Public Messages,
     Speeches, and Statements of the President January
     20, 1953 to January 20, 1961 (Washington, D.C.:
     Government Printing Office, 1961). 8 vols.

Albertson, Dean, ed. Eisenhower As President. New York:
     Hill and Wang, 1963

Branyan, Robert L. and Lawrence H. Larsen. The Eisenhower
     Administration, 1953-1961: A Documentary History
     (New York: Random House, 1971). 2 vols.

McGovern, George, ed. Agricultural Thought in the Twentieth
     Century. Indianapolis and New York: The Bobbs-
     Merrill Company, Inc., 1967

Hildreth, R. J., ed. Readings in Agricultural Policy.
     Lincoln: University of Nebraska Press, 1968

Porter, Kirk H. and Donald Bruce Johnson, Compilers.
        National Party Platforms 1840-1960. Urbana: The
        University of Illinois Press, 1961
Schoenberger, Robert A., ed. The American Right Wing,
        Readings in Political Behavior. New York: Holt,
        Rinehart and Winston, Inc., 1969

GOVERNMENT DOCUMENTS AND PUBLICATIONS

12 Years of Achievement Under Public Law 480. Economic Re-
        search Service, U.S. Department of Agriculture
        (November, 1967)
Freedom of Communications. Final Report of the Committee
        on Commerce Prepared by Its Subcommittee on Communi-
        cations, Part I, The Speeches, Remarks, Press Con-
        ferences, and Statements of Senator John F. Kennedy,
        August 1 Through November 7, 1960
The Yearbook of Agriculture. 1953-1960

NEWSPAPERS AND MAGAZINES

Bloomington-Normal Daily Pantagraph
Deseret News (Salt Lake City)
Des Moines Register
Minneapolis Tribune
New York Times
Ohio Farmer (Columbus)

356

Prairie Farmer (Chicago)

Progressive Farmer (Kentucky-Tennessee-West Virginia Edition)

Wallaces Farmer (Des Moines)

Washington *Post*

Atlantic

Harper's

Life

Newsweek

The New Republic

Time

BOOKS

Andrews, Stanley. *The Farmer's Dilemma*. Washington, D.C.: Public Affairs Press, 1961.

Anderson, Patrick. *The President's Men, White House Assistants of Franklin D. Roosevelt, Harry S. Truman, Dwight D. Eisenhower, John F. Kennedy and Lyndon B. Johnson*. Garden City: Doubleday and Company, 1968.

Adams, Sherman. *First-Hand Report: The Story of the Eisenhower Administration*. New York: Harper and Brothers, 1961.

Baker, Gladys et al. *Century of Service, the First 100 Years of the United States Department of Agriculture*. Washington, D.C.: Government Printing Office, 1963.

Baldwin, David A. *Economic Development and American Foreign Policy, 1943-62*. Chicago: The University of Chicago Press, 1966.

Bass, Robert H. *Food Versus Force: A Short History of Agriculture in the Soviet Union*. New York: Free Europe Press, 1957.

Benedict, Murray R. *Farm Policies of the United States, 1790-1950*. New York: The Twentieth Century Fund, 1953.

_____ and Oscar C. Stine. *The Agricultural Commodity Programs: Two Decades of Experience*. New York: The Twentieth Century Fund, 1956.

Benson, Ezra Taft. *Cross Fire: The Eight Years With Eisenhower*. Garden City: Doubleday and Company, 1962.

_____. *Farmers at the Crossroads*. New York: Devin-Adair Company, 1956.

_____. *Freedom to Farm*. Garden City: Doubleday and Company, 1960.

_____. *New Horizons in Farming*. Salt Lake City: Deseret Book Company, 1963.

Childs, Marquis. *Eisenhower: Captive Hero*. London: Hammond, Hammond, and Company, 1959.

Coppock, John O. *North Atlantic Policy--The Agricultural Gap*. New York: The Twentieth Century Fund, 1963.

Christensen, Reo M. The Brannan Plan. Ann Arbor: Univer-
    sity of Michigan Press, 1959.

David, Paul T., ed. The Presidential Election and Transi-
    tion 1960-1961. Washington, D.C.: The Brookings
    Institution, 1961.

Donovan, Robert J. Eisenhower: The Inside Story. New
    York: Harper and Brothers, 1956.

Dror, Yehezkel. Public Policymaking Reexamined. San
    Francisco: Chandler Publishing Company, 1968.

Eisenhower, Dwight D. The White House Years. Garden City:
    Doubleday and Company, 1965. 2 vols.

_____. At Ease: Stories I Tell to My Friends. Garden
    City: Doubleday and Company, 1967.

Fenno, Richard F., Jr. The President's Cabinet, An Analysis
    in the Period from Wilson to Eisenhower. New York:
    Random House, 1959.

Findley, Paul. The Federal Farm Fable. New Rochelle, New
    York: Arlington House, 1968.

Freeman, Orville L. World Without Hunger. New York:
    Frederick A. Praeger Publishers, 1968.

Frier, David A. Conflict of Interest in the Eisenhower
    Administration. Ames: Iowa State University
    Press, 1969.

Gerson, Louis L. John Foster Dulles. New York: Cooper
    Square Publishers, Inc., 1967.

Goldberg, Roy A. <u>Agribusiness Coordination: A System</u>
     <u>Approach to the Wheat, Soybean, and Florida Orange</u>
     <u>Economics</u>. Boston: Harvard University School of
     Business Administration, 1968.

Hadwiger, Don F. <u>Federal Wheat Commodity Programs</u>. Ames:
     The Iowa State University Press, 1970.

Hammond, Paul Y. <u>The Cold War Years</u>. New York: Harcourt,
     Brace and World, 1969.

Helfrich, Harold W. Jr., ed. <u>The Environmental Crisis</u>,
     <u>Man's Struggle to Live With Himself</u>. New Haven and
     London: Yale University Press, 1970.

Higbee, Edward. <u>Farms and Farmers in an Urban Age</u>. Phila-
     delphia: Twentieth Century Fund, 1963.

Hughes, Emmet John. <u>The Ordeal of Power: A Political</u>
     <u>Memoir of the Eisenhower Years</u>. New York:
     Atheneum, 1963.

James, Dorothy Buckton. <u>The Contemporary Presidency</u>. New
     York: Western Publishing Company, 1969.

Kendrick, Alexander. <u>Prime Time, The Life of Edward R.</u>
     <u>Murrow</u>. New York: Avon Books, 1969.

Kessel, John H. <u>The Goldwater Coalition, Republican</u>
     <u>Strategies in 1964</u>. Indianapolis and New York:
     Bobbs-Merrill Company, Inc., 1968.

Kirschner, Don S. City and Country, Rural Responses to
Urbanization in the 1920s. Westport, Conn.:
Greenwood Publishing Corporation, 1970.

Krock, Arthur. Memoirs, Sixty Years on the Firing Line.
New York: Popular Library, 1968.

Larson, Arthur. Eisenhower: The President Nobody Knew.
New York: Popular Library, 1968.

Lyon, Peter. Eisenhower: Portrait of the Hero. New York:
Little, Brown and Company, 1974.

MacNeil, Neil. Dirksen: Portrait of a Public Man. New
York and Cleveland: The World Publishing Company,
1970.

Martin, Joseph, as told to Robert J. Donovan. Joe Martin,
My First Fifty Years in Politics. New York:
McGraw-Hill Book Company, 1960.

Mathews, Donald R. U.S. Senators and Their World. New
York: Random House, 1960.

Matusow, Allen J. Farm Policies and Politics in the
Truman Years. Cambridge, Mass.: Harvard University Press, 1967.

Mayer, George H. The Republican Party 1854-1964. New York:
Oxford University Press, 1964.

Mazo, Earl. Richard Nixon: A Political and Personal
Portrait. New York: Harper and Brothers, 1959.

McCune, Wesley. _Ezra Taft Benson, Man With a Mission_.
Washington, D.C.: Public Affairs Press, 1958.

Meyer, Frank S., ed. _What Is Conservatism_? New York:
Holt, Rinehart and Winston, 1964.

Mooney, Booth. _The Politicians: 1945-1960_. Philadelphia
and New York: J. B. Lippincott Company, 1970.

Morrow, E. Frederick. _Black Man In the White House: A_
Diary of the Eisenhower Years by the Administrative
Officer for Special Projects, 1955-1961. New York:
Coward-McCann, Inc., 1963.

Nelson, Lowry. _American Farm Life_. Cambridge: Harvard
University Press, 1954.

Nixon, Richard. _Six Crises_. New York: Doubleday and
Company, 1962.

_____. _The Challenge We Face_. New York: McGraw-Hill
Book Company, 1960.

Paarlberg, Don. _American Farm Policy: A Case Study of_
Centralized Decision-Making. New York: John Wiley
and Sons, 1964.

_____. _Great Myths of Economics_. New York and Cleve-
land: The World Publishing Company, 1968.

Parmet, Herbert S. _Eisenhower and the American Crusades_.
New York and London: The Macmillan Company,
1972.

Peabody, Robert L. and Nelson W. Polsby, eds. New Perspec-
tives on the House of Representatives. Chicago:
Rand McNally and Company, 1969.

Richter, Edward J. and Berton Dulce. Religion and the
Presidency, A Recurring Problem. New York: The
Macmillan Company, 1962.

Ripley, Randall. Power in the Senate. New York: St.
Martin's Press, 1969.

Rossiter, Clinton. The American Presidency. New York:
Harcourt, Brace and Company, Inc., 1956.

Rovere, Richard H. Affairs of State: The Eisenhower Years.
New York: Straus and Cudahy, 1956.

_____. Senator Joe McCarthy. Cleveland and New York:
The World Publishing Company, 1966.

Schapsmeier, Edward L. and Frederick H. Schapsmeier.
Henry A. Wallace of Iowa: The Agrarian Years,
1910-1940. Ames: The Iowa State University Press,
1968.

_____. Prophet in Politics: Henry A. Wallace and the
War Years, 1940-1965. Ames: The Iowa State University Press, 1970.

Schickele, Rainer. Agricultural Policy, Farm Programs and
National Welfare. Lincoln: University of Nebraska
Press, 1954.

Schriftgiesser, Karl. <u>Business and Public Policy, The Role</u>
<u>of the Committee for Economic Development: 1942-</u>
<u>1967</u>. Englewood Cliffs, New Jersey: Prentice-Hall,
Inc., 1967.

Schultze, Charles L. <u>The Distribution of Farm Subsidies:</u>
<u>Who Gets the Benefits?</u> Washington, D.C.: The
Brookings Institution, 1971.

Soth, Lauren. <u>Farm Trouble</u>. Princeton: Princeton University Press, 1957.

Stein, Herbert. <u>The Fiscal Revolution in America</u>. Chicago
and London: The University of Chicago Press, 1969.

Street, James H. <u>The New Revolution in the Cotton Economy</u>.
Chapel Hill: University of North Carolina Press,
1957.

Sulzberger, C. L. <u>A Long Row of Candles, Memoirs and</u>
<u>Diaries</u>. New York: The Macmillan Company, 1969.

Sundquist, James L. <u>Politics and Policy: The Eisenhower,</u>
<u>Kennedy, and Johnson Years</u>. Washington, D.C.:
The Brookings Institution, 1968.

Talbot, Ross B. and Don F. Hadwiger. <u>The Policy Process in</u>
<u>American Agriculture</u>. San Francisco: Chandler
Publishing Company, 1968.

Thomson, Charles A. H. and Frances M. Shattuck. <u>The 1956</u>
<u>Presidential Campaign.</u> Washington, D.C.: The
Brookings Institution, 1960.

Toma, Peter A. The Politics of Food for Peace, Executive-
    Legislative Interaction. Tucson: The University
    of Arizona Press, 1967.

Tweeten, Luther. Foundations of Farm Policy. Lincoln:
    University of Nebraska Press, 1970.

Whalen, William J. The Latter-day Saints in the Modern
    World: An Account of Contemporary Mormonism. New
    York: The John Day Company, 1964.

Wilcox, Walter W. The Farmers in the Second World War.
    Ames: Iowa State University Press, 1947.

SIGNED ARTICLES

Appleby, Paul H. "An Administrative View," Journal of Farm
    Economics, XXXVI (February, 1954), 8-12.

Breimyer, Harold F. "Agriculture As Van and Rear in Insti-
    tutional Change," Journal of Economic Issues, IV
    (March 19, 1970).

DeVoto, Bernard. "The Easy Chair," Harper's, Vol. 210
    (May, 1955), 8.

Eisenhower, Dwight D. "Campaign Speech at Lexington,
    Kentucky," Vital Speeches, XXIII (October 15,
    1956), 2 ff.

_____. "Some Thoughts on the Presidency," Reader's
    Digest, Vol. 95 (November, 1968), 49-55.

Egerer, Gerald. "The Political Economy of British Wheat, 1920-1960," _Agricultural History_, XL (October, 1966), 295-310.

Fletcher, Max E. "Liberal and Conservative: Turn and Turnabout," _Journal of Economic Issues_, II (September, 1968), 312-322.

Graebner, Norman A. "Eisenhower's Popular Leadership," _Current History_, XXXIX (October, 1960), 230-236, 244.

Hammar, Conrad H. "Agricultural Economists and Farm Policy," _Journal of Farm Economics_, XXXIX (November, 1957), 881-893.

Handlin, Oscar. "The Eisenhower Administration: A Self-Portrait," _Atlantic_, Vol. 218 (November, 1963), 67-72.

Hardin, Charles M. "The Republican Department of Agriculture--A Political Interpretation," _Journal of Farm Economics_, XXXVI (May, 1954), 210-227.

Hibbs, Ben. "'Ike': The Last Years of a Great American," _Reader's Digest_, Vol. 95 (July, 1969), 111-116.

Hudson, Michael. "Epitaph for Bretton Woods," _Journal of International Affairs_, XXXIII (1969).

Leddy, John M. "GATT--A Cohesive Influence in the Free World," _Journal of Farm Economics_, XL (May, 1958), 228-237.

Martin, Harold H. "Elder Benson's Going to Catch It!" _The Saturday Evening Post_, Vol. 225 (March 28, 1953), 22-23, 110, 112-113.

McCalla, Alex F. "Protectionism in International Agricultural Trade, 1850-1968," _Agricultural History_, XLIII (July, 1969), 392-343.

Murphy, Donald R. "How Will the Corn Belt Farmers Vote," _The New Republic_, Vol. 139 (October 6, 1958), 6.

Novak, Robert D. "Reports: Washington," _Atlantic_, Vol. 225 (April, 1970), 4-14.

Paarlberg, Don. "Status of the National Rural Development Program to Date," _Journal of Farm Economics_, XXXIX (May, 1957), 261-270.

Paul, Rodman W. "The Mormons As a Theme in Western Historical Writing," _The Journal of American History_, LIV (December, 1967), 511-523.

Penn, Raymond J. "USDA Reorganization and BAE," _Journal of Farm Economics_, XXXVI (February, 1954), 16-18.

_____. "Federal Agricultural Price and Income Policy, 1955-59," _Journal of Farm Economics_, XLI (May, 1959), 184-193.

Rasmussen, Wayne D. and Gladys L. Baker. "A Short History of Price Support and Adjustment Legislation and Programs for Agriculture, 1933-65," _Agricultural Economics Research_, XVII (July, 1966), 69-73.

Reid, Bill G. "The Agrarian Tradition and Urban Problems,"
    The Midwest Quarterly, VI (Autumn, 1964), 75-86.

Rhodes, Richard. "Ike: An Artist In Iron," *Harper's*,
    Vol. 241 (July, 1970), 70-77.

Richter, Jay. "The Next President and Southern Agriculture,"
    Progressive Farmer, Vol. 75 (October, 1960), 25.

Ripley, Randall B. "Power in the Post-World War II Senate,"
    The Journal of Politics, Vol. 31 (May, 1969), 465-
    492.

Rossi, Manlio Doria. "Agriculture and Europe," *Daedalus*,
    Vol. 93 (Winter, 1964), 335-357.

Rossiter, Clinton. "The New American Conservatives,"
    Harper's, Vol. 214 (April, 1957), 75-82.

Schnittker, John A. "The Farmer in the Till," *Atlantic*,
    Vol. 224 (August, 1969), 43-45.

Schwenger, Robert B. "Synthesis of Trade and Agricultural
    Policy in GATT," *Journal of Farm Economics*, XL
    (May, 1958), 238-248.

Smith, Mervin G. "Low Income--That's the main 'farm prob-
    lem,'" *Ohio Farmer*, Vol. 226 (August 20, 1960), 5,
    18.

Taylor, Henry C. "The Reorganization of the Economic Work
    of the USDA," *Journal of Farm Economics*, XXXVI
    (February, 1954), 12-14.

Thomson, Jim. "Congress Has Little to Show for Nine Months of Legislation," Prairie Farmer, Vol. 131 (September 19, 1959), 80.

Tolley, Howard R. "Dismemberment of the BAE," Journal of Farm Economics, XXXVI (February, 1954), 14-16.

Tontz, Robert L. "Membership of General Farmers' Organizations--United States, 1874-1960," Agricultural History, Vol. 38 (July, 1964), 143-156.

Tunley, R. "Everybody Picks on Benson," American Magazine, XLVII (June, 1954), 26-27, 106-110.

Wells, O. V. "Agricultural Economics Under the USDA Reorganization of November 2, 1953," Journal of Farm Economics, XXXVI (February, 1954), 1-8.

Wheeler, Leslie A. "The New Agriculture Protectionism and Its Effect on Trade Policy," Journal of Farm Economics, XLII (November, 1960), 797-810.

White, William S. "Who Really Runs the Senate?" Harper's, Vol. 213 (December, 1956), 35-40.

Wooten, Paul. "20 Years of Farming," The Farm Quarterly, Vol. 21 (Spring, 1966), 56-59, 145-146.

UNSIGNED ARTICLES

"A New Prophet," Newsweek, LXXV (February 2, 1970), 71.

"Agriculture: Bawls and Bellows," Time, LXI (February 23, 1953), 25.

"Agriculture: See It Now?" _Time_, LXVII (February 6, 1956), 18.

"Apostle At Work," _Time_, LXI (April 13, 1953), 25-28.

"Behind the Committee Doors: The Senate Questions Ike's Cabinet," _The New Republic_, Vol. 128 (February 2, 1953), 10-12.

"Drop Benson or Else," _The New Republic_, Vol. 138 (March 10, 1958), 2.

"Dwight D. Eisenhower, 1890-1969," _Newsweek_, LXXIII (April 7, 1969), 2-7.

"Farmers Like a Man Who Stands by His Convictions," _Life_, Vol. 44 (June 2, 1958), 79-82.

"Flies in the Barn," _Time_, LXXV (March 28, 1960), 21-22.

"Long Knives for Ezra," _Time_, XXXIV (December 21, 1959), 12.

"Mr. Speaker: The Dynamo of Capitol Hill," _American Magazine_, CLIX (April, 1955), 24, 102-103.

"Resigned to Duty," _Life_, Vol. 34 (December 28, 1959), 11.

"The Congress: Joseph and Ezra," _Time_, LXVII (March 5, 1956), 19.

"The Farm Problem: Men on a Margin," _Life_, Vol. 47 (December 14, 1959), 101-11.

"The Heavy Overhang," _Time_, LXVI (November 7, 1955), 25.

"The Real Farm Income," _The NFO Reporter_, IX (October, 1965), 4.

INDEX

Adams, Sherman, 40, 44, 70, 81, 136, 137, 153, 154, 195
Agricultural Act of 1949, 5, 71
Agricultural Act of 1954, 84-86, 163, 166, 242
Agricultural Act of 1956 (Soil Bank), 125, 132, 139
Agricultural Act of 1958, 208
Agricultural Adjustment Act of 1938, 87
Agricultural Trade Development and Assistance Act (1954), 98, 105, 112,
   187, 229, 238
Aiken, George, 42, 53, 59, 161
American Farm Bureau Federation, 35, 81, 133, 148, 153, 244
Anderson, Clinton, ix-xi, 4, 211
Andresen, August H., 69, 162, 198
Benson, Ezra Taft
   Agricultural Act of 1954, 84
   Agricultural Act of 1956 (Soil Bank), 125
   Agricultural Act of 1958, 208
   agricultural experience, 14
   Agricultural Trade Development and Assistance Act (1954), 98
   American Institute of Cooperation, 32
   book, Freedom to Farm, 260
   Cache Valley, Idaho, 24
   dump Benson movement, 61
   education, 21-23
   evaluation, 274-276
   farewell to Eisenhower (1961), 268
   first report of Rural Development Program, 144
   Food and Fiber Bill (1958), 203
   Food for Peace program, 236
   General Statement on Agricultural Policy, 38
   home life, 27-29
   modern agriculture, 224
   Mormon background, xvii
   Nixon accepts 1960 farm plank, 251
   nomination for Secretary of Agriculture, 15
   political philosophy, 217
   proposals to eliminate subsidies and acreage allotments (1959), 222
   St. Paul, Minnesota speech, 40
   selects staff, 46-48
   trade missions (1955), 100
   trade missions (1957), 197

Benson (cont.)
    trade missions (1959), 232
    trade missions (1960), 258
    USDA reorganization, 51
Brannan, Charles, 5
Brannan Plan, 5
Burdick, Quentin N., 241
Butz, Earl L., 48, 49, 108, 148, 264
Carlson, Frank, 6, 12, 13, 40
Coke, Earl J., 47
Commodity Credit Corporation, 55, 65, 76, 77, 116, 152, 165, 241, 252
Cooley, Harold D., 169
Coolidge, Calvin, 2
Davis, John H., 48, 52, 117
Dewey, Thomas E., 1
Dirksen, Everett M., 12, 91, 118, 199
Dulles, John Foster, 105, 109
Eisenhower, Dwight D.
    advice to Nixon (1960 campaign), 244
    Agricultural Act of 1954, 84
    Agricultural Act of 1956 (Soil Bank), 125
    Agricultural Act of 1958, 208
    agricultural proposals to Congress (1959), 221
    Agricultural Trade Development and Assistance Act (1954), 98
    appoints National Agricultural Advisory Commission (1953), 62
    established Commission on Increased Industrial Use of Agricultural
       Products, 119
    established Interagency Committee for Agricultural Surplus Disposal
       (Francis Committee), 99
    farewell to Benson (1961), 269
    Food and Fiber Bill proposed (1958), 203
    Food for Peace program, 236
    Great Plains Program, 140
    Kasson, Minnesota Pledge, 7-8
    NATO Commander, 1
    Operation Arrowhead (campaign of 1956), 154
    Rural Development Program, 144
Eisenhower, Milton, 13, 16
Ellender, Allen J., 153, 183
Ferguson, Clarence M., 49
Food for Peace, 236, 237
Francis, Clarence, 99, 103, 106, 108, 109, 115, 121, 187
Freeman, Orville, 268
Goldwater, Barry, 213
Hall, Leonard, 42, 137, 196
Hardin, Clifford M., 49
Hauge, Gabriel, 43, 61, 121, 152, 154, 156, 176, 235
Hickenlooper, Bourke B., 42
Hoover, Herbert, 1, 50
Hope, Clifford, 6, 13, 59, 61, 69, 87, 162, 164
Humphrey, Hubert, 176, 236

Interagency Committee for Agricultural Surplus Disposal (Francis
    Committee), 99, 104
Jensen, Ben, 225, 226
Johnson, Lyndon B., 92, 175
Judd, Walter, 113, 114
Kennedy, John F., 79, 175, 255, 267
Kline, Allen, 35, 81, 244
Laird, Melvin R., 194
Lambie, James B., Jr., 99, 105
McCarthy, Joseph, 192
McGovern, George, 191
McKay, David O., 18
McKeller, Kenneth D., 179
McNary-Haugen Bill, 2
Morse, True D., 47, 90, 144, 150
Mundt, Karl, 41, 135, 136, 153, 194, 239
Murrow, Edward R., 240
Myers, William I., 13, 48, 57, 64, 245, 264, 268
National Agricultural Advisory Commission, 48, 57, 59, 62, 118, 131
National Farm Organization, 146, 148
National Farmers Union, 35-36, 205
National Grange, 35, 81, 149, 178, 261
New Deal, xvi, 87, 89
Newsom, Herschel D., 35, 81, 149, 261
Nixon, Richard M., 82, 236, 243, 244, 245, 247, 251, 256, 264, 267
Paarlberg, Don, 47, 57, 176, 235, 236, 246
Parity
    flexible (1948), 4
    formula established (1910-1914), 3
    Kennedy farm plank proposes 90 percent, 255
    modernized (1954), 73
    75 percent level proposed (Food and Fiber Bill, 1958), 203
Patton, James G., 35, 149
Persons, Wilton B., 41, 44, 156, 178
PL 480; see Agricultural Trade Development and Assistance Act (1954), 98,
    99, 105, 112, 182, 187, 229, 235, 238
Production and Marketing Administration, 42
Proxmire, William, 212
Rayburn, Sam, 179
research program, 202
Roosevelt, Franklin D., xvi, 211
Rural Development Program, 144, 166, 189
Rural Electrification Administration, 225
Seaton, Fred A., 13, 60, 265
Short, Romeo E., 52
Shuman, Charles B., 133, 134, 148, 153
Soil Bank; see Agricultural Act of 1956, 125, 132, 139, 150, 166, 170,
    242
Sparkman, John, 40
Staley, Oren Lee, 146

Taft, Robert A., 11
Thye, Edward J., 36, 138, 200
Truman, Harry S., 1948 election, 1, 55, 89, 211
Wallace, Henry A., 211, 265, 276
Watergate, xvii
Young, Milton R., 36, 41, 69, 153